Spokesman for the Kingdom

Volume Two of the Series
Studies in Mormon History

James B. Allen, Editor

This publication is supported
by a generous grant
from Roland Rich Woolley

Spokesman for the Kingdom

Early Mormon Journalism and the *Deseret News,* 1830-1898

Monte Burr McLaws

Brigham Young University Press
Provo, Utah

Library of Congress Cataloging in Publication Data

McLaws, Monte Burr, 1934—
Spokesman for the kingdom.

(Studies in Mormon history; v. 2)
Bibliography: p. 231.
Includes index.
1. Deseret News, Salt Lake City. 2. Church
of Jesus Christ of Latter-day Saints. I. Title.
II. Series.
PN4899.S385D45   071'.92'25   76-48954
ISBN 0-8425-0023-5

Library of Congress Catalog Card Number: 76-48954
International Standard Book Number: 0-8425-0023-5 (hardback)
Brigham Young University Press, Provo, Utah 84602
© 1977 by Brigham Young University Press. All rights reserved
Printed in the United States of America
77   1.5M   19791

Acknowledgments

I am indebted to many institutions and individuals for making this study possible and am happy to acknowledge the much appreciated assistance. Since the newspaper is consciously and unconsciously the best record of its own aims and methods, a special expression of gratitude is due the University of Missouri Library which made the entire *Deseret News* file available to me on microfilm. I thank the libraries of Brigham Young University, the University of Utah, the Utah State Historical Society, and especially the Historical Department of The Church of Jesus Christ of Latter-day Saints for access to all materials under their jurisdiction relating to the subject of this book.

A research grant-in-aid from the Nebraska Humanities and Social Science Development Program and a faculty research grant-in-aid from the Wayne State College Foundation proved helpful in the latter stages of the research.

Of the people who helped in the production of this book I am indebted most to Lewis Atherton who, in directing an earlier version of this work as a doctoral dissertation at the University of Missouri, provided firm yet friendly guidance in both content and style. I also acknowledge with appreciation the continuous sound and very practical recommendations offered by S. George Ellsworth.

For careful and critical perusal of early drafts of the manuscript, I wish to acknowledge colleagues and former colleagues Peter Judd, Ida Domazlicky, and particularly John Corcorhan for his valuable advice on style.

I wish to thank the Brigham Young University Press both for important editorial comments and for bringing the book out under their imprint.

For reading the manuscript and encouraging its publication, I wish to thank Davis Bitton, Thomas Alexander, and Leonard Arrington. More especially I thank James Allen, without whose faithful and conscientious backing the book would not have been published.

Special acknowledgment is due my family: my brother, John Larry McLaws, and my sister, Lyndella Bryant, for their continuous support; my children, Brad, Brent, and Maria, for patient waiting. By far the greatest thanks goes to my wife, Emily, without whose conscientious typing and proofreading of several drafts, practical and friendly criticism of style and content, and constant support of and faith in the author, this book never would have been written.

Contents

Introduction

The story of the Mormons is one of the most fascinating in all American history. . . . It is probably the most important chapter in the history of the trans-Mississippi frontier and . . . is a treasure-house for the historian of ideas, institutions, and social energies." So stated the late Bernard DeVoto, acknowledged scholar of the American West, while lamenting thirty-five years ago the neglect of the Mormon experience by historical writers. One might also bemoan the fact that too few good, honest, and candidly critical biographies of American newspapers have been written. This is particularly true of papers in Utah. This book, primarily a study of the *Deseret News,* a Mormon institution of major importance and interest, is designed to help fill the gap.

Two major studies of the *Deseret News* have preceded this book: Wendell J. Ashton's *Voice in the West: Biography of a Pioneer Newspaper* in 1950 and Arlington Russell Mortensen's doctoral thesis, "The *Deseret News* and Utah, 1850-1867" in 1959. *Voice in the West* is a storehouse of factual information, particularly about pioneer paper manufacturing, the mechanical growth of the *News,* and the lives of its employees, rather than an interpretive study. Written in 1950 by a former managing editor of the *News,* it is a sympathetic official centennial history. More analytical and objective, Mortensen's history stops once the paper became a daily. As suggested in its title, it is in large part a history of early Utah as reflected in the pages of the *Deseret News*. *The First 100 Years: A History of the Salt Lake Tribune, 1871-1971* by O. N. Malmquist is the centennial treatment of the oldest continuously published non-Mormon newspaper in Utah. Malmquist, a retired political reporter of long service on the *Tribune,* in contradication of his book's subtitle has actually written a political history of Utah, a history too frequently based on secondary sources.

This study concentrates on the nineteenth-century life of the *Deseret News,* chief official Utah organ of the Mormons, emphasizing the paper's role as an active agent in Mormondom. However, it is also an interpretive account of local and foreign Mormon journalism from 1830, and also treats gentile newspapers inside Utah and out as their pages related to the Mormons. It deals with press power, reliability, and tactics as well as censorship and control in a theocratic frontier government. In addition to being journalistic history, it reveals a great deal of the political, social, cultural, and intellectual life of pre-twentieth-century Mormonism.

This is a critical study. The *Deseret News* itself properly recognized the need for honest criticism and invited such in its own pages. It recently stated that the press could not afford to become complacent. "And if complacency is to be avoided," it contended, "the press should welcome criticism from the outside as well as from its own ranks." Despite this position, however, and perhaps because the *News* was the official spokesman for the Church, some Mormon readers may find parts of this book a bit unsettling. Nevertheless, even this critical approach has found the Mormons to be a literate, courageous, and practical people—a people who, on the whole, published a newspaper of unique interest that energetically represented them in an honest and sober fashion which has generally done them honor.

The dean of newspaper historians, Frank Luther Mott, stated that the *Deseret News* was the "first successful religious daily newspaper in the English language." Founded in 1850 as one of the first twenty newspapers established west of the Missouri River and north of Texas, the *News* has outlived all its contemporaries except for the Santa Fe *New Mexican.* One of the oldest institutions in the Mormon Church today, it constitutes a living link with the past century, reflecting Mormon history as no other source can. But more than age qualifies the *News* to be the subject of a book. Recognizing the power of the press, Brigham Young assigned the *Deseret News* a key role in building and defending the economic, political and spiritual kingdom he started in the Great Basin.

Although this book is mostly concerned with the *Deseret News,* it recognizes a continuity within Mormon journalism, which began with the founding of the Church in 1830. Patterns established and experience gained in Ohio, Missouri, and Illinois left their mark on journalism in the Great Basin.

The press was important in Utah from the start. Although Mormons went to the desolate regions of the West to find asylum, Brigham Young did not mean for physical isolation to cause intellectual isolation. He ordered that a press be sent to the Great Basin regardless of cost, and a newspaper established to insure communication from the "proper source." Utah's remoteness profoundly affected the life of the *Deseret News.* But problems of newsprint, newsgathering, subscription and capital which generally proved insurmountable for private frontier newspapers never proved fatal to the *News,* both because of the Church's insistence on having a press and because of the fervent support of the paper by most Mormons.

The *News* was not always run by professional journalists; early editors included a judge, a merchant, and a government surveyor. *News* editors regularly appeared more interested in religion than journalism, and a primary qualification seemed to be intimacy with the leadership of the Church. Three served as Brigham Young's private secretary prior to their appointment on the paper. Nevertheless, all the paper's editors were men of letters and some were experienced, gifted writers. Although they were not publicly recognized, assistant-editors often did the actual editorial work, even when very able but overly-extended journalists like George Q. Cannon and Charles W. Penrose were editor. But this is not a study of the editors, nor should it be, for although some were certainly talented, unlike most other newspapers in the early West the Mormon-owned *Deseret News* was never a personal journal but rather the organ of an institution, controlled and dominated by ecclesiastical authority.

Although the *Deseret News* was not immune from some news suppression and editing by Church leaders, even to the extent that one editor was summarily fired, such practices were infrequent.

The editors were either in the Church hierarchy or close to it, and the *News* did not receive or need constant and close supervision. The *News's* motto throughout the nineteenth century was "Truth and Liberty," though in order to protect and perpetuate the Church the whole truth was not always printed. As the organ of the Mormon Church and the official medium through which the views, wishes, and instructions of the Church leaders were expressed and disseminated among the Saints all over the world, the *Deseret News,* less transitory than the spoken word, was a much better means of continuous communication than the classroom, lectern or pulpit. The *News* was a solidifier of opinion, vital in building the Kingdom of God and the Mormon empire in the West.

Along with its function as a "regular" newspaper, the *Deseret News* was filled with Church-related subjects and its columns reflected Mormon theology and values, from millennialism and the "Lost Tribes" of Israel to approved dance styles and women's clothing. Recognizing the power of the press to shape human minds, the *News* tried to issue a wholesome, reliable paper for the entire family. It strongly editorialized against pornography, and almost never admitted to its pages news items of a sensational nature. This caused well-known and respected nineteenth-century western historian Hubert Howe Bancroft to observe that the *News* ranked among the top newspapers in being free from journalistic scandal-mongering and obscenity. However, despite its repeated statement that it was not dependent on a big circulation built on yellow journalism, for financial reasons the pragmatic *Deseret News* was not the completely high caliber journal Mormon leaders would have preferred. Although it offset them by long, disapproving editorial arguments, the *News* saturated its pages with high-paying patent medicine advertisements and ran liquor, tobacco, tea, and coffee advertisements—including those of the Church-owned cooperative store, ZCMI. However, unlike many newspapers of the day, including its local competitior, the gentile-owned *Salt Lake Tribune,* the *Deseret News* was totally free from distasteful advertisements of medications claiming to bring about abortions or birth control and supposed remedies for the treatment of venereal disease.

Contrary to some Mormon hopes, close contact with gentiles was not eliminated by the move to Utah, and the *News* attempted to keep Mormon-gentile conflict to a minimum. To discourage non-Mormon immigration, it played down the mineral resources in the Great Basin. Endeavoring to convince Washington, D.C., of Mormon loyalty and propriety, it exaggerated the positive aspects of Mormondom, as in its unsuccessful attempt to convince the federal troops under General Albert Sidney Johnston of the folly of marching into Salt Lake City. On very sensitive matters, however, like the Civil War, slavery, and abolitionism, or the cover-up of the 1857 Mountain Meadows Massacre, the *Deseret News,* given its reasons for existence, wisely remained editorially uncommitted or virtually silent.

Many Eastern papers and some on the West Coast bombarded their readers with criticisms of the Mormons based on erroneous information coming from their Utah correspondents. Brigham Young correctly did not place the confidence in these "foreign" correspondents that his most recent biographer, Stanley Hirshson, did; it is at best naive for a scholarly historian to put such trust in hearsay evidence culled from newspapers. Yet Hirshson's gullibility illustrates the dimensions of the perhaps impossible task Brigham Young assigned to the *Deseret News* of allaying fears of Mormon rebellion and correcting misrepresentations believed by policy-makers in Washington and by the American people in general.

Because *News* circulation among non-Mormons was limited, it could not have much influence where influence was needed. Therefore, quasi-official Mormon journals, often filled with verbatim quotes from the *News,* were started in Washington, D.C., New York City, St. Louis, and San Francisco. This tactic was soon abandoned, however, and the *News* directly undertook the task of correcting the distorted reports. Maneuvering to increase its influence, it sent complimentary annual subscriptions to the U.S. President, his entire cabinet, all territorial delegates, most members of the House of Representatives, and all but one of the Senators. Other influential people like famous political cartoonist Thomas E. Nast also received free copies of the Church's official newspaper.

Mormons also faced newspaper criticism from Salt Lake City-based journals. This study traces and analyzes such local opposition and Mormon strategy toward it. The official leadership, fearing ideas which ran counter to Church policy in Utah, used every legal effort to suppress newspapers that were founded to oppose Brigham Young's understandable desire for unity and conformity or to attack his authority. The methods used were varied and flexible, including economic sanctions. The initial journalistic line of defense was deliberate silence of the *Deseret News* and reliance on privately Mormon-owned but not Church-affiliated papers. However, because of the ever-increasing popularity of the *Salt Lake Tribune,* the *News* gradually shifted to guarded indirect attacks of its own. Finally, the traditionally sober church paper moved to wide-open frontal exchanges with the *Tribune,* exchanges that reached peaks of personal editorial name-calling that would surprise today's readers. Although this intensely personal journalism subsided, the two papers continued their confrontations into the twentieth century. But today, almost bedfellows, they have combined their printing, circulation, and advertising solicitation into a single corporation.

From 1850, when a *News* "extra" publicly announced to the world that the Mormons officially sanctioned plural marriage, until Church President Wilford Woodruff's 1890 Manifesto declaring the end of polygamy in the Church, the *Deseret News* faithfully and energetically communicated church policy on this principle. Sounding much like the southern apologists for the other so-called "twin relic of barbarism," the *News* argued that polygamy was sanctioned by the Bible, was not unconstitutional, and was sociologically and physiologically superior to monogamy. Although scientifically dated, many of these arguments still make fascinating and insightful reading.

The *News* so vigorously and repeatedly blasted away at federal marshals, judges, and antipolygamy legislation that its editors were some of the first to be imprisoned or forced into exile. In the face of mass Mormon arrests, the *News* was used either openly or subtly to counsel and admonish loyalty to the plural marriage doctrine. It told polygamists to stand on principle, to not compromise in the smallest degree, regardless of consequences. The Church paper heaped praise on those who chose jail over compromise and severely castigated those who abandoned the Principle for freedom. Nevertheless, when the Church eventually saw that polygamy was indefensible before puritanical, gentile America, it started to change its policy. The *News,* as the official Church paper, trying to help Mormons accept the inevitable abandonment of the principle, switched from defending polygamy to defending the "Manifesto" from criticism by some Mormons for the "surrender" to the popular will of America.

A potentially effective agent, the *Deseret News* tried to persuade Congress and the American people generally that Utah deserved statehood. However, gentile opposition to polygamy was only one reason for delaying statehood. Another source of conflict was Mormon control of Utah government. Unlike its policy of openly defending polygamy, the *News* from the very beginning denied all charges pertaining to the Mormon political kingdom. It also consistently claimed to be nonpartisan and made efforts to present itself as such. Its pages, however, reveal that it was indeed the mouthpiece of the Mormon-supported Peoples Party. Writing to the President of the Church on the question of separation of church and state, *News* editor Charles Penrose persuasively pointed out that statehood alone would save the Church and that it would come only after Washington was satisfied the Church was detached from the state. Convinced of the overriding importance of the mission of Mormonism, Penrose insisted that the Church at least give the appearance of giving up control over civil affairs.

For almost fifty years the *Deseret News* defended polygamy and championed Utah statehood. In so doing, its editors displayed both great courage and practical wisdom. At the turn of the century, with the major problems of Mormon-gentile conflict seemingly behind it, the *News* began shifting away from vigorous defensive journalism toward more genteel moralizing.

This book attempts to assess the pivotal role of the *Deseret News* in expressing the concerns of the Latter-day Saints in the nineteenth century, along with examining its journalistic methods, tactics, and achievements. As the best-known spokesman for the Mormon point of view, the *News* was under pressure to explain and defend Church policy. Although the editors, as insiders, sometimes seemingly became overzealous in defending the Church, they nevertheless generally approached their task with commendable integrity and responsibility. The history of the *Deseret News* in the nineteenth century is an important part of the history of the Mormon people themselves.

Spokesman
for the
Kingdom

1
Midwest
Mormon
Journalism

In much of the world, the 1830s and 1840s saw the growth and spread of new political ideas, changes in social concepts, and a revision of religious traditionalism. In America, a wave of optimism and the rise of the common man swept Andrew Jackson to the presidency; but the religious quest for salvation was not so unified. Splinter sects, sectionalism, and pessimism led to slander and competition among the great popular churches of the period. "We must not be surprised, then," wrote William Warren Sweet, "to find in this period a great variety of new interests arising; new and strange sects; new movements in thought, reforms of one kind or another; many of them the result of individual vagaries."[1]

This proliferation of new religious ideas was accompanied by an expanding religious press, established to satisfy the growing appetite of readers disappointed by scanty coverage of religious matters in the secular press and to acquaint the members of inland churches with the developments in their eastern counterparts. More importantly, however, these newspapers were started to propagate and defend controversial ideas.

The first religious weekly newspaper in the United States was initiated in September 1808 by Elias Smith, a contentious minister who had made many enemies in religion and politics. Smith started his *Herald of Gospel Liberty* both to reach a larger audience with his controversial opinions and to reply more effectively to contemporary ministers who used the press to abuse him. Following in the footsteps of *Gospel Liberty,* sectarian newspapers with similar objectives increased so much that by 1833 some one hundred were scattered over the nation.

Every denomination and every school of thought within a denomination felt that it had to have its own organ; often there were more than twenty periodicals for the leading churches. The *Millenial Harbinger,* official organ of the Disciples of Christ, listed in 1838 sixteen different Disciple periodicals extending over the United States, Canada, and England.

Just as political ideas born in Europe relentlessly moved to America, so, too, did religious papers undergo the torturous journey from east to west. In many instances the religious newspaper, important in spreading church doctrine, was first on the scene in the westward moving frontier. Michigan's first newspaper, the Roman Catholic *Michigan Essay,* was started near Detroit on 31 August 1809. The *Shawnee Sun,* the earliest paper in what became Kansas, was a Baptist missionary sheet started in 1835. Oklahoma's first newspaper was the Baptist *Cherokee Messenger,* begun in 1844. Newspapers also played an important role in the frontier history of The Church of Jesus Christ of Latter-day Saints (Mormons), an indigenous American religion founded in western New York in 1830 by Joseph Smith.

Indeed, one might say Mormonism began in the office and printing room of a newspaper. With the laborious task of writing the manuscript of the Book of Mormon behind him, Joseph Smith turned to Egbert B. Grandin, publisher of the Palmyra, New York, *Wayne Sentinel,* for aid in publishing the fruits of his inspiration. Grandin initially declined the opportunity, as did the Rochester *Anti-Masonic Inquirer.* However, after receiving a guarantee of payment through a farm mortgage, Grandin agreed to print 5,000 copies for $3,000. Some of the alarmed citizens of Palmyra, trying to pressure Grandin into disclaiming the agreement, temporarily succeeded in halting the printing when they announced a boycott of the book. Not to be deterred, Joseph Smith and Martin Harris, the owner of the secured farm, countered with assurances of their willingness and ability to pay regardless of the threatened sanction. In the early spring of 1830, the Book of Mormon rolled off the press of the *Sentinel*. In its preface, Joseph Smith publicized the "unlawful measures taken by evil designing persons to destroy" him and his work and declared that he would correct the "many false reports" circulated about the book. From the very beginning he illustrated the role he intended the press to play in the Mormon Church.[2]

This initial difficulty with publishing, the increasing newspaper criticism of Smith and his associates, and the need for maintaining contact with an expanding membership soon made the leaders of this new religion realize the value of the press in building and defending the "Kingdom of God" and its principles and policies.

Mormon Prophet Joseph Smith was, in terms of the average New England education and village culture, the product of a literate background. Beginning as it did with a book, Mormonism had to make its appeal to a literate audience. It is not surprising, therefore, that Smith and his church attracted many gifted and fearless writers who founded and edited periodicals. The Mormon community was equipped not only with a temple and bishop's storehouse, but also with a printing press. Along with elders and bishops, Mormons appointed an official printer to the Church. As with most things, Joseph Smith was responsible for journalism and the appointment of journalists for the Church.

Lack of proselytizing success and problems with their neighbors caused Smith and his followers to move west. Major settlements were established first in Ohio and later in Missouri. In September 1831, Joseph Smith commissioned William Wines Phelps to publish in Independence the first Mormon journal, a monthly periodical to be named *The Evening and Morning Star*. This move followed on the heels of publication of Mormon apostate Ezra Booth's series of critical anti-Mormon letters in the Ravenna *Ohio Star*.[3] Smith obviously intended to counter the many false reports and foolish stories published in the newspapers and widely circulated to curtail the Church's missionary efforts.

Phelps's appointment follows a clearly defined pattern that reveals the close relationship between the Church and its press. Formerly a prominent political figure in Canandaigua, New York, and an editor of a party newspaper there, Phelps operated the Church paper on a stewardship basis. Any profits realized over and above what was necessary for the support of him and his family were to be turned over to the community "Bishop's Storehouse." Church leaders reserved the right to select the editor and to counsel him as to the policy and content of the paper. This relationship is well illustrated, as is Smith's recognition of the paper's importance, in a letter the Prophet wrote to Phelps:

> We wish you to render the Star as interesting as possible, by setting forth the rise, program and the faith of the church, as well as the doctrine; for if you do not render it more interesting than at present, it will fail, and the church will suffer a great loss thereby.[4]

Despite his lack of training in journalism, this concern over the success of the *Star* showed Joseph Smith's astute awareness of the paper's defects. The major weakness was a combination of a poor selection of material, the absence of orderly and simple development, and a turgid style, the vice of almost all American literature of the time. The problems facing the *Star* could in part be traced to an over-anxious editor, intent upon heralding the messages of the new church, unmindful that many of his readers were not familiar with the historical development and ideas of the Church.

Among such ideas was millenarianism. The quest for the millennium goes as far back as Hebrew nationalism and was perpetuated in the New Testament. Although suppressed in Roman Catholicism, it survived with the establishment of religions based on the conviction of the imminence of the second coming of Christ. Millenarianism was completely respectable, both socially and intellectually, far into the nineteenth century. It became a chief motivating force in Mormonism.

The name of the paper—*The Evening and the Morning Star*—like the names of later periodicals in the Mormon Church, depicted the nearness of the end of the world and the second coming. Its prospectus explained that it was "the forerunner of the night of the end, and the messenger of the day of redemption," and concluded, "Therefore, in the fear of him, and to spread truth among all nations, kindred, tongues and people, this paper is sent forth, that a wicked world may know that Jesus Christ . . . will soon appear."[5]

Although the *Star* was politically independent, it contained secular information under the heading "Worldly Affairs." However, almost all this material illustrated some point of Mormon doctrine. Concerned with "signs of the times," the journal faithfully reported earthquakes, storms, plagues, fires, and other natural and man-made catastrophies.[6] For the Mormons, the "Kingdom of God" was to develop, not in consequence of some cataclysmic action of God, but through human effort. Thus Mormon millennialism is related to "the mission of America" and other concepts outside the narrowly defined realm of religion. This responsibility to prepare the Earth by helping to build the "Kingdom" politically, economically, and spiritually was a major mission of the *Star,* as it was to be for all Mormon periodicals. The vigorous pursuit of this mission became a chief cause of Mormon-gentile conflict throughout the nineteenth century.[7]

Heralding the second coming and reporting the fulfillment of prophecy was but one challenge of the *Star.* Phelps acknowledged another role—perhaps the major one—that the church paper was to play: "We promised to correct as many falsehoods as we could, for of all the statements that have been published in the newspapers of the day concerning this church not one has reached us but what in a greater or less degree was untrue."[8] Advancing this goal created havoc for the *Star* and ultimately precipitated its demise.

The smoldering conflict flared up when the *Star* was interpreted by Missourians as favoring abolitionism. A misunderstood editorial by Phelps in July 1833 on the free Negro and the Mormon Church in Missouri ignited the main tinderbox of anti-Mormon complaints —a fear of their political and economic domination of Jackson County.[9] Although Phelps ran a *Star Extra* on July 16 trying to clear up the apparent misunderstanding, Jackson County's "old settlers" decided to raze the printing establishment. They battered down the door and mercilessly threw the editor's wife and sick child into the street. They hurled the press from a second story window, scattering records, paper, and type through the streets, and completely leveled the building—all in less than an hour. Not until the murder of Elijah P. Lovejoy by a rabble at Alton, Illinois, in 1837, along with destruction of his Presbyterian newspaper with antislavery leanings, was so serious an outrage committed again against a religious newspaper.

Publication of the *Star* was suspended for only four issues before it was revived in Kirtland, Ohio. The Church obtained another press, and with Oliver Cowdery, a former schoolteacher and prominent figure in the Church from its inception, as editor, the *Star* continued publication through the remaining ten numbers of volume two, when it was replaced by the *Latter Day Saints' Messenger and Advocate.*

Like the *Star,* the *Advocate* carried religious articles, letters and news from missionaries, conference reports, and notices of marriages, births, and deaths. It also assumed its predecessor's function as

Church defender. In explaining this role, the editor adopted the philosophy of Thomas Jefferson, who stated that as long as reason was left free to combat falsehood, there was little danger from the spread of error. When assailed by the anti-Mormon press, Cowdery chose not to dip his pen in gall and answer "every vile epithet . . . lavished upon" the Church. Rather he proposed to leave the authors alone "till they wasted their own strength or conquered themselves."[10]

Oliver Cowdery was careful about what he put into the *Advocate*. In his first valedictory, he showed how seriously most Mormon editors took their responsibilities as he recognized the permanency of the printed word over transitory speech. "To realize that one year and eight months' labor is now before the public," wrote Cowdery, "that whether truth or untruth has been disseminated in the same, it must remain, and calls for the serious consideration of a candid heart full with the expectation and assurance, that before the Judge of all, and an assembled universe I must answer for the same."[11]

Running from October 1834 to September 1837 the *Advocate* frequently changed publishers and editors. Nationwide economic difficulties, lack of income from advertisements, and chronic nonpayment by subscribers help explain the turnover in proprietorship. However, the first two editors left their posts claiming the paper too often took them away from their regular business. The third change was apparently for reasons of health, while the last resulted from insubordination. Perhaps the difficult times made challenges to Joseph Smith's leadership inevitable. Different forces tried to point the Church in what they thought was the right direction.

W. A. Cowdery and Joseph Smith were the main figures in a controversy over a principle that ultimately created considerable conflict among Church members. W. A. Cowdery, Oliver's brother and the last editor of the *Advocate,* filled the next to last number of the paper with an analysis of the "Panic of 1837" and the failure of the Mormon bank in Kirtland. Together with other disgruntled Saints, he placed the blame for the bank failure on Joseph Smith. Cowdery declared that he was not prepared to censure any man nor say who could have done better under the circumstances, and even granted that the mistakes could "have been errors of the head and not the heart," yet it appeared that he had the Mormon Prophet in mind. Referring to those who thought that Joseph Smith could do no wrong, Cowdery warned his readers against arbitrary authority:

> We will here remark that whenever a people have unlimited confidence in a civil or ecclesiastical ruler or rulers, who are but men like themselves, and they begin to think they can do no wrong, they increase their tyranny, and oppression, establish a principle that man poor frail lump of mortality like themselves, is infallible. Who does not see a principle of popery and religious tyranny involved in such order of things?[12]

In assessing blame for the bank's failure, W. A. Cowdery committed an indiscretion that ended his editorial career. Joseph Smith, the apparent object of such frank criticism, used his position as the head of the Church to discontinue publication of the *Advocate* and start a new paper, the *Elder's Journal*. Published by the president of the Twelve Apostles and edited by the Prophet himself, the new paper soon made clear that there would be a policy change:

> We would say to the patrons of the Journal, that we calculate to pursue a different course from that of our predecessor in the editorial department. . . . We will endeavor not to scandalize our own citizens, especially where there is no foundation in truth for so doing; we consider that when a man scandalized his neighbors, it follows of course that he designs to cover his own iniquity: we consider him who puts his foot upon the neck of his benefactor, an object of pity rather than revenge, for in so doing he not only shows the construction of his own mind but the wickedness of his heart also.[13]

Joseph Smith's stewardship over the content of the Mormon press, aptly demonstrated in his clash with Cowdery, did not end with this incident. Even while the press continued to carry out its various functions, the shadow of the Prophet hovered in the background. He felt that such diligent concern was needed to unify and guide his followers.

That concern conformed with another consideration of the early church. The Mormons saw themselves as a chosen people who, having a covenant with God, enjoyed continuous divine revelation, counterbalanced by an equally fervent awareness of continuous satanic influence. For them, Satan, who realized the nearness of the millennium, a time in which he would be powerless, was making a last desperate attempt to destroy the Church. This belief caused them to regard all opposition as inspired by Satan and all opponents as the devil's co-workers. Such a belief could explain Joseph Smith's reaction to W. A. Cowdery's attack. Of course, other people have had such a belief, but among the Mormons it was especially intense.[14] This concern over potential subversion was an underlying aspect of the direction taken by the new Mormon periodical.

The *Elder's Journal* was more explicitly a Church apologist than its predecessors had been. It proposed to counter the "lying mania" which plagued the Church by publishing the correspondence of traveling elders—thus the name *Elder's Journal*. Sidney Rigdon, counselor to the Prophet Smith and assistant editor of the *Journal*, contended that it had been the way of all Saints, in all times, to give to following generations an adequate account of their travels and experiences to stand as a witness against false and malicious accusations. Drawing on history, he told his readers that the only thing that had saved the name of the medieval European sect known as the Waldenses from infamy and contempt was their writings. He argued that had it not been for the efforts expended to leave to posterity a "true account" of themselves, their enemies would have left the world in perfect ignorance of both their character and religion. "But the course which they took," wrote the editor, "to be their own historians has turned infamy upon the heads of their enemies . . . until their memory is had with reverence among all men, whose approbation is worth having." Rigdon emphasized that the Mormons had a duty to themselves, their children, and the world to do the same, and offered his paper to the public in fulfillment of such a duty.[15]

Despite such a noble aim, the *Journal* had to contend with more immediate practical problems. Since the perennial problem of delinquent subscribers plagued the *Journal*, its editor explained to the elders in the field that they constituted the main prop of the periodical and that the future of the endeavor depended upon them. He asked them to use their influence to obtain new subscribers and to collect and send home to Zion the greatly needed funds. In turn, he pledged to conduct the paper in such righteousness that it would be a trumpet through which they could send their "warning voices, to all nations, kindreds, tongues and people."[16]

Through no fault of its own, the *Journal* was unable to fulfill that pledge. After only two numbers, the *Journal's* publishing house was attached by the Geauga County Court to satisfy a judgment against Joseph Smith and his associates stemming from the bank failure. The Prophet later claimed that the seizure had been motivated by Mormon persecutors who, seeing they could not legally abolish the paper, destroyed the press and printing establishment by fire.[17] In the meantime, Smith felt compelled to flee to Far West, Missouri, where the Missouri Saints had begun to gather. Two more numbers of the ill-fated *Journal* were published there before more trouble between Mormons and Missouri's "old settlers" silenced it.[18]

Under the threat of extermination, the Mormons left Missouri in the winter of 1838-39 and moved across the Mississippi River into Illinois. As religious exiles scattered along the river in and around Quincy, they suffered a difficult winter. Among the wanderers was Ebenezer Robinson, the future editor of the next Mormon periodical. In the spring, Robinson and his fellow-Mormons moved seventy miles upriver, where they founded Nauvoo, a town that soon rivaled Quincy's commercial position and became the largest city in Illinois. Within two months of their arrival, Robinson, along with Joseph Smith's younger brother Don Carlos, issued the prospectus for a new Church paper, the *Times and Seasons.* However, problems of health and finances prevented them from issuing the first number until November.

Following the pattern set in 1831 with the birth of the *Star,* the two editors were permitted to keep any profits in return for representing the Mormon cause. The press itself, which had survived the abortive Far West, Missouri, experiment, belonged to the Church.[19] Robinson conscientiously tried to help establish the "Kingdom" and the "truth" on earth, but at the same time hoped to build a permanent business for himself and his family. However, by the fall of 1841 the Twelve Apostles had enlarged their responsibilities in the developing "Kingdom" growing in Nauvoo, and, dissatisfied with the editorial policy of the *Times and Seasons,* they decided that the official paper should be owned and operated directly by the Church. They threatened to start a competing paper unless Robinson relinquished his duties.[20] Only after a "revelaton" commanding the Prophet to have the Twelve "take in hand the *Times and Seasons*" did Robinson reluctantly sell his business rights to Joseph Smith,[21] who then became the new publisher and editor.

Joseph Smith, denying that he had exercised any direct supervision over the former paper, made clear his future relationship to the *Times and Seasons.* "I alone stand responsible for it," he announced, "and shall for all papers having my signature henceforward."[22] While he assumed responsibility for the editorial column for only seven months, the paper was sufficiently official to make its pages a virtual fiat to members of the Church.

Although one of the major reasons for its creation had been the desire to maintain contact with the scattered Church membership, the journal attempted to carry out its motto "Truth Will Prevail" by detailing the history of the persecutions suffered by those who had braved the Missouri experience. Hoping to gain public sympathy, and to give their plight as wide a hearing as possible, the Church sent copies of the publication to the leading papers in the United States.[23] One such paper, the *Chicago Democrat,* praised the Mormons for their sagacious attempt to profit from persecutions.[24] This exploitation of their difficulties continued while the Mormon press expanded in order to more adequately meet its varied responsibilities.

To enlarge its audience, the *Times and Seasons* increasingly diversified its pages. This was not entirely new. To broaden appeal, the now defunct *Star* had printed one supplement containing advertisements, and its editor, William Phelps, had also published the *Upper Missouri Advertiser,* a weekly that had announced it would "contain sketches of the news of the day, politics, advertisements, and whatever tends to promote the interest of the great West."[25] The *Advertiser* lasted only eleven months, but it illustrated the early Church's pattern of trying to develop a secular newspaper along with its religious periodicals.

Like its predecessors, the *Times and Seasons* provided information on the *times,* emphasizing that it was the *season* for the beginning of the millennial reign of Christ. In a departure from most earlier efforts, however, it carried more general news and more advertisements, including some for patent medicines,[26] though it stated that it would refrain from any interference in political matters.

Within seven months of the start of the *Times and Seasons,* the Mormon press began the tradition of international coverage. The concept of millenarianism, a major motivating factor behind the foreign mission movement, was promulgated in the *Millennial Star,* begun in Manchester, England. Like its contemporaries, the *Star,* first of a long series of foreign periodicals, was imbued with the spirit of Christ's second coming. As the Church's major European press, the *Star's* chief function was to help gain converts to the faith and to encourage their emigration to America—the center of "Zion"—in preparation for the millennium.[27] It succeeded admirably.

The Church's press was continually changing and expanding. A "regular" newspaper was needed. Filled primarily with religious matters, Church journals of this early period, with the exception of the *Upper Missouri Advertiser,* could hardly be described as newspapers. However, Joseph Smith did show an interest in publications of a secular nature. While at Kirtland, Ohio, the Church leader was offered a liberal patronage from influential men in the Jacksonian party if he would publish a political weekly favorable to the administration. He accepted the offer on the grounds that the Church would thereby demonstrate its sincere intention to support the government.[28] For some unexplained reason, however, the project, to be called *The Northern Times,* never went to press. Other Mormons, too, supposedly wanted a "second" paper, and in 1840 it was announced that a nonpartisan weekly paper, *The News,* devoted to literature, art, science, and agriculture, would soon be published in Nauvoo. This project failed because of insufficient subscribers. And though another weekly, the *Nauvoo Ensign and Zarahemla Standard,* was on the drawing board when Don Carlos Smith died in 1841, Nauvoo had to wait until 16 April 1842 for a "regular" weekly paper.

Named the *"Wasp,"* the new weekly intended to supplement the primarily religious content of the *Times and Seasons.* Its editor, William Smith, announced that he alone reserved the "privilege of weighing in a balance the correctness and character of every principle" that came under his observation.[29] However independent from the Church this might sound, the fact remained that, because the editor was both the brother of the Prophet and a member of the Church hierarchy, little separation existed. Declaring that it had no intention of duplicating the Church's monthly *Times and Seasons,* the *Wasp* saw its purpose as emphasizing more general news, thus generating a wider appeal in the community. The early success of this direction can be measured by the increased advertising submitted by local businessmen. But well-meaning as William Smith's declaration may sound, it could not disguise the main purpose of the *Wasp:* improving on the work done by the religious publications. The enormity of the challenge soon became apparent.

The unique provisions of the City of Nauvoo's charter, Joseph Smith's assumption of more and more temporal power, his involvement in politics, and rumors of Mormon polygamy turned the Illinois press, which at first had been sympathetic to the refugees from Missouri, against the Mormon Prophet and his followers. This growing hostility to the Mormons was not an isolated trend, nor were the followers of Joseph Smith alone singled out as objects of criticism. Nativism, a reactionary movement that arose to challenge new immigrants and their cultures, also took upon itself the role of defending "American" traditions. Masons, Roman Catholics, Mormons, and other groups soon fell prey to this anti-intellectual bent.

The Nativist press saw these minority groups as un-American conspirators, and in true crusading fashion set out to destroy the threats "in sensational exposes, [and] in countless fantasies of treason and mysterious criminality. . . ."[30] Nativists attacked the Mormons, as they did the Masons and Roman Catholics, less in terms of rivalry between divine and satanic powers than in terms of a supposed threat of secret conspiracy, an approach that gave Nativists occasion for many irrational acts. At a time when ministers and journalists were decrying the increase in immorality, emphasis given in Nativist literature to "licentious subversives" offered a convenient means of ascribing to minority groups guilt for the ills of society in general. The wrongs of individuals or the nation could be transferred to the enemy, thus allowing Nativist indignation to be vented on small, sometimes disorganized and defenseless groups.

The venom of the attack produced a fiery counterattack by the minority groups. The *Wasp* was conscious of the task before it. In the "Introductory" to the new publication, its editor commented,

> We are a community of people at whom the shafts of slander are levelled and missiles of the wicked unsparingly hurled. The public press is daily teeming with slanders, foul calumnies, and base misrepresentations; and every effort is made, by the base and unprincipled, to turn the tide of popular opinion against us, to misconstrue our movements and desecrate our characters. Shall this state of things be suffered longer to exist without some channel through which we can convey correct information to the world and thereby disabuse the public mind as to the many slanders that are constantly perpetrated against us?[31]

William Smith proceeded to explain that the *Wasp* would endeavor to act defensively in dealing with its opponents, but that when it did speak it would manifest a bold and determined spirit becoming to its station and worthy of its cause. It was not, however, Smith's aim to sink to the *"low scurrility"* that often characterized partisan editors.[32]

Once his desire to defend the Mormon faith was clearly announced, Smith worked to expand its platform. By the end of 1842 the *Wasp* doubled its size and changed its name to the *Nauvoo*

Neighbor, with the promise that it would continue to mind its own business and not interfere with the rights of others "either politically or religiously," and would keep all of its activities in harmony with its new name.[33]

The paper's growth in size was matched by the desire to improve the quality of its content. The *Neighbor* planned to have various sources of news. It announced that it was seeking an exchange agreement with principal European newspapers, that it already had such an exchange with the most important United States weeklies, and that its facilities for obtaining information through traveling Mormon missionaries would make it "second to none in the West."[34]

The editor's dynamic leadership did not stop with these changes. In somewhat of a contradiction to an earlier position, the paper turned its attention to politics and directly supported Joseph Smith's candidacy for the office of U.S. President in the 1844 election Believing him to be a sincere candidate, the *Neighbor's* editor declared that he hoped to bolster support of Smith's aim by sending the *Neighbor* "into every district, city, village and hamlet throughout the length and breadth of the Union." He called upon everyone to obtain as many subscribers as possible and thereby help secure Smith's election. the editor exclaimed, "We have a great and mighty object before us; and union, energy and untiring industry of all will effect its glorious consummation."[35] The little weekly lacked sufficient circulation to significantly influence the election, and with the death of its candidate just eight days after its ambitious statement, the *Neighbor* lost the opportunity to mount a concerted campaign to elevate Smith to the presidency. What it did succeed in doing was to continue the spread of apprehension about the policies and aims of the Mormon Prophet.

From the time that Thomas C. Sharp purchased the *Warsaw Signal* in the spring of 1841, the Mormons had been faced with vitriolic criticism in their immediate vicinity.[36] And a hostile press became the catalyst that touched off a series of events leading to the death of the Mormon Prophet and the Saints' eventual expulsion from their homes in Nauvoo.

Curiously, it was to be a newspaper within the walls of the Mormon city itself, published by formerly high-ranking Saints, that brought Joseph Smith to his death. William Law, a former counselor to Joseph Smith, his brother Wilson, a brigadier-general in the city's army, and several other prominent Church leaders and

businessmen withdrew from the Church and, buying a press, resolved to set up an opposition newspaper. They explained that
they had sought a reformation from within the Church to avoid
exposing Smith's alleged crimes to the public, but that their petitions
had been treated with contempt.[37] In a letter to the editor of the
Warsaw Signal, Francis Higbee, an associate of the Law brothers,
outlined the aims of the anticipated sheet and emphasized that it
would oppose both Smith's political "Kingdom" and polygamy:

> We shall issue the last week in this month. The paper I think
> we will call the *Nauvoo Expositor;* for it will be fraught with Joe's
> peculiar and particular mode of Legislation . . . and a dissertation
> upon his delectable plan of Government; and above all, it shall be
> the organ through which we will herald his *Mormon* ribaldry.[38]

The first and only number of the *Expositor* appeared on the
streets of Nauvoo on 7 June 1844. It attacked the practice of
polygamy, the Prophet's political views, and his candidacy for
the United States presidency. Its editors accused the Prophet of
autocratic methods, and declared, "We will not acknowledge any
man as king or lawgiver to the Church."

The Church now had to defend itself from internal as well as
external criticism. As mayor of Nauvoo, Smith had the city council
declare the *Expositor* a public nuisance and order its destruction.
Within three days the city marshall, John P. Green, backed by the
city militia, had successfully executed the order, including confiscation of all available copies of the sheet.

Contrary to the judgment of George R. Gayler, the destruction
of the *Expositor* was not "the most serious blunder committed
by the Mormons since their arrival in Illinois . . . ."[39] Smith had
to silence the apostate newspaper by force and run the risk of
repercussions from seeming to trespass on the rights of a free
press, or it would have prematurely exposed his plans and seriously
jeopardized his dreams for a political "Kingdom."[40]

News of the *Expositor's* suppression intensified the existing anti-
Mormon feelings throughout the State, especially in Hancock
County where the *Warsaw Signal* hastily but emphatically issued
a call to arms:

> We have only to state that this is sufficient! War and extermi-
> nation is inevitable! CITIZENS ARISE, ONE and ALL!! Can you
> stand by, and suffer such INFERNAL DEVILS! to ROB men of
> their property right, without avenging them? We have no time to

comment! Every man will make his own. LET IT BE WITH
POWDER AND BALL.[41]

The *Expositor's* publishers sued for a writ against Joseph and
Hyrum Smith on the charge of riot—a writ that eventually brought
the two brothers to their violent deaths.[42] To the Church leaders,
the destruction of the opposition press seemed necessary to the
salvation of the "Kingdom." Ultimately the death of the Smith
brothers probably bought valuable time for the Saints, for if they
had been driven from Nauvoo at that time rather than in 1846,
they would have been insufficiently prepared to cross the Mississippi
and seek new homes in the West.

In the leadership crisis following the death of Joseph Smith,
Brigham Young, president of the Council of the Twelve, used
the two Church papers to help secure in the minds of the saints
his claim that the Twelve Apostles were the proper heirs to Joseph
Smith's authority. Brigham Young was challenged in this position,
but the papers followed the strategy of not discrediting, and therefore not publicizing, the challengers by frontal attacks. Rather, they
sought to build confidence in Brigham Young and the Twelve by
minimizing the challenges and giving the readers a feeling of
harmony between the members of the Church and their new leader.[43]

Although the Mormons remained in Illinois almost two years
after the martyrdom of their Prophet, his death marked the beginning of the end of Nauvoo. By 1845 county and state authorities
would not, or could not, guarantee the security of the Mormon
city against an ever-increasing number of depredations.[44] Most
Illinois citizens got their impression of the Mormons from newspapers so filled with subjective, prejudicial arguments that it was
impossible to find an impartial view. Thus the Mormons were
forced to leave their homes in Illinois. Though it is difficult to
properly assess the blame, the anti-Mormon press, which constantly
and relentlessly called for expulsion, has been credited by at least
one student with playing the major role.[45]

The *Nauvoo Neighbor,* whose chief mission had been that of
Church apologist, apparently came to the same conclusion. In its
final issue it confessed its inability to pacify the Church's enemies
and correct misrepresentations being made about the Mormons:

> It may be thought by some that this step of discontinuing the
> *Neighbor,* is premature, but when it is understood that the people
> of the United States gloat themselves upon *"public opinion,"* and

that opinion, is put in motion and reiterated by men who could whisper, *sub rosa,* that "it was well that Joseph Smith was killed, for he would revolutionize the world with Mormonism," it will be considered a wise move, for why need we expend money and time, to warn a nation that already is grating its teeth at us, and menacing a threat by a conventional nod, *to be gone* or we will blot you out from under heaven?[46]

Four months after the *Neighbor* suspended publication, the *Times and Seasons,* bitter about the treatment received by the Church from the "old settlers" of Illinois and state and national authorities, wrote its own obituary. It announced that all was in preparation for the great move of the Saints beyond the borders of the United States. "It is reduced to a solemn reality," wrote the editor, "that the rights and property, as well as the lives and common religious belief of the Church of Jesus Christ of Latter-day Saints, *cannot be protected* in the realms of the United States. . . ." Continuing, the editor indicated that the migrants would stop somewhere between the Mississippi and the Pacific, where they themselves would become the "old-settlers," and concluded, "May God continue the spirit of fleeing from false freedom, and false dignity, till every Saint is removed to where he can sit under his own vine and fig tree without having any to molest or make afraid. *Let us go—Let us go."*[47]

The exodus from Nauvoo has to be explained in both positive and negative terms. Although the Mormons, in keeping with the expansion impulse of the 1840s, fled *to* the Rocky Mountains to build an empire, they also fled *from* the unquestionably inhospitable and severe treatment they had received in the Midwest. The ever-rising tide of persecution that the Mormon press had failed to counteract forced them out of the permanent location of "Zion" and to temporary asylum where they expected trouble only from Indians and wild animals. Even Brigham Young, the builder of the Great Basin, hoped to return to Missouri to establish the "Kingdom" and to be buried there if his hopes should be realized.[48]

The restless history of the Mormons in Ohio, Missouri, and Illinois explains the transitory nature of their early publications and to a large degree also documents the failure of their press to allay the fears of non-Mormons and to convince their enemies, both internal and external, that their motives were acceptable. However, these early Mormon periodicals provided guidance to the Church membership as well as a record for study by future historians. Like the Waldenses, the Mormons were their own historians. Their journals and newspapers remain as evidence of a literate people battling for their convictions, and constitute rich source material for anyone seeking to determine if their literature, like that of the Waldenses, vindicates a persecuted religious minority. These Midwestern publications also set the general patterns of nineteenth-century Mormon journalism and gave Mormons valuable experience in the rudiments of journalism and the power of the press, experience that would later be used in the Great Basin.

Footnotes

1. William Warren Sweet, *The Story of Religions in America* (New York: Harper and Brothers, 1930), pp. 374-75.
2. The Book of Mormon (Salt Lake City, Utah: The Church of Jesus Christ of Latter-day Saints, 1976), pp. iii-iv.
3. Joseph Smith, Jr., *History of the Church of Jesus Christ of Latter-day Saints,* Period I: History of Joseph Smith the Prophet, by Himself, ed. B. H. Roberts, third edition (Salt Lake City, Utah: Deseret Book Company, 1948), 1: 217.
4. Quoted in Elbert A. Smith, "Forerunners of the Saints' Herald," *Saints' Herald* 52 (26 January 1910): 81.
5. *The Evening and the Morning Star,* June 1832 (hereafter referred to as *Star).*
6. For example, *see Star,* July 1832.
7. Klaus J. Hansen, *Quest for Empire: The Political Kingdom of God and the Council of Fifty in Mormon History* (East Lansing: Michigan State University Press, 1967), pp. 18, 149-50.
8. *Star,* July 1833.
9. Richard L. Bushman, "The Mormon Persecutions in Missouri, 1833," *Brigham Young University Studies* 3 (Autumn, 1960): 12-14.
10. *Latter Day Saints' Messenger and Advocate,* February 1837 (hereafter referred to as *Advocate).*
11. Ibid., May 1835.
12. Ibid., July 1837.
13. *Elder's Journal,* November 1837.
14. Franklin D. Daines, "Separatism in Utah, 1847-1870," *Annual Report of the American Historical Association for 1917,* 58 (1920): 334.
15. Prospectus of *Elder's Journal,* in *Advocate,* August 1837. The persecution of the Mormons, though not as extensive and intensive, nor carried on for nearly as long, was much like that of the Waldenses. This is especially true with the Utah period.
16. *Elder's Journal,* August 1838.
17. Ibid., July, 1838.
18. The press was buried in Far West to protect it from Mormon enemies.
19. This was the same press used in Far West, Missouri, to print the *Elder's Journal.* It was exhumed by Smith and Robinson and carried to Illinois. *See* Robinson's "Valedictory," *Times and Season's,* 15 February 1842.
20. Smith, *History of the Church,* 4: 454, 463. Apostle Willard Richards, later the first editor of the Utah Church paper *Deseret News,* was to pro-

cure a press and type and publish a paper for the Church if Robinson refused to turn over the *Times and Seasons.*

21. Smith, *History of the Church,* 4: 503, 514.

22. The *Times and Seasons,* 15 March 1842.

23. The *Times and Seasons,* 15 October 1841, boasted that the paper circulated in every state and territory of the United States as well as in parts of Canada and Europe.

24. *Chicago Democrat,* 25 March 1840.

25. *Star,* August 1832. Little space was ever given in the *Star* itself to advertisements beyond those publicizing the Church's own publications.

26. Of the five advertisements in the 15 November 1840 issue, four were notices of patent medicines kept in stock by the *Times and Seasons* editors themselves. Patent medicine advertisements appeared only four other times after November 1840, soon after which all notices disappeared permanently.

27. The *Millennial Star* was published continuously for 130 years, from 1840 through 1970, when it was suspended as a result of a consolidation of Church publications.

28. The *Times and Seasons,* 1 June 1845.

29. *Wasp,* 16 April 1842.

30. David Brion Davis, "Some Themes of Counter-Subversion: An Analysis of Anti-Masonic, Anti-Catholic, and Anti-Mormon Literature," *Mississippi Valley Historical Review* 47 (September, 1960): 207.

31. *Wasp,* 16 April 1842.

32. Ibid.

33. *Nauvoo Neighbor,* 9 May 1843.

34. Ibid.

35. Ibid., 19 June 1844. In addition to the *Wasp* and the *Neighbor,* the Church had two other weeklies in the 1840s—the *Prophet* and its successor, the *Messenger,* which published continuously from May 1844 to February 1846 in New York City. Primarily religious newspapers, they carried a fair amount of general news, and the *Prophet* was used to publicize Smith's presidential candidacy in New York, Boston, and Philadelphia.

36. Warsaw was located fifteen miles south of Nauvoo.

37. *Nauvoo Expositor,* 7 June 1844.

38. *Warsaw Signal,* 15 May 1844.

39. George R. Gayler, "The 'Expositor' Affair. Prelude to the Downfall of Joseph Smith," *Northwest State College Studies* 25(1 February 1961): 11.

40. The commonly held notion that the order to destroy the *Expositor* was illegal and infringed on a free press is convincingly refuted by Dallin H. Oaks in "Suppression of the *Nauvoo Expositor,*" *Utah Law Review* 9 (Winter 1965): 862-903.

41. *Warsaw Signal,* 12 June 1844.

42. Both Joseph Smith and his older brother Hyrum were killed 27 June 1844 in Carthage, Illinois. Two men who shared their prison cell and almost their fate were John Taylor, the editor of the *Times and Seasons* and the *Nauvoo Neighbor,* and Willard Richards, the Prophet's secretary and later the first editor of the *Deseret News.*

43. The *Times and Seasons,* September and October 1844. Brigham Young did not hold a monopoly on the recognition of the value of the press. Sidney Rigdon, his most serious immediate challenger, started publishing in October 1844 his *Messenger and Advocate* in Pittsburgh, Pennsylvania, in an attempt to strengthen his claims of leadership. Colonel George M. Hinkle, Church excommunicant since 1839, issued the first number of *The Ensign* (Buffalo, Iowa), 15 July 1844. Of the many schismatic groups resulting from the death of Smith, almost all took advantage of the press. For a listing *see* Loy Otis Banks, "Latter Day Saint Journalism," pp. 486-91.

44. Robert B. Flanders, *Nauvoo: Kingdom on the Mississippi* (Urbana: University of Illinois Press, 1965), p. 306.

45. Helen Fulton Snider, "Mormonism in Illinois: An Analysis of the Non-Mormon Press Materials 1838-1848" (unpublished master's thesis, State University of Iowa, Iowa City, 1933), p. 157.

46. *Nauvoo Neighbor,* 29 October 1845.

47. The *Times and Seasons,* 1 February 1846. Actually the *Times and Seasons* issued its last number 15 February 1846.

48. *Deseret News,* 3 September 1877.

2

Problems
of
Isolation

In Missouri and Illinois the Mormons looked for tranquility
and a permanent settlement in which to practice their beliefs. They
found neither. Refugees in a country that traditionally provided
a haven for refugees, this growing religious throng, like their
European ancestors before them, looked westward for a Utopia.
Unlike their adventurous predecessors who set out to cross a hostile
sea without a sure destination, the Mormons at least had a new
home to welcome them—the valley of the Great Salt Lake. The
site was not selected at random. During his lifetime Joseph Smith
had shown great interest in the West, and had indicated that one
day the Saints would go to the Rocky Mountains. While the first
prophet was not destined to lead the trek, his successor Brigham
Young took up Smith's dream of the western residence. When
it became obvious that the Saints would have to leave Nauvoo,
Young studied all available information and decided on the Great
Basin. The Mormons prepared to cross the Great Plains. The sus-
picion, hatred, and violence that had characterizeed the Mormons'
Midwest experience were replaced by the uncertainties of settling
a strange land: hard work and deprivation, with the ultimate hope
of peace to practice their religious beliefs without harassment.

Anti-Mormon opposition became so bitter that the planned spring exodus from Nauvoo turned into a winter escape. The first company of Mormon refugees crossed to the Iowa side of the Mississippi on 4 February 1846, just eleven days before the Church's *Times and Seasons* shut down its press. In the weeks and months to come, thousands more would follow. Brigham Young, establishing supply bases along the way, led some 15,000 exiles across Iowa to the Missouri River. Planning for their own needs and those of future arrivals, they cultivated large tracts of land and built hundreds of dwellings. By the spring of 1847, two "cities" had sprung into existence on the banks of the river, Kanesville (Council Bluffs, Iowa) on the east and Winter Quarters (Florence, Nebraska) on the west.

As with earlier Mormon settlements, a newspaper quickly followed the establishment of Kanesville. Called *The Frontier Guardian,* the new journal published its first issue on 7 February 1849. Its editor, Apostle Orson Hyde, who had recently returned from England where he had headed the *Millennial Star,* declared that the *Guardian* would devote itself to the topics of religion, prophecy, literature, art, and science, and strongly advocated the establishment of common schools along the frontier. The settlements on the Missouri, however, were never intended to be more than jumping-off stations for the Saints moving farther west. When Hyde sold the newspaper in February 1852 after most Mormons had left Kanesville for the Great Basin, it had been the spokesman of the Church in the Midwest for three years.

The Salt Lake Valley was largely an unknown area. Noted Western explorer John C. Fremont led Mormons to believe that the Great Basin was surrounded by lofty mountains and filled with rivers and lakes without outlet to the sea, unexplored deserts, and savage tribes. Temperatures often soared above one hundred and sometimes toppled to as low as thirty-two degrees below zero. Indeed, when the first Mormons to enter the valley questioned aged and seasoned pioneer Jim Bridger about the fertility of the soil, he said he would give $1,000.00 if he only knew there could be a single ear of corn grown there.

Once the Mormons were on the scene they observed that some sections of the basin abounded in rich black sandy soil and that rain was not totally absent. Nevertheless, the region was excessively dry and certain parts proved sterile and barren. It was not a site to arouse universal delight.[1] Why should the harassed Mormons choose such a site for their new home when other west-bound pioneers bypassed it for the more inhabitable environs of California and Oregon? The answer is not difficult to comprehend.

Having failed to permanently erect a Kingdom within American society, Mormons felt that only by limiting their contacts with gentiles could they hope to achieve freedom to practice their religion. They sought a place no others would covet, a place where, as one of their hymns declared, "None would come to hurt or make afraid."[2] Young reasoned that attractive areas like California and Oregon would draw large numbers of gentiles. He therefore resisted strong and repeated appeals to settle on the Pacific Coast and chose instead the seclusion he felt was necessary for the growth of the religious Kingdom.

Even before the exodus from Illinois, Mormon leaders laid careful plans to cope with the harsh reality of their isolation. Physical seclusion was not meant to carry over into intellectual isolation or into depriving the Saints of the Church's official written word. In the interest of providing his followers with proper and needed reading, Brigham Young pleaded with immigrating Mormons to bring with them books about the world's affairs. More significantly, he commissioned W. W. Phelps, editor of the first Church periodical, to raise money for the purchase of printing equipment to publish his own books and to establish a newspaper.[3] This task, like those delegated to other builders of the new sanctuary, was to prove a difficult one.

Armed with letters of introduction from Brigham Young, Phelps accepted the challenge. In one letter Young explained that those who planned to follow him to the Rocky Mountains could not be exalted in the next life without knowledge because it was through obedience to knowledge that they received their blessings. The extent of a Saint's knowledge helped determine the degree of his exaltation. Young trusted that his statement of this principle would be enough to persuade the Saints to help Phelps get the necessary equipment to provide their children with books and themselves with new and inspiring reading.[4] If the Saints wanted this "Intelligence of Eternity" to flow from the "proper source," Young insisted, they would have to receive Phelps and assist him in his "Journey of noble Enterprize."[5]

When Phelps received this assignment, he was living with Young and the Mormons at Winter Quarters. He could easily have bought a press in St. Louis or Cincinnati—but he was broke. He therefore undertook a "mission" to the east coast, where he collected enough money from the faithful to enable him to buy a small Ramage hand press in Boston. By November 1847, Phelps had the press back in the Mormon settlements on the Missouri River, ready for transportation to the mountains the following spring. Brigham Young, however, felt compelled to give priority to people over machinery, and as much as he wanted to have printing equipment in the new location, it was left behind. In a letter from Chimney Rock, Nebraska, on his second trip to Utah, Young explained his actions to the anxious Church leaders of the small but growing settlement in the Salt Lake Valley:

> You must not be disappointed in not seeing the printing presses, type, paper, mill irons, mill stones, carding machines, etc., as I had fully calculated on the teams that you sent from the valley bringing them on. We have the poor with us; their cry was urgent to go to the mountains, and I could neither close my ears nor harden my heart against their earnest appeals. . . . I am disappointed in not bringing the presses, etc., but I can not avoid it; it is out of my power to do everything. . . .[6]

Church authorities in the Great Basin, while aware of the reasons for the delay, continued to ask that the printing press and materials be forwarded from Winter Quarters.[7] But transportation remained an acute problem in the impoverished settlements of western Iowa. The difficulty was finally solved by a general donation of goods and money from local Mormons. In May 1849, three ox-drawn wagons, loaded with Church property, including a printing press, type, glue, stationery, ink, and 872 bundles of newsprint, left for the West under the supervision of Howard Egan, a trusted and experienced overland wagon boss.[8]

Egan carried with him a letter to Brigham Young from apostles Orson Hyde, George A. Smith, and Ezra T. Benson, that foreshadowed the attitude the Church paper in Utah would have toward reporting on national political events. The letter explained that some fifteen bundles of poor quality printing paper had been kept in Iowa because they were hardly fit even for the printing of politics. The apostles also expressed the hope that they would soon receive from Salt Lake City a neatly printed newspaper filled with instruction and counsel for the scattered Saints.[9]

After more than a thousand miles of rivers, mountains, and deserts, and approximately ninety days and nights punctuated by the threat of disease, Indians, bad weather, and hundreds of "forty-niners," Egan and company arrived in the Salt Lake Valley.

The printing material for a newspaper was finally in the Basin, ready to spread the Church's message to the Saints.[10]

Running parallel with the task of propagating the faith was that of forming a new government. Between the end of the Mexican War and the Compromise of 1850, when Utah received its territorial status, Brigham Young organized and set in motion the "State of Deseret." The word *deseret*, taken from the Book of Mormon and interpreted as meaning *honey bee*, motivated the adoption of the beehive (symbolizing cooperative industry) as the emblem of almost everything Mormon in the Great Basin. When Egan's press, which found its home in the gable-roofed adobe mint in Salt Lake City, published its first issue of a newspaper on 15 June 1850, it naturally was called the *Deseret News*.[11]

On most frontiers the printing press, stimulated by a spirit of speculation and optimism, appeared very early among the institutions of civilized life. It served as an important unifying element of urban culture and as a catalyst for changing an undisciplined frontier group into a responsible and disciplined entity. Mormon settlements, unlike those of most frontiers, were by their nature close-knit, compact, and founded by people motivated almost solely by religion, much like those of their Puritan ancestors. In Utah, the Church not only was the first institution to develop, but also was by far the most powerful and influential element in the society. Indeed, the Utah printing materials and press, because of the isolated nature of the Great Basin, did not even arrive until two years after the first town was founded.

Once on the scene, the Church press encountered problems never acute in the Mormon Midwest publication experience. Prior to the Utah period, Mormon troubles had centered around their gentile neighbors. Now, with such enemies left behind for a time, their struggle against men was replaced by their struggle with nature. Not only had the difficulty of finding, purchasing, and transporting the printing press been intensified by the remoteness of Utah, but the effects of isolation continued to shape and permeate the very life and development of the *Deseret News*. These journalistic Mormon pioneers had to struggle with the difficulty of gathering news, the scarcity of supplies and materials needed to print the paper, and an audience often financially unable to subscribe to the fledgling enterprise.

News gathering, a major function of any newspaper, was to exasperate the *Deseret News*. Unlike most newspapers, its "local" news came from scattered communities throughout the Great Basin, instead of from a single town. National and foreign information was even more difficult to come by. Willard Richards, the first editor of the *Deseret News,*[12] explained to Mormons that because they were so removed from the East they could not hope to see everything at once despite the fact that they lived on the tops of the mountains. He assured his readers that he gathered up old and current news items as fast as possible.[13]

As fast as possible was at best a rather slow process in early Utah. One source said the information used in the columns of the first issue of the *News* arrived in Salt Lake City by wagon from the Missouri River after thirty-nine hurried days of travel.[14] During the winter, travel was slower still, and Utah sometimes had no contact with the outside world for months. "News, very scarce at this season of the year," wrote Richards in December 1850, "all foreign news frozen."[15] The California mail in 1852 was delayed as much as fifty days in crossing the Sierras.[16]

Methods of obtaining news were many and varied, and the *News* used them all, from traveling agents to pioneer passers-by. As with earlier Mormon newspapers, the *Deseret News* was showered with correspondence from missionaries serving from one end of the globe to the other. Its editor encouraged the "brethren" in Utah and those "in the world" to furnish communications and correspondence for the *News,* promising that they would thereby enrich its columns with a variety of style and an amount of information "attainable in no other way."[17] As was the common practice with all early newspapers, the *News* had a large number of exchanges, including newspapers from all over the world, and filled its columns with "clippings" from these.[18] While such news was most welcome, it was something that could not always be relied upon.

News editor Willard Richards reported that he did not receive regular files of exchange papers from the East. This was not a simple problem of transportation—as he claimed that the postmaster at Laramie retained for his own use newspapers and magazines bound for Salt Lake City. The editor complained that this disjointed and unreliable service kept him ignorant of world events simply because he was only able to read an occasional paper. Lamenting, Richards feared he would remain uninformed until, as he wrote, "the lightning rods, railroad cars, and balloons run daily and hourly between the mountains and vallies, with fewer stopping places on the route, where the transports are liable to be picked by the crows, black crickets and gulls."[19]

The United States Government postal service was deserving of some criticism. Utah was supposed to receive regular monthly government mail deliveries, but it generally took two months for mail to arrive, and on at least one occasion communications were nine months late. The *News* described this chronic problem as "gross injustice, miserable mismanagement, . . . foul corruption and fogyism." In a heated editorial it further explained that the despicable manner in which 50,000 isolated citizens were supplied with the mail was a disgrace to the government and a matter of great inconvenience, disappointment, and loss, fully appreciated only by those who had experienced it, as had the inhabitants of Utah.[20] The *News* hinted as early as 15 October 1853 that if "UNCLE SAM, Bro. JONATHAN, or anybody" would send it regular mails, it would attempt to put out a daily paper, but concluded, "till then be satisfied, we can do no more."

In fact, a solution was at hand, but government action negated it. The Brigham Young Express and Carrying Company (the "YX Company"), a Church cooperative, had been organized in 1857 to provide quick and regular passenger, freight, and mail service. Its efficiency could be measured by its first mail delivery between Salt Lake City and Independence, Missouri, a feat accomplished in twenty-six days. Had the venture been allowed to continue, it might very well have solved some news-gathering problems. But alas, Washington's fear of Mormon disloyalty led to the cancellation of the YX Company's federal mail contract before it was even six months old. With this communal effort to overcome problems of isolation nipped in the bud, the *News* did not grow into a "regular" daily for another ten years. However, with the coming of the pony express in 1860, mail began to arrive quite regularly about every ten days, and by mid-October of 1861 the *News* was printing daily "Extras," (*The Pony Dispatch*), which some have considered to be the first daily paper in Utah.[21]

Even though the *News* expressed satisfaction with the Pony Express for the time being, its real hopes lay in the coming of the telegraph, which reached Utah in 1861 and made the Mormon capital just a wire's tick from New York, Washington, and San Francisco. Maintaining this shrunken distance between Young's remote empire and the outside world, however, proved difficult. In addition to the problems created by deep snowfalls, immigrants caught in snowstorms burned telegraph poles to keep from freezing, while other travelers apparently used the wire as a ferry cable across rivers. Indians, not always superstitious of the wires, were known to destroy the lines for various reasons, and herds of buffalo could play havoc with the new communication system.[22] Consequently, telegraph wires in early Utah were often dead for days and sometimes weeks at a time.

The communication problems, however, hampered the production of the *Deseret News* less than the scarcity of newsprint. Within five months after the first issue, the weekly had to become a semi-monthly for a while because of "lack of paper."[23] The uncertain and inadequate supply of foolscap caused the newspaper to suspend publication for periods of time ranging from a week to as much as three months.[24] Once it cut the number of pages it published from eight to four, asserting that "Half a loaf [was] better than no loaf."[25]

To overcome this continual threat to the very life of the paper, a problem caused by the sheer distance from the outside world and complicated by snow, mountains, Indians, and undependable freighters, the Church developed a successful local paper industry which became the first effective paper mill in the trans-Mississippi West.

The ingredients for this new endeavor were found among the faithful. Rags constituted the raw material for paper manufacturing, and the Church and its newspaper carried on a joint effort to furnish the mill with a steady supply. The *Deseret News* cried, "RAGS! RAGS!! RAGS!!! Save your rags, everybody in Deseret save your rags; old wagon covers, tents, quilts, shirts, etc., etc., are wanted for paper. . . ."[26] Reminiscent of American Revolutionary times, when saving rags was urged as a duty, Mormon bishops were asked to instruct their respective wards (congregations) as to the need for rags and, further, to see that they were forthcoming.[27] Brigham Young sent George Goddard, a rather prominent merchant and Church stalwart, on a "rag mission." For over three years, from Franklin, Idaho, in the north to Sanpete, Utah, in the south, Goddard foraged weekdays from house to house soliciting rags, and on Sundays preached "rag sermons." In fact, his first speech in the Salt Lake City Tabernacle was a "rag discourse," backed up and enlarged upon by talks from Young and his counselor Heber C. Kimball.[28] In a later Tabernacle discourse, Young explained the value of rags and severely criticized those Mormon women who wasted them. He accused the female Saints of preferring to throw their rags away instead of saving them. Young questioned whether or not there was a mother in the community that thought she was so well off that she did not need the extra money from saving rags. Answering himself, he charged that many of them would rather steal beef and other things they need than stoop to pick up rags to make paper on which to print the *Deseret News*.[29]

The paper manufactured locally was generally coarse in texture and dark gray in color, making the print on it difficult to read in candlelight,[30] a feature not uncommon among Western newspapers. The *News* explained that the color of the paper resulted from the inability to bleach dark rags at the factory. It announced, "dark grey is better than no paper," but threatened that the poorer of the two alternatives would soon be the case if all *News* patrons and non-*News* patrons alike did not gather up and bring in their rags.[31] The demand quite often outstripped the supply.

The *News* was forced at times to import newsprint, even though it preferred to patronize the Church mills in spite of the fact that the Church paper cost more than paper from the East.[32] The benefits of manufacturing paper directly in Utah were considered incalculable by the *News*. It would not only keep thousands of dollars from leaving Utah, but would make paper more readily available and, if necessary, purchasable on credit. Suggesting an additional advantage, the *News* claimed that but a quarter as much printing had been done as would have been done if paper were manufactured in Utah.[33] Though it did not overcome the paper shortage that killed many individually owned papers in the West, the Church, through efforts like the paper mill, made significant inroads in that problem.

Another problem was that the *Deseret News,* like most early newspapers of the nineteenth-century American West, was produced on a hand press.[34] Occasional squawkers about slow production were quickly reminded that the *News* lacked a power press, such as was used in eastern American cities, and that with a hand press it was a full day's work for a good pressman to strike off enough papers to supply even those subscribers who called for their paper directly at the office.[35] However, increased subscriptions eventually enabled the Church to secure what was a rather rare item in the early West—a steam press.[36] This power press printed eighteen times as fast as the old manual press.[37]

The improvement speeded printing, but securing readers remained a constant concern. Subscribers are a major source of support for any newspaper, but on the frontier they were difficult to obtain. In the beginning of publication of the *News,* most bishops of the Church acted as its emissaries, but the paper soon asked that all Church officials, including the Council of the Twelve and the Seven Presidents of Seventies, consider themselves agents and use every opportunity to encourage subscription.[38]

Not all agents were Church officials, however, and these were paid what one Church leader called a "liberal per centage for a very small amount of time and attention. . . ."[39] In criticizing slothful *News* representatives in 1859, the editor said that if they were good businessmen like they should be they could devise ways of increasing their number of subscriptions and thus, through the 20 percent they got for their labors, make a "handsome profit. . . ."[40] A later editor used a different approach, appealing to the strong religious commitment among Mormons. He agreed that an agent's commission was "no great business item," but quickly emphasized that all persons connected with the *News* had one great object and end: to serve, which they had never attempted to reduce to a matter of money.[41]

Church officials, who considered the *News* invaluable to the people of Utah, strongly encouraged increasing circulation. Heber C. Kimball, first counselor of Brigham Young, emphasized that although the paper contained interesting and instructive local and foreign news items, its most important function was to make counsel and teachings of the Church hierarchy available to the public. For this Church leader, a single sermon was worth more than the cost of many copies of the newspaper. In his argument Kimball hit upon what was perhaps the most significant aspect of the *News.* He explained that because memories were often undependable and because comparatively few could assemble in the Tabernacle to hear Church leaders, the printed word, which could be read and pondered on again and again and handed down from generation to generation, was of priceless value.[42]

The Church could have been proud of their efforts to build subscription. *News* circulation rose from about 220 in 1850 to 667 a year later and, growing at a phenomenal rate, reached 4,000 by 1856.[43] However, because of the importance of the paper, ecclesiastical leaders hoped that each head of family in Utah Territory would take at least one subscription to the paper.[44] Consequently, the *News* used many kinds of inducements to build subscription. At first it promised any person who would send in four subscriptions for six months at the regular rate, free copies for the same length of time.[45] Later, however, and rather contradictorily it condemned what it called "The Gift Enterprize System" for subscription recruitment and said that the proper thing would be to reduce the rates rather than make subscribers pay for the copies that went to agents for their services.[46] The *News* invited all those who loved their own history, the teachings of the "only TRUE theologians" of the day, and current events to take the Church paper, "that intelligence may illume our happy vales as broadly, as fully, and as freely as does the genial radiance of the bright beams of an unclouded morning's sun."[47] The editor even suggested to farmers who doubted they could afford the *News* that they keep one more hen than usual as an easy way of raising the necessary cost.[48]

In this struggle to grow, the *News* claimed that it practiced no deception and resorted to no subterfuges to induce subscription, preferring instead to stand on its own merits.[49] In fact, at one point the *News* condemned the *Christian Advocate* for playing upon the fears and sympathies of religious people in an attempt to increase subscription. The *Advocate,* according to the *News,* explained to a patron who failed to resubscribe and pay his $2.70 that his mother had read the paper even before he was born and had long gone to paradise. Then it stressed, "This year's *Advocate* may guide your feet safely to the same heaven. Brother can you afford to . . . quench this light for $2.70?"[50]

Despite the *News's* criticism of the *Advocate's* tactics, its own most common inducement to increase subscription was to arouse its patrons' sense of duty. Many newspapers, especially those on the frontier, expected and received a certain amount of support from the people acting out of obligation. For example, the Boulder, Colorado, *County News* explained that Boulderites should patronize their town paper because it was a mining and agricultural paper devoted to their own interests.[51] "It has been taken for granted," wrote the *News* editor in accounting for why his paper was not filled with constant duns to patrons, "that every Saint would subscribe, and do the best he could about payment, as he would do upon a mission, in paying tithing, or in performing any other duty pertaining to salvation."[52] The editor was convinced of this policy and could not understand why some Mormons read papers other than the *News.* The mere fact that it was owned by and conducted for the Church was cause enough for them to take it and pay for it, if for no other reason than to support the Church of which they professed to be members.[53] Noting that from its inception the *News* had advocated Mormon principles, the paper explained that all Latter-day Saints should feel an obligation to do their part in sustaining it.[54]

The *News* had many other reasons why a patron should take the paper, besides his duty as a Church member. The editor in 1872 felt it "Hardly Suitable" to publish a list of "Seven reasons why every family in Utah should take the *Deseret News*," sent in by one "H. T. K.," claiming that "modesty" forbade such action.[55] However, a successor to the editorial chair felt no such compunction in 1891 and under the bold letters "WHY THE DESERET NEWS SHOULD BE SUBSCRIBED FOR IN PREFERENCE TO ANY OTHER PAPER" he listed eleven rather interesting and insightful reasons.

> 1. It is the Organ of the Church of Jesus Christ of Latter-day Saints, and the views, wishes and instructions of the Church Authorities are expressed, and given to the Saints.
> 2. It may always be depended upon as advocating . . . the right side of every question proper for public journals to treat upon.
> 3. It is devoted to the interest of the Latter day Saints. . . .
> 4. It is not published for speculation. . . .
> 5. It is doing its utmost to establish home industries. . . .
> 6. There is no danger of any subscriber . . . failing to get what he subscribes for. . . .
> 7. It is now printed throughout in new and readable type. . . .
> 8. It is free from objectionable advertisement. . . .
> 9. Its tone is not regulated by public opinion. . . .
> 10. It never nauseates its readers by palming off columns of self-praise for news items.
> 11. The NEWS practices no deception. . . .[56]

These arguments made in 1891 would have made sense to most Mormons of any period of time. For quite understandable reasons, however, the influence of such arguments on circulation in early Utah would not likely have been profound. Utah's remote location contributed greatly to the local cost of living, and the common excuse given for not taking the *News* was that its rates were so high people could not afford it. Mark Twain, in reporting his two-day visit in Salt Lake City in 1861 explained, "We had learned that we were at last in a pioneer land, in absolute and

tangible reality. The high prices charged for trifles were eloquent. . . ." Reflecting on costs encountered before reaching the
Basin, he continued, "We had always been used to half-dimes
and 'five cents' worth' as the minimum of financial negotiations;
but in Salt Lake if one wanted a . . . peach, or a candle, or a
newspaper, or a shave, or a little Gentile whiskey . . . twenty-
five cents was the price, every time."[57]

At first the Church paper cost its readers fifteen cents a copy
or five dollars a year. The annual rate rose to six dollars in 1853,
but by 1867 had returned to five. These rates were high when
compared to eastern U. S. newspapers, and the readers of the
News complained. Even though it came out daily except Sunday
in 1851, the *New York Times* sold for only one cent a copy and
four dollars a year. Ten years later, after doubling in size and
adding a Sunday edition, the *Times* charged its readers seven
dollars per annum. The *Minnesota Democrat* of St. Paul, a "frontier" weekly, though much less isolated than the Great Basin
frontier, cost only two dollars a year in the midnineteenth century.

On 6 March 1852, the *News* admitted its price was high, but
rightly insisted that it was at least as cheap and maybe cheaper,
in proportion to cost, than other things in the Territory. *The
Owyhee Avalanche,* an Idaho weekly the size of the *Deseret News,*
charged its patrons twice as much as did the Mormon newspaper.
In answer to the complaints that it was more expensive than the
popular weeklies in the East, its foreman, Arieh C. Brower, presented a few facts in a letter that he felt the "wise" ought to
hear. The type in the East was set by boys and girls, explained
Brower, "at a scanty pittance per week," and the paper was printed
by steam at a rate of 20,000 to 60,000 sheets per hour, making
the cost of production "inconceivable." Through various kinds of
inducements, argued the foreman, circulation of Eastern papers
was swelled to hundreds of thousands and every cent had to be
"paid in *cash,* in *advance."* And paper in the East cost from two
to three dollars per ream while in Utah it was as high as ten
dollars.[58]

Mormons were not unique in their concern about the cost of
subscription. As a rule few early settlers anywhere could afford
to buy a newspaper, and in many cases a newspaper was such a
rarity that it was passed among friends until its lines became il-
legible before it was thrown away.[59] Naturally, the *News* was
normally opposed to readers' borrowing. It claimed that it was

possible for every family to have a newspaper of its own if it wanted it, and reported hearing complaints that patrons' papers were often worn out by their neighbors before the subscriber had an opportunity to read them. "When your neighbor asks for your newspaper to read during the night," wrote the editor on 20 March 1852, "ask him to lend you his horse to ride through the night, and he will see at once that your request is the most reasonable, inasmuch as he is able to buy a newspaper, and you are not able to buy a horse." However, four years later the *News* editor changed his view: "It is presumed that all can be accommodated," he wrote, "at least through the neighborly principle of loaning."[60] This turn in philosophy did not result from a substantial growth in subscriptions—instead, a shortage of supplies that reduced the number of copies printed in 1858 perhaps best accounts for this temporary shift.

Though money was scarce and subscription rates were high, it was a matter of priorities, and Church leaders as a rule had little patience with those who persisted in the idea that they could not manage to purchase the *News*. To the exclamation, "Well really, br. Smith, I cannot afford it," Apostle George A. Smith replied, "Cannot afford it? How much does your tobacco cost you a year?"[61] *News* foreman Brower merely questioned, "Shall the Saints value the instructions of the servants of God with money? Or murmur to bear their burdens of the Kingdom?"[62]

The continual efforts of Mormon authorities to stimulate reading in the Great Basin were considerably undermined by the common frontier characteristics of low incomes and little leisure time. However, though this problem of subscription, acute in any frontier society, was by no means overcome, it was unquestionably alleviated by the appeal the Church-owned *News* made to the sense of duty of a rather uniquely dedicated people.

As a matter of fact, faced with the problems of subscriptions, communication, and newsprint, it is almost unbelievable that the *Deseret News* survived at all. Early frontier newspapers had a tremendously high death rate, double that of papers in the first part of the twentieth century. Actually, any newspaper that survived more than a few years in the West was a unique institution.[63] Utah's newspaper casualty rate at times approached 90 percent.[64] In a 5 January 1893 article discussing newspaper longevity, the *News* explained that Salt Lake City was entitled to the unique distinction of being the "newspaper cemetery and journalistic rocky road" of the Territory. Although editors started newspapers with intention of permanence, the *News* explained why they so often failed:

> [They] make their appearance, fling their banners to the breeze, boldly proclaim their principles, and then start in with sleeves rolled up to mould, carve and polish public opinion. And they all do stay—as long as they can. Full soon they find out that they did not begin with money enough and that the sheriff is too persistent and importunate a fellow to be held at arm's length continually.

The *News* claimed Napoleon had said that the three things needed most in conducting a war were, first, money; second, money; and third, money. Concluding its article the Church paper commented that the same could well be said of newspapers.

Where did the *Deseret News* obtain its financing? One source of capital, of course, was subscription. Unfortunately, however, not all newspaper customers were paying customers. Delinquent subscribers were the bane of newspaper publishers all over nineteenth-century America, including Utah. Lamenting this fact *News* editor Albert Carrington told his Mormon patrons, "It is rather singular that occasion for comments on breaking promises should be found among those whose faith requires their yea to be yea and their nay to be nay, but so it is."[65] Carrington announced in 1864 that the *News* was seriously hampered by the numerous petty accounts on its books which had accumulated to the "useful" sum of $51,000, and stated, "Readers, do you wonder that at times we feel sore?"[66]

Had the *News* subscription been limited to those with cash only, the paper would have had few customers indeed. Cash was scarce on any frontier, and, struggling to keep the wolf from the door, newspapers offered to take almost any variety of produce except "poor babies."[67] The *News* explained that it would accept as payment for the paper virtually everything in the provision line, at market prices.[68] At one point its list of acceptable articles included "Butter, Cheese, Eggs, Fowls, Ducks, Geese, Snipes, Prairie-chickens, Bears, Molasses, Pork, Mutton, Wood, Poles, Corn, Oats, Shingles, Lumber . . . and every good thing. . . ."[69] The *News* announced in 1856 that laborers could pay for the paper by working on the Big Cottonwood Canal and presenting to Judge Elias Smith, who was also the *News* business manager, a certificate of hours.[70] Next best to cash were items that helped the Church operate the *News,* and it was common to see such requests as "Glue wanted immediately. Save all your cattle's feet and pates, and make glue. Printers' rollers cannot be made without glue; will you make us some?" and "Will some of our friends bring us a little tallow to light our midnight hours, while we are searching after news for their pleasure? How can we work without light?"[71]

Another essential requirement in the functioning of the *News* was some kind of pay for its workers. In many Church-controlled enterprises in Utah all officers except the secretary and treasurer were required to serve without pay.[72] This was even true to some extent with common employees who were told not to ask, "How much shall I have for my labor?"[73] *News* employees were paid, but rarely in cash. In 1856 it was said that the laborers on the newspaper were rationed on half a pound of "sickly looking" bread stuff per day, and they were sinking for want of nourishment.[74] Calling for food to feed his employees, the editor emphasized to subscribers that printers, like everybody else, required the common necessities of life and that because very few of them were vegetarians they preferred, when possible, not to live on bread alone.[75]

The scarcity of money in Utah in the 1850s was acute, and the barter system, although declining in use, remained rather common throughout the nineteenth century. Utah journalist E. L. T. Harrison, commenting on the cash that would result if an unrestricted mining policy was initiated in the Territory, claimed in 1869 that twice as many people in Utah would take a newspaper but for the trouble and expense of paying in kind.[76] The *News* accepted payment in a variety of forms even in the 1870s, though to a lesser degree, and continued to pay employees at least partly in kind.[77]

However, there were certain indispensable items necessary to run a paper that could be purchased only with cash, and at one point the editor explained that if cash was not forthcoming, "Deseret" would soon remain without the *News*. "We are ever ready and willing to do all we can to comfort, bless, edify and instruct and do good to the Saints," explained the editor, "but, we are not sufficiently versed in Chemistry to convert the *earth* into Gold. . . ."[78]

One principal source of cash income for frontier newspapers was government printing. Between July 1851 and 1 January 1855, the *News* earned from this source and presented bills to the government for as much as $13,476.55[79] However, the *News* was not always willing to take government work. It refused the commission to print the Laws of the First Session of the 32nd Congress because the suggested rate would not even pay for the cost of labor and newsprint, and the editor also asserted that the Laws would crowd out matter that would be more important and interesting to most of his subscribers.[80] Another helpful source of money for western newspapers was job printing, an area the *Deseret News* was involved in almost from its beginning and in which it considered itself a leader among Western papers.[81] In addition to government and job printing, money grants or subsidies were also a source of financial assistance for newspapers in the West. This was especially true in Mormon Utah.

Investigation of ownership and operation of the various Mormon enterprises founded in the last half of the nineteenth century reveals that the Church played a major role in the entrepreneurial promotion of Utah's economic development. Not bound to any fixed concept of capitalism, the Mormons tried any combination of Church and private enterprise that seemed necessary to achieve their intended goals. Even theoretically private ventures were channeled by Church sanctions in efforts to guarantee that every enterprise would help build the "Kingdom."[82] However, almost none of the enterprises that Young and the Church helped sponsor and support survived more than a few years.[83] On the other hand, the *Deseret News,* entirely owned and financed at this time by the Church and always considered indispensable, survived and eventually prospered.

In spite of its difficulties in getting started and its problems with newsprint, communications, and money, the *Deseret News* was never in any real danger of having to close. The editor made this indelibly clear when he wrote on 5 March 1856 that "profit or no profit, a Church paper will continue to be printed." Much later, emphasizing that Utah citizens should subscribe to the *News,* the editor claimed that unlike hundreds of newspaper ventures, a *News* subscriber need not worry about failing to get what he subscribed for because of failure and a suspension of publication.[84]

Even when the hard times of the 1850s rendered it difficult to sustain the various Church projects, Apostle D. H. Wells explained that the *Deseret News* was one of the few business operations the Church must keep in motion.[85] This willingness of the Church to underwrite the *News* demonstrated the value attributed to it, and made it one of the few Church or Utah institutions which has spanned the more than 125 years from 1850 to the present. Of course, the *News* was not the only journal in need of this kind of financial help. In order to stay alive many newspapers in western settlements had to be subsidized, some perhaps to a greater extent even than the Mormon organ. In many cases local merchants and businessmen gave their hometown paper such needed support.[86] In Salt Lake City this help came from the Church.

Not all religious newspapers have had the permanency of the *Deseret News.* Those that concentrate strictly on religious news seem generally to fulfill their particular purpose. However, the successful Church-supported paper that deals with general news and seeks a nondenominational audience is a rarity.[87] Nevertheless, the *News* not only attempted, but in a large measure succeeded in its dual role as religious and secular paper. Although *The Christian Science Monitor* is unquestionably the most successful of this breed of papers in the United States, the *News* has the distinction of being the first successful religious daily in the English language.[88]

The dual role of the Mormon paper was not apparent in its initial edition. The very first issue of the *News* centered on news reporting. No religious articles or sermons appeared. However, although it continued to cover local, national, and international news, it quickly began taking on the trappings of a religious journal. In its third issue it started printing the texts of the speeches of Church leaders delivered in the Bowery on Sundays,[89] and in November 1851 it renewed the *Times and Seasons'* earlier serialization of the history of the Prophet Joseph Smith.[90] In fact, by 1857 this direction of the *News* had gone so far that John Hyde, an ex-Mormon schoolteacher in Utah, wrote in his history of the Church that the Mormons published a weekly paper at Salt Lake City almost totally occupied by the autobiography of Joseph Smith and discourses of the hierarchy.[91] These sermons often occupied the whole of page one and much of the second page. This coverage of sermons, however, slacked off to such a degree that by the end of the Civil War the *News* wrote, "Notice.—Sabbath-Meetings, Theatricals and several other items are unavoidably crowded out this week."[92] But it was not until much later that the policy of regularly publishing speeches of the hierarchy began really to change. By 1866 they had gradually disappeared altogether except at the time of the Church's annual and semi-annual conferences in Salt Lake City and, before the end of the century, these were only being briefly summarized.

The gradual disappearance of Church sermons suggests the general trend of the *News* away from the dual role it played during the nineteenth century to the almost strictly secular paper of today. But, the *News* never lost its unmistakable identity as a Church paper. John Q. Cannon, an assistant editor of the *News* in 1881, explaining that he had to write a marriage announcement for the paper, recorded in his diary, "It was quite a difficult matter because of the circumstances, her husband being a Gentile, and it would not do to gush over it in a Church paper."[93]

But as early as 1856 the *News* had expressed a desire to separate religious and secular news. This was to be accomplished by the publication of two papers. Although the Church had sponsored two papers in Independence, Missouri, and again in Nauvoo, Illinois, Brigham Young apparently felt that he could not afford, on a frontier that was a good deal more difficult than the one Smith had faced, to subsidize more than one newspaper. *News* editor Albert Carrington explained in 1856 that when subscriptions increased substantially and payments were promptly made, another paper could be started. When that time should arrive, he concluded,

> the Church paper can be thrown into a still more convenient form for binding, be confined more exclusively to doctrine, history and elders' correspondence, and the world and its affairs find more ample space in a paper devoted to that kind of matter. As it now is, it must all be mixed up, history, geographical, scientific and other articles, and so forth and so on.[94]

A year later Carrington re-emphasized that until subscribers, realizing that capital was needed to finance publication, paid more cash no second Mormon paper could profitably be printed in Utah. Indeed, a strictly Church paper of the kind Carrington described did not, for whatever reason, appear until 4 April 1931, nearly seventy-five years later. Still published today, the new paper was called the *Church News* and, as today, was a supplement to the Saturday edition of the *News*.[95]

The modern achievement of the long-desired goal of two Church newspapers came, despite the difficulties of the depression-ridden 1930s, in a period of Mormon history much less harsh than that of early Utah. When Salt Lake City was extremely isolated, with acute problems with communication, newsprint, subscriptions, and capital, the *News* not only could not be divided, but also had considerably less influence after the Civil War. However, these difficulties, usually insuperable to individually managed frontier news-papers, never proved fatal to the *Deseret News* because of the rigidly prescribed cooperative efforts directed by the powerful Mormon Church.[96] Although incapable of totally offsetting the compelling influences of its secluded habitat, the theocratic Mormon society did alter the ordinary frontier newspaper pattern. The *News* survived, and as the official organ of this religious society would be employed to build and strengthen the Mormon "Kingdom" in Utah.

Footnotes

1. As quoted in Milton R. Hunter, *Brigham Young the Colonizer* (Salt Lake City: Deseret News Press, 1940), p. 11.

2 William Clayton, "Come Come Ye Saints," *Hymns: The Church of Jesus Christ of Latter-day Saints* (Salt Lake City: The Church of Jesus Christ of Latter-day Saints, 1948), p. 13.

3. The press used by the *Times and Seasons* apparently became encumbered with legal property ownership disputes resulting from the evacuation of Nauvoo. *See* Brigham Young, Camp of Israel, Winter Quarters, 1 April 1847, letter to Messrs. Babbit, Heywood and Fullmer, Brigham Young Collection, LDS Church Historical Department.

4. Ibid.

5. Brigham Young, Camp of Israel, Winter Quarters, 1 April 1847, letter to the Saints in the United States and Canada, Brigham Young Collection, LDS Church Historical Department.

6. Andrew Jenson, comp., "Journal History of the Church" (unpublished day-by-day history of The Church of Jesus Christ of Latter-day Saints from 1830 to the present), 17 July 1848, LDS Church Historical Department (hereafter referred to as "Journal History").

7. George A. Smith and Ezra T. Benson, Salt Lake City, Utah, letter to Orson Pratt, "Journal History," 20 December 1848.

8. "History of Brigham Young" (unpublished history by Brigham Young and others, 1847-1877), 7 May 1849, LDS Church Historical Department. John D. Lee, a close friend of Brigham Young who crossed the plains with Egan, found him careless with his language, apt to drink to excess, yet absolutely fearless; Juanita Brooks, *John Doyle Lee: Zealot, Pioneer Builder and Scapegoat* (Glendale, California: Arthur H. Clark Co., 1962), p. 132.

9. Orson Hyde, George A. Smith, and Ezra T. Benson, Kanesville, Iowa, 7 May 1849, letter to Brigham Young and Council, Brigham Young Collection.

10. "Journal History," 7 August 1849.

11. During the ten months between its arrival in Salt Lake City and the publication of the *Deseret News* the press was busy printing legal documents and laws pertaining to the State of Deseret.

12. A heavy man of forty-five in 1850, Richards was born in Massachusetts, where he taught school, lectured, and studied medicine. He was a first cousin to Brigham Young and joined the Mormons in 1836, becoming Joseph Smith's private secretary, historian of the Church, Nauvoo city recorder, and an Apostle. Prior to assuming responsibility for the *News,* he had edited the *Millennial Star* and had worked on the *Times and Seasons.*

13. *Deseret News* [Salt Lake City], 1 October 1853, hereafter referred to as *News*.
14. Wendell J. Ashton, *Voice in the West: Biography of a Pioneer Newspaper* (New York: Duell, Sloan and Pearce, 1950), pp. 120-21.
15. *News*, 28 December 1850.
16. Elias Smith, diary, 30 May 1852, Utah State Historical Society Library, Salt Lake City, Utah.
17. *News*, 19 September 1855.
18. Ibid., 31 May and 12 July 1851; 28 September 1854.
19. Ibid., 31 May 1851.
20. Ibid., 12 September 1855.
21. J. Cecil Alter, *Early Utah Journalism: A Half Century of Forensic Warfare, Waged by the West's Most Militant Press* (Salt Lake City: Utah State Historical Society, 1938), p. 298.
22. Elias Smith, diary, 16 March 1862, *See also* Ashton, *Voice in the West*, p. 121.
23. *News*, 19 October 1850.
24. Ibid., 2 March 1864.
25. Ibid., 31 March 1858.
26. Ibid., 30 November 1850.
27. Ibid., 13 February 1861.
28. As quoted in Leonard J. Arrington, *Great Basin Kingdom: An Economic History of the Latter-day Saints, 1830-1900* (Cambridge: Harvard University Press, 1958), p. 115. *See News* 29 May 1861 and 14 May 1862.
29. Brigham Young, "The Order of Enoch," discourse given 9 October 1862, Salt Lake City, Utah, as published in *Journal of Discourses by Brigham Young, his two Counsellors, and the Twelve Apostles*, 15:222 (*hereafter referred to as Journal of Discourses*).
30. *News*, 12 October 1854.
31. Ibid., 10 August 1854.
32. Ibid., 10 December 1869.
33. Ibid., 13 February 1861.
34. Jackson E. Towne, "Some Suggestive Characteristics of Early Western Journalism," *Arizona and the West* 1 (Winter 1959): 355.
35. *News*, 12 December 1855.
36. Towne, "Some Suggestive Characteristics of Early Western Journalism," p. 355.
37. Ashton, *Voice in the West*, p. 126.
38. *News*, 1 July 1850 and 5 March 1853.
39. Heber C. Kimball, "The 'Deseret News,' Its Value. . . ," discourse given 15 March 1857, Salt Lake City, Utah, in *Journal of Discourses*, 4: 293.
40. *News*, 16 March 1859.
41. Ibid., 7 October 1863.
42. Kimball, "The 'Deseret News,' Its Value," *Journal of Discourses*, 4: 293-94.
43. *News*, 19 August 1851; Daniel H. Wells, "Duty of Sustaining and Upholding the First Presidency in All Their Operations, Etc.," discourse given 9 March 1856, Salt Lake City, Utah, in *Journal of Discourses*, 7: 94.

44. *News,* 4 March 1857; Wells, "Duty of Sustaining and Upholding the First Presidency," *Journal of Discourses,* 7: 94.
45. *News,* 15 November 1851.
46. Ibid., 29 March 1869.
47. Ibid., 5 March 1856.
48. Ibid., 2 October 1852.
49. Ibid., 10 February 1891.
50. As quoted in *Christian Advocate* [New York City], 31 January 1878.
51. David F. Halaas, "Frontier Journalism in Colorado," *The Colorado Magazine* 44 (Summer 1967): 190.
52. *News,* 5 March 1856. However, as seen later, scolding delinquent subscribers was not too uncommon.
53. Ibid., 4 January 1866.
54. Ibid., 10 February 1891.
55. Ibid., 23 May 1872.
56. Ibid., 10 February 1891.
57. Mark Twain, *Roughing It* (New York: Harper and Brothers, 1871), pp. 121-22.
58. Arieh C. Brower, Great Salt Lake City, Utah, December 10, 1853, letter to Dr. W. Richards, editor of the *News,* Willard Richards Collection, LDS Church Historical Department. Although Brower's letter did not appear in the *News,* the paper printed similar information on 8 February 1856.
59. Everett N. Dick, *The Sod House Frontier, 1854-1890: A Social History of the Northern Plains from the Creation of Kansas and Nebraska to the Admission of the Dakotas* (Lincoln, Nebraska: Johnsen Publishing Company, 1954), p. 418.
60. *News,* 31 March 1858.
61. George A. Smith, "Raising Flax and Wool—Home Manufactures—Church Literature . . . ," discourse given 7 April 1867, Salt Lake City, Utah, *Journal of Discourses,* 11: 364.
62. Arieh C. Brower, Great Salt Lake City, Utah, 10 December 1853, letter to Dr. W. Richards, editor of the *News,* Willard Richards Collection.
63. Dick, *The Sod House Frontier,* p. 426; Alter, *Early Utah Journalism,* p. 11; William A. Katz, "The Western Printer and His Publications, 1850-1890," *Journalism Quarterly* 44 (Winter, 1967), 710.
64. Alter, *Early Utah Journalism,* p. 9.
65. *News,* 16 November 1864.
66. Ibid., 23 March 1864. Because pay for mail subscription is by law required in advance, the contemporary *News* has no delinquency in that category. However, it does have delinquent payment of an average of about $1,000 per year, or 0.5 percent of the total subscription; C. M. Graham, secretary to William B. Smart, editor and general manager, *Deseret News,* Salt Lake City, Utah, 9 October 1974, letter to author.
67. Dick, *The Sod House Frontier,* pp. 425-26; Frank Luther Mott, *American Journalism: A History of Newspapers in the United States through 260 Years, 1690-1950* (New York: Macmillan Company, 1950), p. 203.
68. *News,* 25 March 1863.

69. Ibid., 15 November 1851.
70. Ibid., 4 June 1856.
71. Ibid., 10 January 1852 and 13 December 1851.
72. Arrington, *Great Basin Kingdom,* p. 299. *See* David Calder, Salt Lake City, Utah, 13 March 1877, letter to Brigham Young, David Calder Collection, LDS Church Historical Department.
73. *News,* 1 April 1857.
74. Wells, "Duty of Sustaining and Upholding the First Presidency," *Journal of Discourses,* 7: 95.
75. *News,* 25 March 1863.
76. *Utah Magazine* 3 (16 October 1869):376-77.
77. Joseph Beecroft, diary, 27 August 1870, LDS Church Historical Department; *News,* 16 March 1859.
78. *News,* 16 October 1852.
79. Statements on books and financial records, Joseph Cain Collection, LDS Church Historical Department.
80. Willard Richards, Salt Lake City, Utah, 30 October 1852, letter to J. M. Bernhisel, Willard Richards Collection.
81. *News,* 21 November 1867.
82. Leonard J. Arrington, "Religious Sanction and Entrepreneurship in Pioneer Utah," *Utah Academy of Science, Arts, and Letters* 30(1952-53): 130.
83. Arrington, *Great Basin Kingdom,* pp. 112-28. These included such industries as pottery, sugar, wool, iron, and lead.
84. *News,* 10 February 1891.
85. Wells, "Duty of Sustaining and Upholding the First Presidency," *Journal of Discourses,* 7:94.
86. Halaas, "Frontier Journalism in Colorado," p. 203.
87. Erwin D. Canham, *Commitment to Freedom: The Story of the Christian Science Monitor* (Boston: Houghton Miffin, 1958), p. 46.
88. Mott, *American Journalism,* p. 288.
89. *News,* 29 June 1850. The Bowery was an unwalled shelter shaded by a roof of boards or brush constructed to accommodate large Church gatherings in early Salt Lake City.
90. Ibid., 15 November 1851.
91. Ibid., 5 July 1865.
92. Ibid., 5 July 1865.
93. John Q. Cannon, diary, 16 March 1881, typewritten copy, Brigham Young University Library, Provo, Utah.
94. *News,* 5 March 1856.
95. Ibid., 4 March 1857. As of September 1974, the *Church News* had a total world circulation of 110,317, far exceeding that of the *News,* which was just over 75,000.
96. Frederick Jackson Turner, who emphasized the development of individualism as a product of the American Frontier, also explained that unusually harsh and desolate areas of land would produce and require cooperative efforts; Frederick Jackson Turner, "Contributions of the West to American Democracy," *The Turner Thesis, Concerning the Role of the Frontier in American History,* ed. George Rogers Taylor (Boston: D. C.

Heath and Co., 1956), p. 27. Although Utah was such an area of land, Mormon notions of cooperatives were not born there, but rather were carried with them across the plains; Arrington, *Great Basin Kingdom,* pp. 62-63.

3

The Deseret News
as a
Kingdom-Builder

B oth internal and external opposition to the extension of Joseph Smith's power into temporal affairs split the Church and led to the Mormon expulsion from Illinois. The majority of the Saints, however, accepted the leadership of Brigham Young in both ecclesiastical and civil affairs, and followed him to Utah. Those who remained behind formed various splinter groups, but most eventually found their way into the highly democratic Reorganized Church of Jesus Christ of Latter Day Saints. With an initial absence of significant external opposition and virtually none from within, Brigham Young built an empire in Utah that dwarfed that of his predecessor.[1]

"The will and dictation of the Almighty" was to govern this western Mormon Commonwealth.[2] Apostle George A. Smith told the Saints, "What we do we should do as one man. Our System should be Theo-Democracy—the voice of the people consenting to the voice of God."[3] Instead of popular sovereignty there was divine sovereignty. The people did not confer the authority and, therefore, could not take it away. Their voice was but a sanction in support of what God chose.[4]

In any society, and especially in one like this "theo-democracy" of early Utah where a well-disciplined directorate stood at the helm, there are a number of ways to communicate the will of the directors. The theater, school, lectern, pulpit, and newspaper all serve as aids in transmitting and implementing policies of the leadership. To this end all these devices were enlisted by the Church hierarchy with varying degrees of success.

The Deseret Musical and Dramatic Association was organized the same year that the first issue of the *Deseret News* appeared. Its purpose was to entertain, improve the culture, and exemplify Church doctrine, but it had little influence. Schools also began early, and a university had even been founded by 1850, but they were less successful than had been hoped.[5] (At times the *Deseret News* came to their rescue, as when, during shortages of textbooks, the paper served as reading material in the schoolrooms.[6]) Organized lectures by well-read men such as Joseph Young, Orson Pratt, and Parley P. Pratt were often held in Salt Lake City, along with the weekly Sunday sermons of Church leaders and thinkers. But the group attending organized lectures was relatively small. The General Conferences, held twice a year, motivated Saints outside Salt Lake City to visit the center of Zion to hear their leaders speak from the pulpit. However, Apostle Erastus Snow said in 1877 that in spite of the fact that these conferences had been held regularly since Utah was first settled, only a small number of the Mormons had been able to attend.[7] Even in Salt Lake City itself many residents, for various reasons, chose to remain at home.[8] For those that did go, the transitory nature of the spoken word substantially weakened the impact of the message. Of all methods of communication used, however, the newspaper was the most important. Brigham Young once told the *News* editor that it would be better to print two columns of the *Deseret News* than to publish schoolbooks.[9]

Church leaders exercised control over all social institutions within the Great Basin that promised to become powerful enough to influence public opinion to any degree. When cultural and social societies formed by individuals acting independently of the Church showed signs of too much autonomy, they were taken over by the Church and subordinated to its purposes. One proposal for an independent newspaper to be devoted to scientific and literary affairs never got beyond the talking stage, for "its friends," wrote John Hyde, "are afraid the Church might become so fond of it, as to hug it to death, as it has their literary institutions."[10] Book committees were appointed by the Church hierarchy to ap-prove or disapprove certain publications,[11] and Church authorities judged one book to be so filled with inaccuracies that they announced publicly that all copies should be "gathered up and destroyed."[12]

There were, of course, many books and pamphlets printed and circulated among the Mormons in Utah; but the *Deseret News,* filled with everything imaginable, provided the most readily available reading material. And, like nearly all early economic and social institutions in Utah, the *News* was owned and controlled by the Mormon Church and Brigham Young.

Brigham Young publicly denied charges that he censored the *Deseret News,*[13] but he quite often involved himself with its operation and publication. Ed Howe, a non-Mormon who later became a noted newspaperman in Kansas, worked several months as a typesetter for the Church paper in 1871 and 1872. Howe declared in his autobiography that he had never seen as fascinating a town as Salt Lake City nor enjoyed life anywhere more than when in the Church capital. He then related a story showing Brigham Young's relationship to the *News,* besides giving a unique glimpse into the character of the Mormon prophet:

> One day he came into the *News* office, the occasion being publication of some sort of church report, and he called at the composing room with the business manager, looking up some detail. I had worked on the report, and produced the copy they were looking for. The prophet seemed to question some of the figures, and wanted to see whether I had followed copy. It turned out that I had, and there was no correction. "You're right, and I'm wrong," he said, patting my shoulder, which I thought a good deal from the head of the Mormon church.[14]

A much more important source than Howe in showing Brigham Young's supervision of the *Deseret News* is the paper's own editor. In a letter to Young explaining the newspaper's contents and layout, Willard Richards wrote, "If my President has any improvement to suggest, my ears are open, & I shall be happy to hear."[15] An undated note from Richards to Young reveals even more specific control.

> Beloved Bro. I send you, at the earliest moment, a proofsheet of News No 5. Should you think any of the Editorial too spicy, or incorrect, please mark it. You will find Typograph Errors but probably you can get the meaning. I would particularly refer to page 2. *"Things as they are."* But the whole is before you. Your[s] Truly, in haste.[16]

This relationship between the Church leader and the Church paper was succinctly expressed in an admonitory letter from Richards to a *News* reporter, George D. Watt: "My course has been dictated and controlled by my President; and when you find fault with my course you find fault with my President. . . . The word of Bro Brigham, is Bro Willard's law, and he is governed by it in all his doings. . . ."[17]

Because the editors were either Church leaders themselves or closely associated with them, it was not necessary to have continuous and intimate monitoring of the *News* by Brigham Young. Most decisions, in fact, seem to have been made by the editors themselves, although at times they were decided in conjunction with the President and his associates.[18] Because of this close relationship, disagreement between the *News* and the Church was virtually nonexistent, and the coming of a new editor, an occasion which generally resulted in radical policy shifts in most western newspapers,[19] affected the *News* very little. When Albert Carrington took over the editor's chair in 1854, he opened his salutatory by writing, "changing editors changed neither views nor politics . . . ," and concluded, "We design facing the music under the same banner, [and] pursuing the same policy. . . ."[20]

There is little question not only that the Church exercised its control over the *News,* but also that such control had clear reasons. During the Civil War, anti-Democrat and Copperhead placards which read, "The freedom of the press is subordinate to the interests of a nation," were commonplace in the streets of the North.[21] The *Deseret News* apparently operated from the beginning under a similar standard; and, although its motto throughout the nineteenth century was "Truth and Liberty," for the sake of the Kingdom the whole truth was not always printed. For example, Lyman W. Porter of Morgan County, Utah, sent the *News* editor a letter in which he complained against claim jumpers of land that he and his neighbors had been cultivating for ten to twelve years. He explained that Mormon "Brethren," assisted by a "President of a Stake" who himself was "a much interested Party" were even taking land that others were living on. "We have quite a Number of apostates in the County," wrote Porter, but "none of them as yet, have had a Sufficient amount of Gaul [as Church leaders] to Jump their Neighbores Land." Concluding his letter he noted: "Some of the Bretheren have been heard to say, if that [claim jumping] is Gospel, they have a bout got through with

Mormonism."[22] Porter's letter was one-sided, and may have distorted the truth, but maintaining the proper image of Church leaders was a very important factor in keeping a people united and dedicated, and the excerpts quoted above would have disturbed some Saints. The *News* editor, therefore, discreetly scratched them out and wrote to the Church president, "Dear Brother:—Enclosed I send you a letter read today from Brother Lyman W. Porter, of Porterville, a portion of which I have published and the whole of which I thought might interest you."[23] Although the editor prudently kept parts of the letter from his readers, he apparently felt that the Church authorities would want to know about the situation described by Porter.

Maintaining an acceptable image with the outside world was also important and the Church tried to avoid printing anything in the *News* that might unduly offend or present an undesirable picture to those beyond the borders of Utah. Most sermons of major Church figures were published in the columns of the *News,* but not until after they had been carefully edited and revised.[24] Brigham Young explained that because these sermons were read by tens of thousands outside Utah, he often omitted the "sharp words" when he had them printed.[25] Heber C. Kimball's speeches were so fiery that at times editor Albert Carrington had to clip the "music" out of them.[26]

In a sermon he delivered at the time federal troops were en route to Utah in 1857, Kimball explained how such inflammable rhetoric was treated by the *News*:

> To gratify some who cry, "oh, don't say anything, brother Heber, —don't say anything, brother Brigham, to bring down the United States upon us," we have at times omitted printing some of the remarks that might offend the weak-stomached world, and we have made buttermilk and catnip tea to accommodate the tastes of our enemies; but the poor devils [federal troops, etc.] are not pleased after all. Would they come any quicker if we told them that they were poor, miserable, priest-ridden curses, who want a President in the chair that dare not speak for fear those hell-hounds be on him?[27]

Thus for the good of the cause the *News* at times was restricted in what it could print. It has been said, however, that a tightly controlled press is a dead press. This may be true when referring to a newspaper in a democracy, but the *Deseret News* which operated in a theo-democratic system where virtually everything existed for and was used by the Church to obtain certain ends, was very much alive. Even though there was some suppression and shaping of news, in the Mormon theocratic Kingdom few felt themselves unjustly coerced.

As Kimball said, the *News* was "controlled for the mutual benefit of all who . . . were interested in building up the kingdom of God on the earth."[28] Unlike most other papers, the *News* was not primarily an economic enterprise. "It is not published for speculation," wrote the editor in 1891, "and never has been . . . ; the profits, if any there be derived from it, being advocated to extending its sphere of usefulness, and benefitting the community."[29]

Thus the *News,* not solely after money, sought to bless the Church and its members by helping to build the Kingdom in a variety of ways. For many in the United States, news was considered history, and the important thing was to get it down in print in permanent form. This far-reaching and long-lasting concept of Kingdom building was strongly evident in Mormon thought, and the first issue of the *News* articulated the notion very well:

> A paper that is worth printing is worth preserving; if worth preserving, it is worth binding; for this purpose we issue in pamphlet form; and if every subscriber shall preserve each copy of the "News," and bind it at the close of the volume, their children's children may read the doings of their fathers, which otherwise might have been forgotten; ages to come.

Since the *News* hoped to be a storehouse of information for present and unborn generations and to serve as a means for quickly retrieving knowledge for them, it announced in its second issue that a general index would be published. Heber C. Kimball assured the Saints that if they would take care of the paper and hand it down to their children generation by generation, copies would still be extant in the millennium. "Such publications," he declared, "are not going to be burned up, according to my faith they will go into the resurrection."[30] Unfortunately, few took to heart the admonition to preserve the *News.* Early Mormon historian and creative writer Edward Tullidge wrote that the *News* itself provided an example of how virtually the whole early record of a colony could become lost in thirty or forty years, "seeing that scarcely a volume of this first issue survives."[31]

But the *News* was interested in more than just recording history. Although not primarily a proselytizing tool of the Church, it explained that its editorials did attempt to spread the Gospel.[32] Referring to a speech by George A. Smith, counselor to Brigham

Young, which contained a summary of the early history of the Church, the editor explained that the *News* containing this sermon would be good to send to friends, both Mormon and Gentile.[33] Responding later to what he had described as an interest among Americans and others in the teachings of the Church, the editor declared that the manifestation of this spirit of inquiry had led to an extended circulation of the *News* and would possibly be "the means of bringing many people to the knowledge and obedience of the truth."[34] The *News* expressed confidence that the printing press could effect much more good than missionaries, whose time was spent in verbal proselytizing, and do it more expediently, but that it could only be a great instrument of good if "properly guided and controlled." When "under the control of pure, truthful influences," wrote the editor, and "used for the amelioration, redemption and elevation of mankind," then and only then would its full power and value as a missionary be completely known and understood.[35]

To assist in this proselytizing, it was essential that the *News* have a wide distribution. Foreman of the *News* office Arieh C. Brower, in a letter to the editor dated 10 December 1853, wrote what he hoped would be printed in one of its columns. Brower stated that he longed for the time when the "organ of the Kingdom of God" would be fully appreciated, and when its "circulation shall not be limited by the confines of these mountains, but extend through every nation, Kindred, tongue, and people on the globe."[36] Brower's dream of having his letter published was never realized, and the *News* never reached the alleged circulation of Arthur E. Howard's *The Salina* [Utah] *Sun,* which claimed to go "everywhere," even to "hell" if its publisher did not use common sense.[37] But it became, almost from its beginning, both national and international in its circulation.

The *News* had agents in Idaho, Arizona, Wyoming, Nevada, and New Mexico. Travelers passing through Salt Lake City often purchased copies of the *News* to send to their relatives and friends in the Midwest and East. The *News* also followed the common practice of sending newspapers to libraries throughout the United States, although it questioned the value of sending free copies to "minor cities."[38] Indeed, the *News* circulated in the United States from Maine to Louisiana and California, and to many major cities in between.

Its circulation was not confined to the borders of the United

States. Copies of the first issue of the *News* were immediately sent to England,[39] and by 1853 Messrs. Dudell and Dixon, editors of *Dixon's Recorder* in Hong Kong, expressed a desire to receive it on an exchange basis.[40] The *News* received by exchange the *Independent,* a New Zealand newspaper; and, according to Henry Allington's letters from Karori, that part of the South Pacific got regular delivery of the Utah paper.[41] In 1875 the *Deseret News* was found among the seventy odd journals on deposit in the Paris reading room of the *New York Herald.*[42] Even before Brower had given utterance to his longing, the *News* had begun its journey to the four quarters of the world—to a much broader circulation than it has today. Indeed, in 1974 the *Deseret News* had only one subscriber outside the United States, and that was in Canada.[43] Illustrating this earlier broad circulation the following list of "Foreign Agents" locations appeared in the Church paper's issue of 28 May 1853:

1. Lahaina, Sandwich Isles [Hawaii]
2. Liverpool, England
3. Dublin, Ireland
4. Paris, France
5. Hamburg, Germany
6. Berlin, Prussia [Germany]
7. Copenhagen, Denmark
8. Iceland
9. Christiania [Oslo], Norway
10. Stockholm, Sweden
11. Rangoon, Burma
12. Calcutta, Hindoostan [India]
13. Gibraltar, Spain
14. Canton DeVand [Vand], Switzerland
15. Genoa, Italy
16. Malta
17. Kingston, Jamaica
18. British Guiana
19. Cape Town, Cape of Good Hope [Republic of South Africa]
20. Sidney, Australia
21. Hobart Town, Van Diemans Land [Hobart, Tasmania]
22. Bombay, Hindoostan [India]
23. Canton, China
24. Siam, Siam [Thailand]

Wide circulation was important for purposes other than prose-lytizing. Like the newspapers mentioned in the five cities in Richard Wade's *Urban Frontier,* the *News* linked its readers to the places and things they had known before. "We here, although far from you," wrote George Nebeker from the Hawaiian Islands to the *News* editor, "feel the parental cords which bind us to our homes and friends in Utah."[44]

More important in terms of building the Kingdom than national and international communications, at least in the beginning, was the *News's* influence in binding together those in the Great Basin itself. Although it was founded and remained in Salt Lake City except for a brief period in 1857, the *News* was never just a city newspaper. By the time the first issue came off the press on 15 June 1850, over thirty other towns and villages in adjacent and distant valleys had been settled by the Mormons, and before Brigham Young's death in 1877 this number had reached over 350.

Unlike other colonizers in the United States, the Mormons did not expand gradually as the pressure of population demanded. Instead, under Young's direction they settled strategic points throughout the West, starting what they at first hoped would become a sovereign empire encompassing present-day Utah and Nevada, nearly all of New Mexico and Arizona, and parts of Colorado, Wyoming, and California, including a seacoast harbor at San Diego, allowing freedom of the seas for a Mormon navy.

The *News* tended to follow the Mormon flag. From the very beginning, subscribers from "distant parts" of the valley could obtain their papers from agents near their homes. A list of agents printed in the paper's first issue revealed that even then the *News* circulated fifty miles west of Salt Lake City in Tooele Valley and as far south as Sanpete Valley, about 150 miles from Salt Lake. In March 1852 the editor reported that in Springville, a settlement over fifty miles south, not one family in Bishop Johnson's congregation was without the Church paper. (But he noted, "We understand this city [Salt Lake City] is more destitute of the *News* than any other portion of the Territory."[45]) The *News* reached even the extremities of the growing Empire. Its editor emphasized that the paper could go to settlements without post offices nearly every week by private transportation.[46] Apostle George A. Smith, then in charge of the settlement in Parowan, Iron County, some 200 miles from the Mormon capital, reported to the editor in 1851 that a copy of the *News* had been received and that the residents of Parowan were then looking "anxiously" for another issue.[47] By 1855 the Church's paper was distributing some 1,600 copies through the mails to subscribers outside Salt Lake City. Of a total circulation figure of 4,000 in 1856 it seems that some 40 per cent was being received by Mormons outside the City.[48]

Settlement of the extensive Great Basin Kingdom had isolated Mormons from Eastern centers of population, from each other in distant towns in the Mountain West, and, more importantly, from the Church center at Salt Lake City. This made the *News* an indispensable agency of communication.[49] Like the perceptive French observer of early America, Alexis de Tocqueville, the Mormons realized that the press afforded an essential means of interchange between people who never came into immediate contact with each other.[50]

Perhaps the most important single way the *News* maintained this needed contact with settlers outside the capital was in publishing the sermons of the Church leaders, a policy it has followed virtually from its inception. In 1867 the *News* announced it would regularly include one sermon in each Saturday issue to provide valuable Sunday reading for all the Saints outside Salt Lake City as well as for those in the city who were detained at home for one reason or another.[51] Publication of these sermons in the *News,* as well as the lectures and weekly Church speeches, made them available to a much larger audience in a form that was less transitory than the spoken word and more likely to impose upon the mind the conviction of their immutability.

News editorials and sermons by General Authorities buttressed one another and frequently concentrated on the achievement of their common goals. Often editorial space was partially or completely given over to texts of sermons. In one such instance the editor asserted his conviction that foreign Saints would profit from reading speeches given at a recent conference in Salt Lake City quite as much as those in attendance had profited from hearing them.[52]

All the *News* editors asked in return for the liberal space devoted to printing Church sermons was that its patrons read and digest the precious information. "The discourses alone furnish *more* really valuable truth than can be gleaned from all the 'outside' papers in the world," declared the editor in 1855, "and your attention is called to them lest some, in the hurry of worldly cares, pass by the rich treasures of heaven, so bounteously placed within their reach. . . ."[53]

Of course, there was much more in the *News* than Church sermons. It carried notices and announcements of virtually every scheduled meeting. A Pittsburgher visiting Salt Lake City in 1849 told of a Church service where the coming Mormon 24th of July celebration was announced and described in detail. By necessity, before 1850 such notices were given at public meetings,[54] but with the coming of the *Deseret News,* such announcements were more commonly made through its columns.

The *News* was filled with notices of local and regional Church services. It listed Church officials and gave times when they would receive callers. It printed Church excommunications, although only on a selective basis: the editors felt that generally such publicity further alienated the offender, but when a case "needs publication" it was to be made through the official organ of the Church after proper consent from the First Presidency had been received.[55]

Official calls and releases of particular missionaries laboring in the United States and elsewhere were sometimes made through the pages of the *News*. In 1870 it announced that Elder Samuel Savery, who was traveling in the state of New York, was not in a "proper condition of mind . . ." and served notice that he was thereby recalled and requested to discontinue his labors in the ministry.[56] This method of missionary administration became a little confusing and hard to follow at times. David King Udall, a London missionary in 1877, seeing in the *News* that he had been called to fill a mission to Arizona, noted in his diary, "I am willing to respond but it seems strange that I am called to fill another mission before I am released from this one."[57]

The Church paper answered theological inquiries from its subscribers, sometimes in a tone more humorous and scolding than profound. In a letter to Apostle Parley P. Pratt, Andrew Silver asked what caused the banishment of Satan from God, to which Pratt answered, "I either was not present at the banishment of Satan, or have forgotten the particulars. The probability is, that he wished to go to a warmer climate for his health." To this the editor added, "Quite possibly he searched so deeply after the 'mysteries' of the kingdom, that he neglected his duties as many do at the present day."[58]

The official Church journal contained more than strictly religious information and observations. It commented on items of public interest, from the danger of letting a child play with a fork to the benefits to be derived from newly invented farm machinery and the Homestead Act. Described by Jules Remy and Julius Brenchley, European naturalists who visited Salt Lake City in 1855, the *News* contained all that would be found in a regular newspaper and more:

> sermons, editorial articles, facts and events occurring throughout the world, historical fragments, biography, poetry, fables, allegories, curious anecdotes, narratives of travellers and missionaries, political and religious correspondence, description of machines and objects,

scientific discoveries, sketches of manners, accounts of battles, culinary and other recipes, hints to farmers and gardeners, perplexing enigmas, ambitious anagrams turning most frequently on the names of their leaders, finally advertisements, notices, marriages, as so many savory morsels.[59]

It was "very difficult," wrote the two naturalists, "without having seen it, to conceive the quantity of matter crowded into its pages. . . ."[60] Although it did serve the numerous functions of a regular newspaper, its primary role, like that of all institutions in Utah, was to build the Kingdom of God.

In some ways, the *News* shared the goal of building with other western newspapers. Throughout the nineteenth century, from the Ohio Valley to the Far West, editors bellowed optimistic refrains describing their towns; each was billed as the "garden spot of the world." Appropriately named sheets like the *Herald, Advertiser,* and *Bugle* sounded to the world the virtues, real or imagined, of their community. By presenting a favorable image of a particular town to the outside world and acting in a sense like a local chamber of commerce, the paper attracted people and capital. *The Owyhee Avalanche,* an Idaho newspaper, declared in August 1866 that its main purpose had been to tell the outside world about the advantages of Owyhee as a place for both the worker and investor. Indeed, "puffing" the West and particularly the paper's own hometown was probably the principal reason for a newspaper's existence.

But as the *Deseret News* worked to build the Mormon Kingdom, it discouraged the immigration of certain kinds of people, and never overplayed the physical glories of Utah. In fact, the *Deseret News,* serving as a tool to support Brigham Young's policy of isolation from divisive ideas and peoples, used much of its space to refute glowing descriptions of Utah. Referring sarcastically to the Sacramento *Union,* it wrote, "Health, wealth, beauty (of course) and the hub of the nation! Good for Utah! If that does not bring the population what will?"[61] In an 1875 editorial entitled "Exaggeration about Utah," the *News* editor, after listing some overstatements, concluded,

Everybody knows that spoken in such strains these representations are falsehoods. This is not the most delightful climate in the world. . . . This is a hard climate to work in, a hard climate to rear children in. It is easy to be sick here, and it is often difficult to be otherwise. The mortality, if not large, is not excessively small, and it is especially severe on infants. . . . The mountains are not covered with timber; iron, coal, and precious metals can not be found everywhere and anywhere for the digging. The valleys that are well watered are few, and the acres of unclaimed rich soil can not be picked up by the million. Irrigation is necessary to satisfactory soil culture, and only in a few places is water for irrigation abundant and readily available. . . .

It is not fair, it is akin to swindling, to delude people by representing this region as other than what it really is. There are certainly other parts of the world which surpass it in general fertility, natural resources, pleasant and healthful climate, and beauty of landscape. It has its advantages, and other regions have theirs.[62]

Brigham Young knew that no empire could be built without people, but recalling Mormon "persecutions" in the Midwest he set out to fill the Great Basin with his own followers. He hoped that control by occupation would insure that never again could physical force be effectively used against the Mormons.[63] Such a goal, of course, required a very large and imaginative immigration program, for in 1850 Utah had few attractions. Faced with the task of making it and the "peculiar people" that lived there sound appealing, the Mormon propagandists displayed a vision and an enthusiasm which paid off in tens of thousands of immigrants.

The propaganda campaign was made not in the United States or by the *Deseret News,* but in England and Europe by Church mission journals like the *Millennial Star* in Liverpool and *Stjerne* in Scandinavia. As William Mulder said, *"Stjerne* served Utah as the railroad and land commission circulars served other states," and over 25,000 Scandinavians migrated to Utah between 1850 and 1900.[64] How were these and others persuaded to join distant and outcast communities in Utah? It was not by "puffing" the physical attractions of the Basin or by promising wealth and comfort to those who would cross the Atlantic and then the Great Plains. Rather, it was through convincing prospective converts that Mormons were a chosen people of God, that in due time all people would convert to Mormon doctrine, that Daniel's prophecy would be fulfilled, and that a universal Kingdom of God would be established.[65] Thus the Mormon foreign press sought to attract the proper kind of people to fill up the Great Basin Kingdom.

However, the task of encouraging those already there to remain fell to the Church's local journal. Although the *Deseret News* was born a full year after the great California Gold Rush began, Church leaders quickly used it to help keep the Saints from dashing off to the gold fields, decimating the budding empire. Aimed at Mormons who might consider leaving, the second issue of the *News* declared that San Francisco had more suffering and deprivation than had ever been known in New York or Philadelphia, that thousands were actually starving and unemployed, and that the whole of California was overcrowded with unsuccessful and disheartened miners.[66]

The *News* also invoked the power of the Church in support of its efforts to curb gold fever. A lengthy editorial "To the Saints" instructed bishops and local Church leaders to seek out those planning to abandon their farms, warn them against such wickedness, and, if they did not repent, cut them off from the Church. "For they that are not with us," wrote the editor, "are against us, and the counsel is to all, raise all the grain you can, and promote domestic manufactures by all the means in your power, and quit your thirsting after gold or the gods of this world. . . . Do you want to become God-like?" asked the editor. "Then do as He has done, and think no more of going to the gold diggings . . . till you have made a printing press, a steam engine, and a cotton gin. . . ."[67]

Church historian B. H. Roberts praised Mormon decisions to remain in their humble pioneering settlements in a semi-desert region instead of participating in the mad rush for riches outside Utah, saying it was "one of the marvels of those times, and will be in all time to come.[68] The *News,* though not solely responsible, played a major role in this achievement. Later it would be used to keep the Saints from abandoning their fields for Utah's own mineral wealth.

The *News* helped Brigham Young in other ways. In order to maintain the isolation that he had found in the Great Basin and to achieve independence from the hostile gentile world, the Mormon leader considered it necessary to create a self-sustaining economy.[69] The pre-Civil War *News* did its utmost to establish home industries by building its own paper mill and type foundry. It also became · a major instrument of the Church in implementing its economic policy. In 1852 the *News* launched a series of editorials advocating home industry. They continued off and on for the entire year,[70] and in 1853 the *News* expressed its determination to continue to contend for domestic manufactures until home enterprises either gained a reasonable competition with their competitors or drove foreign supplies from Utah markets.[71] However, the major push for home industry and cooperative enterprise in Utah came after the Civil War, with the *News* continuing to serve as champion.

To build a Mormon Kingdom in early Utah, Brigham Young was convinced that he had to keep the people at home as well as make them, insofar as possible, self-sufficient. To do this, and to weld them together in a unified community, communication was essential. *News* editor George Q. Cannon, next to Brigham Young perhaps the most powerful man in Utah, wrote, "in this universally reading age it is as impossible to build up a new country without the influence of printers' ink as it would be to teach school without books."[72] The *Deseret News,* as the official spokesman of Mormondom and the instrument *ex cathedra* by which the views, desires, and instructions of the Church hierarchy were articulated and disseminated among the Mormons, was described by one observer as "the law and the prophets" to most residents of Utah and the *Moniteur Universal* of the Church.[73] As the best available means of constant communication in Utah, the *News,* speaking in timeless printed form, played a vital role in building the "Kingdom of God" and the empire envisioned by Brigham Young.

Footnotes

1. See Robert B. Flanders, *Nauvoo: Kingdom on the Mississippi* (Urbana: University of Illinois Press, 1965), pp. v-vi; Klaus J. Hansen, *Quest for Empire: The Political Kingdom of God and the Council of Fifty in Mormon History* (East Lansing: Michigan State University Press, 1967), pp. 156-58.

2. Brigham Young, "Human and Divine Government—The Latter-day Kingdom, &c.," discourse given 31 July 1859, Salt Lake City, Utah, in *Journal of Discourses,* 6:342.

3. Quoted in Hansen, *Quest for Empire,* p. 40.

4. Hansen, *Quest for Empire,* p. 39.

5. William J. McNiff, *Heaven on Earth: A Planned Mormon Society* (Oxford, Ohio: Mississippi Valley Press, 1940), pp. 66, 151-52.

6. *News,* 23 November 1854.

7. Erastus Snow, "Conferences . . .," discourse given October 13, 1877, Provo, Utah, in *Journal of Discourses,* 19:130.

8. *News,* 8 June 1872.

9. "History of Brigham Young," 7 December 1858.

10. John Hyde, Jr., *Mormonism: Its Leaders and Designs* (New York: W. P. Fetridge and Co., 1857), p. 131.

11. John Nicholson, Salt Lake City, 5 December 1892 and 24 January 1893, letters to Presidents Wilford Woodruff, George Q. Cannon, and Joseph F. Smith, John Nicholson Collection, LDS Church Historical Department.

12. *News,* 23 August 1865. The book was Lucy Mack Smith, *Biographical Sketches of Joseph Smith the Prophet and His Progenitors for Many Generations* (Liverpool, England: S. W. Richards, 1853).

13. *News,* 28 January 1863.

14. Edward Howe, *Plain People* (New York: Dodd Mead and Co., 1929), pp. 99-100.

15. Willard Richards, Salt Lake City, 9 April 1853, letter to Brigham Young, Willard Richards Collection, LDS Church Historical Department.

16. Willard Richards, Salt Lake City, undated letter to Brigham Young, Willard Richards Collection, LDS Church Historical Department.

17. Willard Richards, Salt Lake City, 25 September 1852, letter to George D. Watt, Willard Richards Collection, LDS Church Historical Department.

18. "History of Brigham Young," 7 May 1849.

19. William B. Rice, *"The Los Angeles Star," 1851-1864: The Beginnings of Journalism in Southern California,* ed. John Walton Caughey (Berkeley: University of California Press, 1947), p. 53.

20. *News,* 8 June 1854. Similar statements were made at each change of editor.

21. Frank Luther Mott, *American Journalism: A History of Newspapers in the United States through 260 Years, 1690-1950* (New York: Macmillan Company, 1950), p. 358.

22. Lyman W. Porter, Porterville, Morgan County, Utah, 5 May 1886, letter to *News* editor, George C. Lambert Collection, LDS Church Historical Department.

23. George C. Lambert, Salt Lake City, Utah, 7 May 1886, letter to President John Taylor, George C. Lambert Collection.

24. John Q. Cannon, diary, 22 January 1881, typewritten copy, Brigham Young University Library, Provo, Utah; Richard F. Burton, *The City of the Saints and Across the Rocky Mountains to California* (second edition; London: Longman, Green, Longman and Roberts, 1861), p. 282.

25. Brigham Young, "Joseph Smith's Family—Bashfulness in Public Speaking . . . ," discourse given 2 August 1857, Salt Lake City, in *Journal of Discourses,* 5:99.

26. Ibid.

27. Heber C. Kimball, "Organization—Destruction of Zion's Enemies . . . ," discourse given 2 August 1857, Salt Lake City, in *Journal of Discourses,* 5:132.

28. Heber C. Kimball, "The 'Deseret News,' Its Value . . . ," discourse given 15 March 1857, Salt Lake City, in *Journal of Discourses,* 5:292.

29. *News,* 10 February 1891.

30. Kimball, "The 'Deseret News,' Its Value," *Journal of Discourses,* 4:294.

31. Edward W. Tullidge, *The History of Salt Lake City and its Founders* (Salt Lake City: Tullidge, 1886), appendix p. iv.

32. *News,* 5 March 1856; 28 November 1866; 8 March 1866.

33. Ibid., 13 June 1874.

34. Ibid., 20 January 1875.

35. Ibid., 12 March 1870.

36. Arieh C. Brower, Salt Lake City, 10 December 1853, letter to Willard Richards, Willard Richards Collection, LDS Church Historical Department.

37. J. Cecil Alter, *Early Utah Journalism: A Half Century of Forensic Warfare, Waged by the West's Most Militant Press* (Salt Lake City: Utah State Historical Society, 1938), p. 245.

38. H. G. Whitney, Salt Lake City, 20 December 1902, letter to President Joseph F. Smith, H. G. Whitney Collection, LDS Church Historical Department.

39. Willard Richards, Salt Lake City, 31 July 1850, letter to Levi Richards, Willard Richards Collection (typewritten copy), LDS Church Historical Department.

40. Juanita Brooks (ed.), *On the Mormon Frontier: The Diary of Hosea Stout, 1844-1861* (Salt Lake City: University of Utah Press, 1964), 2:483.

41. *News,* 20 July 1870; 11 January 1872.

42. Ibid., 13 October 1875.

43. C. M. Graham, secretary to William B. Smart, editor and general manager, *Deseret News,* 9 October 1974, letter to author. The weekly

Church News, carrying strictly Church information, does circulate through-out the world today.

44. *News,* 21 November 1867.
45. Ibid., 6 March 1852.
46. Ibid., 29 February 1860.
47. Ibid., 12 December 1855. Jules Remy and Julius Brenchley, European visitors in Salt Lake City in 1855, commenting on the *Deseret News,* wrote that without witnessing it, it was hard to conceive "the avidity with which it is read"; Jules Remy and Julius Brenchley, *A Journey to Great Salt Lake City* (London: W. Jeffs, 1861), 2:190.
48. *News,* 12 December 1855.
49. Indeed, Willard Richards wrote in 1852 that the paper was the "only channel of communication" to the people in the valleys at that time. Willard Richards, Salt Lake City, 25 September 1852, letter to George D. Watt, Willard Richards Collection, LDS Church Historical Department.
50. Alexis de Tocqueville, *Democracy in America,* ed. Phillips Bradley (New York: Vintage Books, 1945), 1:195.
51. *News,* 21 December 1867.
52. Ibid., 16 April 1853; *see also News,* 26 March 1856.
53. Ibid., 1 March 1855.
54. Dale L. Morgan, "The Changing Face of Salt Lake City," *Utah Historical Quarterly* 27 (July 1959): 218.
55. *News,* 11 November 1893.
56. Ibid., 13 September 1870; *see also News,* 19 March 1856.
57. Pearl Udall Nelson (ed.), *Arizona Pioneer Mormon: David King Udall, His Story and His Family, 1851-1938* (Tucson: Arizona Silhouettes, 1959), p. 42.
58. *News,* 11 January 1851.
59. Remy and Brenchley, *A Journey to Great Salt Lake City,* 2:189-90.
60. Ibid.
61. *News,* 12 August 1872.
62. Ibid., 26 July 1875.
63. Franklin D. Daines, "Separatism in Utah, 1847-1870," *Annual Report of the American Historical Association for 1917,* 58(1920): 335.
64. William Mulder, "Image of Zion: Mormonism as an American Influence in Scandinavia," *Mississippi Valley Historical Review 43 (June 1956):* 19, 24-25.
65. Ibid., p. 38. Mormons explain the second chapter of Daniel to mean that God's Kingdom will ultimately replace all man-made kingdoms of the Earth.
66. *News,* 29 June 1850.
67. Ibid., 7 February 1852.
68. B. H. Roberts, *A Comprehensive History of the Church of Jesus Christ of Latter-day Saints, Century I* (Salt Lake City: Deseret News Press, 1930), 3:346.
69. Leonard J. Arrington, *Great Basin Kingdom, An Economic History of the Latter-day Saints, 1830-1900* (Cambridge: Harvard University Press, 1958), p. 112.

70. *News,* beginning 24 January 1852.
71. Ibid., 22 December 1853.
72. Ibid., 24 May 1873.
73. Remy and Brenchley, *A Journey to Great Salt Lake City,* 2:190.

4

The Deseret News and Gentile Conflict: 1850-1869

By moving to Utah the Saints hoped to escape close contact with Gentiles, the source of so much grief for them in the Midwest. They were never able to achieve that purpose in full. Although problems resulting from such contact became more numerous and explosive after 1869, the nineteen years before the railroad reached Utah were by no means void of trouble. The *Deseret News* showed early collisions and, assisted at times by other Mormon periodicals, also sought to reduce the potential for harm to the Mormon cause.

When the Mormons left Illinois in search of refuge from the Gentiles, the Great Basin was Mexican territory, though by the time they arrived it had become a part of the United States. Whether the Saints preferred to settle on Mexican rather than American soil is uncertain, but whatever the ownership of the land they fully intended to govern themselves. Consequently, when Mormon emmissaries visited Washington in 1849 to ask for territorial organization, Thomas L. Kane, an Eastern defender and confidant of the Mormons, pointed out that such a status would result in outsiders being appointed to office and thus inevitable conflict. "You do not want corrupt political men from Washington strutting about you," Kane told them,[1] and he urged them to apply for immediate statehood. This they did, but statehood was a political impossibility at this early date, and the Mormons finally welcomed the territorial status granted 7 September 1850. However, the creation of Utah Territory marked the beginning of the Mormon struggle against carpet bag government, a struggle in which the *News* followed a definite strategy.

It might be expected that a local newspaper would cover and make extensive comment on the appointment of new government officials, the inauguration of a new territorial administration, and the problems that might arise. However, the policy of the *Deseret News* was one of guarded response. It first ascertained the attitude of the new officers. If they proved friendly, it made favorable comment, but if they were antagonistic the *News* generally ignored them.[2]

The first Utah territorial appointees included both Mormons and Gentiles, and Brigham Young was appointed the first governor. Some of the Gentile officials, however, soon antagonized the Mormons, creating an atmosphere of disharmony, and Brigham Young immediately took action to curtail their power and influence. This led to charges of Mormon tyranny and caused several of the appointees, later dubbed "runaway officials," to abandon their assignments. Although hundreds of residents knew of the conflict, the *News,* feeling that no purpose would be served in discussing the subject for its Utah readers, almost completely ignored it.[3]

Ministering as a federal judge in Utah between 1855 and 1857 was W. W. Drummond, a libertine who flaunted his mistress in the faces of the Saints while sanctimoniously criticizing Utah polygamy. He became the object of intense Mormon contempt, yet little reference was ever made to him in the pages of the Church paper. Territorial governor Stephen S. Harding (1862-1863) antagonized the Saints by accusing them of disloyalty, criticizing their religious practices, and attempting to limit the jurisdiction of their courts; but the *Deseret News* avoided giving the slightest hint of such difficulties until just before his departure. The *News,* which generally let Territorial appointees speak for themselves by publishing their speeches, did not even print Harding's December 1862 message to the legislature. The speech was apparently excluded because it boldly criticized Mormon political and military power and called for the abolition of polygamy. After Harding was replaced as Governor in June 1863, a change the *News* welcomed,[4] little about federally appointed officials appeared before 1870, and of that most was favorable.

As with its policy of usually ignoring the anti-Mormon rhetoric of gentiles in Utah, the *Deseret News* also tended to overlook criticism printed in Eastern newspapers. Much of what Eastern journals published about the Mormons came from letters from travelers in Utah and California.[5] However, the *New York Times* had a correspondent in Utah at least by May 1852 and so received most of its knowledge about the Mormons from its own special agents.[6]

It is true that at times the *News* openly attacked editors of outside papers for what it considered to be gross misrepresentations. For example, it accused a *New York Times* reporter named Simonton of treachery, calling him a "double-dyed Iscariot" who intruded upon the citizens of Utah and accepted their hospitality for the sole purpose of lying about their domestic practices.[7] However, it was generally the *News's* policy in this earlier period to ignore criticisms from the East on the grounds that it would be a waste of time to recognize such "slandering twaddle."

The policy of silence was partially based on the optimistic principle that reflective men would observe and compare contradictory statements in other newspapers and recognize that they were filled with accusations made by perjured witnesses.[8] But there were other important reasons for the *News's* muted policy. One editor insisted that if ignored, Church opponents would do a better job of defeating themselves than if harassed by the *News*.[9] Late in 1858 Brigham Young wrote to a close friend in Philadelphia that it was the policy of the *News* generally to exclude from its pages "agitating topics." Young reasoned that treating subjects of this kind in detail would attract unwarranted attention to issues best left alone and would prove "more injurious than beneficial. . . ." Apparently referring to the rather limited circulation of the Mormon paper in the East, and more specifically in Washington, D. C., the Mormon leader explained that "at any rate . . . the appearance of that class of articles in the 'News' could have but little influence in quarters where influence will be most effective in producing correct political and social action." Young was quick to add, however, that this guarded "view of home policy does not, of course, have any bearing upon what it may be deemed proper to handle in papers outside Utah nor upon when nor how; neither is it known how long the present course in publishing may be best for the 'News' columns."[10]

Because the *News* followed this policy, the Church's main line of defense was Mormon newspapers outside Utah whose influence it was hoped would be more effective because of their locations. Not many years after the establishment of the *Millennial Star* in England in 1840, other foreign journals, initially modeled on the *Star,* began to appear. It was not long before the Church was issuing journals in Germany, Sweden, Holland, Switzerland, France, Wales, Denmark, India, and Australia.[11] These were essentially proselytizing journals.

By the middle of the 1850s the Church had also established four "newspapers" in the United States specifically to advocate and defend both Mormonism and the actions of its adherents in Utah. Orson Pratt, sent by Brigham Young to Washington, D.C., to start a periodical in 1852, published the *Seer,* a sixteen-page monthly that for over eighteen months frankly and boldly advocated and defended Mormonism, particularly the recently proclaimed doctrine of plural marriage. In his prospectus, Pratt expressed a hope that President-elect Franklin Pierce, members of Congress, heads of the departments of the national government, governors and legislative assemblies of the states and territories, ministers of all religious denominations, and the people of the republic in general would patronize his periodical.[12]

Less than a year after Pratt's departure for the nation's capital, John Taylor was sent on a similar mission to New York City. Every week for two and a half years he edited and published *The Mormon* at an office directly across the street from both the *New York Herald* and the *Tribune.* The location apparently indicated that Taylor intended to confront Utah critics directly. *The Mormon,* which carried the motto, "It is better to represent ourselves than to be represented by others," expressed confidence in the power of the press and proclaimed its desire to be the "true representative of Mormonism in the world."[13]

Responding to bitter anti-Mormon attacks made by some New York papers, editor Taylor resorted to language that the *Deseret News* would avoid for another twenty years. Identifying the *Sun* by name, the editor bluntly declared, "Your malicious slanders only excite contempt for those base enough to utter them. . . . Talk to us with your hypocritical cant. . . . Pshaw! It's nauseating to every one not eaten up with your corrupt humbuggery and pharisaical egotism. . . ." Concluding his criticism of the *Sun* and other anti-Mormon papers, Taylor made a prediction that has since been essentially fulfilled: he explained that the Mormons would survive and prosper "long after their malicious slanderers shall have sunk to oblivion in the filth of their own corruptions."[14]

The *St. Louis Luminary,* a weekly paper edited by Erastus Snow, was established in Missouri in 1854 to do in the Midwest what the *Seer* and *The Mormon* were doing in the East. The paper announced that it existed primarily to answer false accusations against both the Mormons and Utah and that it would devote itself to the "exposition of the favorable side of Mormonism."[15] Commenting on the St. Louis paper, the *News* articulated the policy that Brigham Young would later outline in the previously mentioned Philadelphia letter. "The *Luminary* does, and will treat on many topics which it would be impolitic to discuss in the *Deseret News,* on account of our great distance from the scene of action, [and] the uncertainty of the mails. . . . ," wrote editor Carrington in 1855; "hence subscribers will find most of the matter in the *Luminary* and *News* different, on account of difference of locality, and immediate policy. . . ."[16]

Early in 1856, George Q. Cannon founded at San Francisco, California, the weekly *Western Standard,* which had as its motto, "To correct Misrepresentation we Adopt Self-Representation."[17] The *Standard's* prospectus announced that it was sanctioned by the leaders of the Church, that it would be devoted to the interests of Mormonism, and that it would be a medium through which the public could derive "correct information in relation to its objects and progress."[18] It stressed at the end of its first volume the apparent need of a press in San Francisco "to defend the truth and its advocates from the slanders and scurrilous reports which have been so freely circulated respecting them. . . ."[19]

These papers, which served with varying degrees of succcess and lengths of time throughout most of the 1850s did not, of course, constitute the only defense of Mormondom. The *Deseret News,* despite its official policy of restrained comment and its handicapped location, did use its pages to try to curtail Mormon-gentile conflict. Coupled with the tactic of virtually ignoring the anti-Mormon federal appointees and the lies of outside newspapers, the *News,* acting as apologist for the Church, presented the Saints in strictly positive, if not always convincing, terms. For example, prominent Utah visitors who had good things to say

about the Mormons got considerable space in the pages of the
News, whereas those who were critical generally were ignored.[20]

In spite of their policy of isolation and self-sufficiency, the
Mormons, like people everywhere, desired to appear in a good
light, particularly when they felt that such a picture provided
the only means of persuading Eastern policy makers that there
was no need to interfere in Utah affairs. The *Deseret News* tried
hard to convince the East that Salt Lake City, despite disadvantages
of geographical location and "fierce opposition" from the four
quarters of the world, was rapidly becoming one of the most
beautiful cities on earth, with a population that would soon be
sufficiently sinless to associate with those of the perfect biblical
city of Enoch, as well as with the angels and just men of all
periods.[21] "Our streets are not rendered dangerous by brawls,
riots, rapes and murder," declared the *News,* "nor are our nights
hideous through the blasphemy and revelings of debauchees."[22]

Criticized by gentiles outside Utah for not reflecting in its
pages the correct state of local affairs and the true tone of public
opinion in the territory, the *News* observed that because the
"world's newspapers" were so generously sprinkled with details
of crime it was difficult to accept a paper that did not participate
in such sensationalism:

> But how can we gratify readers by printing the commission of
> crimes, when there are few or no serious crimes committed?
> . . . How can we home-chronicle the corrupt, conflicting and de-
> structive moves and designs of caucuses, conventions and cliques con-
> trolled by supremely selfish and rotten professional politicians? when
> Utah has no such disorganizing classes of far worse than useless
> population.[23]

Listing qualities that Utah possessed, editor Carrington declared
that the territory contributed little to the corruptions swelling the
Earth's record, "not even enough," he wrote, "to make her news
spicy and interesting to the corrupt taste of a perverse generation. . . ."[24]

To the *News,* the Gentile world was different from the peaceful Mormon community. On 3 September 1857 the *News* reported that bloody riots in New York City for the previous
forty-eight hours had resulted in seven persons being killed and
twenty-five or thirty wounded.[25] A year later the *News* asserted
that cities in the United States willingly admitted that crime of
every description was on the upswing in their midst—while they

piously advocated that manners, law, and morals be taught to Utah at the point of the bayonet.[26] The *News* confessed that some comparatively small misdemeanors like "Sunday street spinning" (loitering in streets) and "fruit . . . pilfering" occurred in the Mormon capital, but quickly asserted that in comparison with the "constant enormities" committed in all cities outside Utah these minor infractions would hardly be noticed.[27]

An excellent illustration of the policy of giving a favorable view of the Mormon cause is the *News's* coverage of the Mountain Meadows massacre. The massacre, which took place in southern Utah on 11 September 1857, resulted in the slaughter of all 120 adults of a California-bound Arkansas wagon train. It was the work of certain misguided and enraged Mormons, acting in concert with Indians and proceeding without the direction or knowledge of Mormon leaders in Salt Lake City.[28]

The Church paper at first ignored the disastrous event, even though papers outside the territory filled their columns with accounts of the slaughter less than a month after it happened.[29] When the *News* did break its silence in December 1857, its only comment was that nearly all California editors were "blowing and striking in perfect phrenzy" about the massacre and blaming Mormons for what Indians had done.[30] Despite proddings from non-Mormon Utah newspapers, the *News* maintained a general editorial silence until 1869, when its editor denied charges that the *News* was saying nothing because it could not prove the Mormons innocent. At that time the editor placed full blame on the Indians and explained that Mormon troops, sent to protect the gentiles, had arrived too late.[31]

The reason for such action on the part of the Church paper seems plain. Regardless of who was responsible for the tragedy, their antagonists believed that Mormons were involved in this sort of activity: indeed, President Buchanan had ordered 2,500 troops to Utah on 28 March 1857 to enforce federal law and insure the peace. Therefore, since the *News* hoped to dispel gentile suspicions rather than enhance them, it decided not to publicize the incident, especially at a time of impending invasion by federal troops.

The massacre occurred while United States soldiers were marching toward Utah, which aggravated the Mormons perhaps as much as during the earlier Missouri persecutions. The pages of the *Deseret News,* although unintentionally, may have contributed to this aggravation and helped provoke the carnage of the ill-fated

Arkansas migrants. Contact between Mormon and gentile frequently led to conflict, and Church leaders never let their followers forget that fact. The *News* recapitulated the tragedies and trials that the Saints had suffered in the Midwest and constantly reminded its Mormon readers that they were martyrs to diabolical oppression.[32]

It is likely that the Saints' anti-gentile feelings were intensified by the serialized account of the life, sufferings, and death of Joseph Smith, then currently appearing in the *News,* which was the source of almost all news for residents of southern Utah at that time.[33] In addition, news of the murder of Apostle Parley P. Pratt in Arkansas reached Salt Lake City in late June 1857.[34] Because of the semi-monthly mail service to San Bernardino, there is little question but that Mormons in the south read the account of Pratt's death prior to the eleventh of September. In its account, the *News* made no attempt to incite its readers; in fact, it emphasized that it had no reliable details of Pratt's death. Nevertheless, the mere announcement of the murder of that popular leader must have aroused Mormon anger against gentiles, particularly those from Arkansas.

At the time, the *News* was printing speeches that approved of blood atonement, and its editorial columns were filled with arguments favoring capital punishment, which may have indirectly encouraged revenge for the assassination of Smith and the murder of Pratt.[35] Taken together, the *News* may have unknowingly served to arouse some Mormons to a state of emotional excitement that contributed to the massacre.

Lurid accounts of Church-inspired murder, treason, and polygamy focused the nation's attention on the "Mormon Empire." In 1856 the Republican party platform even included a plank attacking polygamy as one of the "twin relics of barbarism," slavery being the other. Like the Southerners, Mormon Church authorities felt that the federal government was the major source of their problems, and consequently they tended to support the doctrine of states' rights. Earlier, however, Mormons in the Midwest had blamed the states' rights principle for preventing the federal government from coming to their rescue. "States rights," declared Joseph Smith, "are what feed moles. They are a dead carcass—a stink, and they shall ascend as a stink offering in the nose of the Almighty."[36] However, once in Utah, where they were the "old settlers," Mormons changed their opinions about the relationship of states to the central government. They sought statehood as an escape from federal control. As one historian has phrased it, "to Brigham Young . . . the 'stink' . . . became incense."[37]

With a fairly strict policy of restraint and a limited circulation, the Mormon newspaper could not deal adequately with the Church's differences with Washington, even though the *Deseret News* was pragmatic and its policy not totally inflexible. At times some large Eastern dailies reprinted portions of the Church's official paper, thereby increasing its influence.[38] This increased exposure for the *News* possibly accounts for the editor's declaration that, when necessary, the paper would not hesitate to attack enemies of the Mormon cause.[39] "When necessary" apparently meant when anti-Mormon commentary began to have influence in the East. The "run away officials" were only ignored while in Utah. When they returned to Washington and began spreading stories of Mormon rebellion, the *News* spoke out.[40] Justice Drummond was not neglected by the *News* when in 1857 he returned to the national capital to persuade government authorities that Brigham Young's people were misbehaving.[41] Indeed, the *Deseret News,* in an attempt to curtail Mormon-gentile conflict, began early sustained editorial defense of polygamy and the doctrine of states' rights.

Though ultimately the *News* defended polygamy from every imaginable position, at first it was inclined to assert that the institution was of no concern to those who lived outside Utah. More in favor of popular sovereignty than "popular institutions" (i.e., brothels), the *News* editor declared that Mormons, regardless of the consequences, would continue quietly to practice what they preached without fear of annoyance, though he warned that the Saints knew their constitutional rights and would oppose any attempt at infringement.[42]

More critical for Mormons and their newspaper in the 1850s than the defence of polygamy was the issue of states' rights and self-determination, denied to the Mormons under the federal territorial system. Although the *News* seldom attacked territorial officers personally, in 1857, incensed by the approaching United States Army, it called certain officers of the federal government "rotten political pigmies" and referred to their actions as "the cesspool of their corruptions."[43]

The Church paper had much to say on the subject of the territorial system, consistently aligning itself with advocates of popular sovereignty. Technically, under the territorial system the federal government had full control over a territory, and could even abrogate the laws of the territorial legislature. This seldom happened, but the passing of federal laws for the territory and the appointment of non-Mormon federal officials seemed to violate the Mormon desire for local sovereignty. In 1874 the *News* eulogized former President Millard Fillmore for having set up Utah Territory in 1850 and praised him for having appointed Mormons as well as gentiles to office. It characterized him as having been more imbued with the fundamental principles of American Government than any president since his time.[44] In 1854 the paper supported the Kansas-Nebraska Bill for not binding residents of the two territories in regard to slavery, and declared that territories would now have the right to settle their problems as they preferred, "without troubling Congress, or any other power that has nothing to do with the matter."[45] Almost all *News* comments on the issue of the territories closely reflected the thinking of the champion of democracy, Thomas Jefferson, who argued for self-government at every stage of territorial development.

The *Deseret News* advocated the idea that territories be left alone as long as they stayed within the bounds prescribed by the Constitution.[46] We . . . think," complained the editor in 1858, "most sincerely and patriotically that territories with their present institutions are mere satires, bitter, degrading, homespun satires, on a republican government."[47] If it was too progressive for the United States government to let citizens in territories elect their own officers to the extent accorded the states, then the *News* asked that at least appointments be made in accordance with the known wishes of the ruled.[48]

Continuous criticism of the territorial system by the *News* did not hasten the advent of statehood for Utah. Indeed, with Buchanan's order to send a federal army against the Mormons, it was obvious that the *Deseret News* had failed in its early propaganda campaign to convince Eastern citizens and lawmakers that Utah was free from crime and treason and ready for home rule. However, the Church journal did not admit defeat easily. Hoping to convince the President that Utah was not in rebellion, the *News* filled its editorial columns with long and plaintive arguments, some logical, others emotional and frantic. Bitter and enraged, its editor argued the impropriety and wanton wastefulness of Buchanan's 1857 venture and angrily condemned the federal government:

From the dawn of our Government until now there never has been so outrageous, unconstitutional, illegal, inhuman and in every way occasionless, unjustifiable and wanton a waste of the people's treasure to compass their oppression and destruction, as is to be found in the sending of troops to Utah.

It is most readily obvious to all that the administration of our Government is becoming rotten even to loathing, when anonymous liars and a whoring, lying, venomous late associate justice [Drummond] can incite the expenditure of millions of public treasure in an unjust, outrageously wicked and illegal movement against a peaceful and known zealously loyal people.[49]

Chafing under what it considered persecution of a religious minority, it was hard for the Church paper to understand why an army was being sent against Utah, where, according to the *News,* all "was peace, industry, law, order, virtue, and sobriety," while no federal troops were sent to Nebraska and California where the laws, as it declared, were openly defied and where out-and-out insurrection and rebellion prevailed. "Why are not troops sent to New York, Baltimore, Washington and other cities," questioned the editor, "where the civil authorities are wantonly flouted and blood lawlessly shed by violence reddens their streets?" He answered, sarcastically, "oh they   are not 'Mormons'!"[50]

Armies had expelled the Mormons from their land before, but this time they were not budging. The *News* warned all politicians, editors, and priests who advised sending troops to Utah that the Saints had been forced from their homes for the last time and would doubtless prefer "absolute extermination" to being scattered again.[51] Chronicling the history of persecution "from Noah to Missouri," the editor of the *News* cautioned that although Christ taught that it was necessary that offenses come to people, he also said, "but WO TO THAT MAN BY WHOM THE OFFENCE COMETH."[52] The national government was not intimidated, and federal troops drew closer to the Great Basin.

Attempting to demoralize the soldiers, the *News* urged the troops to turn back, not to "aid corrupt demagogues" in Washington, and to realize it was impossible to penetrate the Mormon defenses.[53] If outsiders felt that someone must come to fight the Saints in Utah, the *News* suggested that the invading force be made up of the priests, editors, letter-writers, politicians, and spectators who had caused the anti-Mormon uproar in the States.[54]

Anticipating the worst from the impending invasion, the Church took steps to insure that its paper would continue publication. In

April 1858 Brigham Young ordered George Q. Cannon to move a press to Fillmore about 150 miles south of Salt Lake City, to publish four issues of the *News* there.[55] At the same time a second press was sent even farther south to Parowan, where the *News* apparently was either to publish alternately with the Fillmore press or regularly if Fillmore had to be evacuated.[56] This would insure that the Church's communication with the outside would not meet the fate of the *Evening and the Morning Star* at Independence, and that the *News* would be regularly sent to California and the East coast.

Complying with Young's order that no apology be made for its removal,[57] the *News* gave no explanation, and only the appearance of Fillmore City in its masthead communicated the paper's new location. No issues were printed in Parowan.[58] Although Albert Carrington's name continued to head the editorial columns of the *News*, Cannon, who had only recently returned from successfully editing and publishing a Mormon California weekly, seems to have done the actual editorial work for the four months that the Church paper issued from Fillmore.[59]

Bloodless harassment of U. S. troops by the Mormons delayed the army from entering the Salt Lake Valley until after a peaceful settlement was achieved in the winter of 1858. Once past the crisis of the "Utah War," the *News* resumed publication in Salt Lake City on September 8, its circulation cut by two-thirds and its size by one-half.[60] More importantly, contact with federal troops, who remained in Utah until the Civil War, began the erosion of the relative isolation the Mormon empire had enjoyed and "contaminated" its residents with the "forbidden ways" of the gentile.[61]

But even though the Civil War took the troops out of Salt Lake Valley, it brought other strains to Mormon-gentile relations. At the time of Abraham Lincoln's first election to the presidency, a *Deseret News* editorial, "Prospective Dissolution," declared that the impending Civil War between the North and the South would give the United States Congress sufficient business without concerning itself with Utah.[62] But this was only wishful thinking on the part of the Church paper, for the Mormons really feared that an outbreak of hostilities between North and South would increase Mormon conflict with the federal government. As a communications link between the East and the West, Utah was of strategic importance. A national government which had sent an army to the Great Basin in 1857 to enforce federal law could certainly be expected to again send troops to insure the loyalty of Brigham Young's kingdom.

In a letter of 30 August 1862 to Secretary of State William H. Seward, Utah Governor Stephen S. Harding warned of Mormon disloyalty and recommended that a military force be stationed in the territory to prevent treason. By October 1862 Colonel Patrick Edward Connor and his "California Volunteers," on orders from Washington, had marched through the streets of Salt Lake City with fixed bayonets, loaded rifles, and cannon and, with their artillery aimed directly at the residence of Brigham Young, had encamped on a hill overlooking the city.

In the light of certain statements printed in the official Church newspaper, Harding's distrust of Mormon loyalty seemed justified to federal officials. The attack on Fort Sumter and its surrender were described by the *Deseret News* as very important events in the history of the collapse of the American Union.[63] A month before Sumter it argued that the outcome of a civil war would be the utter destruction of the United States and that nothing could save it.[64] This attitude stemmed from interpretation of certain Mormon prophecies. Before as well as during the civil conflict, *News* editorials continually explained that the War had been foretold by Joseph Smith, that it was inevitable, and that it was the manifestation of God's wrath upon the people in consequence of their iniquities and abominations.[65] The editor wrote in 1862, "We . . . believe that all things will be brought about and accomplished in the way and manner, and at the time predestined for their occurrence, and have no desire to make things move differently."[66]

Not only did the *News* predict and accept the notion of the dissolution of the Union, but also in the early days of the conflict it seemed to reflect a pro-Confederate position on slavery and states' rights. Commenting on the Republican Convention of 1860, the *News* warned that any party which attempted to raise a political structure based on abolition of the so-called "twin relics" would regret having tampered with "polygamy or any other institution of Heaven."[67] Whether the *News* was implying that slavery, like polygamy, was directed of God is not clear but evidence seems to suggest that this was the case. As a matter of fact, Brigham Young, in his much-publicized interview with Horace Greeley, editor of the New York *Tribune,* supposedly said as much when he explained that Negro servitude was "of divine institution."[68] Responding to the criticism of outsiders that such an attitude was contrary to the spirit of the Constitution, Young angrily replied "it is none of their damned business what we do or say here."[69] Although Brigham Young felt that Negroes should be treated with kindness, he held that it was necessary that they be servants,[70] a paternalistic attitude not unlike the traditional view in the South.

Despite these seemingly natural Mormon inclinations to favor the Southern cause during the Civil War, historians have disagreed as to the allegiance of the *Deseret News.* Hubert Howe Bancroft maintained that the Mormons, and particularly their official organ, were not adverse to the Union cause.[71] A more recent historian of Utah, Gustive O. Larson, concluded that the *News* reported the War objectively, rarely commenting editorially until the summer of 1864 when it definitely turned pro-Union.[72] On the other hand, T. B. H. Stenhouse, who was an assistant editor of the *News* during the war years, wrote that it was "intensely 'Copperhead' . . . ,"[73] and Edward Tullidge, a contemporary of Stenhouse, seems to have agreed with him.[74] Agreeing with none of these, a more recent student of the subject has concluded that it would be very difficult to determine where the paper stood with respect to the War.[75]

Difficult but perhaps not impossible. Let us return to the question of chattel slavery. The Mormon press advocated a qualified institution of slavery; indeed Joseph Smith, editorializing in the *Elder's Journal* of July 1838, said Mormons did "not believe in setting the Negroes free." Both Smith and Brigham Young expressed the belief that blacks were meant to be servants and although they ought not be maltreated they were to remain as servants until God willed otherwise.[76] It is true that in campaigning for the United States presidency in 1844 Joseph Smith called for the abolition of slavery, an apparent change from his earlier position. But if his position on slavery seems somewhat ambivalent, he and the Church press, always proponents of states' rights, consistently took a hard stand against ignorant, if well-meaning, radical, preaching abolitionists of the North. Writing an article for the April 1836 *Messenger and Advocate,* Smith explained:

> I do not believe that the people of the North have any more right to say that the South shall not have slaves, than the South have to say the North shall.
> And further, what benefit will it ever be to the slaves for persons

to run over the free states, and excite indignation against their masters in the minds of thousands and tens of thousands who understand nothing relative to their circumstances or conditions? I mean particularly those who have never traveled in the South, and who in all their lives have scarcely seen a Negro. . . . When I see persons in the free states, signing documents against slavery, it is no less in my mind, than an army of influence, and a declaration of hostilities against the people of the South. What course can sooner divide our nation?

Note that even Smith's campaign statement which appeared in the 15 May 1844 issue of the *Times and Seasons,* advocating freeing blacks, reflects what may have been his overriding concern—states' rights and wild-eyed Northern abolitionists. "Petition also, ye goodly inhabitants of the slave states, your legislators to abolish slavery by the year 1850 or now," explained the Mormon Prophet, "and save the abolitionist from reproach and ruin, infamy and shame." Later, still critical of certain types of abolitionists, the *Deseret News,* commenting on Lincoln's Emancipation Proclamation, declared that the announcement resulted from the agitation of fanatical and insane radicals.[77]

But the Mormon attitude on slavery is best revealed in an unusually candid editorial written by Albert Carrington on 5 January 1859. His attitude reflects the thinking of the intensely practical Abraham Lincoln as well as Mormon theology. Carrington explained that because slavery was a well-rooted system by the time the U.S. government was organized, federal authorities had the responsibility to restrict it to its "proper limits"; and, without infringing on the rights of the free citizens, prevent it from spreading. Carrington felt that returning the blacks to Africa was impractical, and that freeing them and giving them full franchise was "impolitic and absurd." The editor declared that absolute and irrepealable natural laws made whites and Negroes distinct and that amalgamation was both forbidden and unnatural. Carrington agreed that it had been wise to outlaw the foreign slave trade and to adopt laws that would moderate the treatment of those already enslaved, but hastened to state his conviction that everything possible had now been done to ameliorate the harshness of slavery. The *News* editor said that Mormons disliked any system which made chattels of the bodies or souls of any human, but they also opposed freeing what he called "a horde of hereditary bondsmen" to possibly become, at their will, governors, lawmakers, and heads of departments of the federal government.

Sounding now more like Jefferson Davis than Abraham Lincoln, Carrington went on to explain that he had heard eloquent speeches on both the sufferings of Southern slaves and on their emancipation. "We have heard all these, too, in cities and towns and villages," he wrote, "where slavery in its most galling bitterness, wore the transparent mask of freedom. We have seen old men and matrons weep over the rehearsal of poor old 'Uncle's' agony," continued the editor, "while their children, male and female, dragged the heavy coal truck deep, deep down in the earth, goaded by the curses and lashes of the worst of task masters." Concluding his criticism of abolitionists, Carrington asked that the Dred Scott decision allowing slavery in any state or territory be enforced, and that the people regulate their own domestic institutions.

Seven months after Carrington's editorial, Horace Greeley visited Salt Lake City. In a speech to the Deseret Typographical and Press Association, Greeley criticized the Mormons for refusing to condemn Southern slavery: "I never have heard, from the lips or the journals of any of your people, one word in reprehension of that gigantic national crime and scandal, American chattel slavery." He recognized that Mormons were forceful in speaking of the wrongs they themselves had suffered, but asked, "What are they all to the perpetual, the gigantic outrage involved in holding in abject bondage four millions of human beings?" Greeley described this silence as obstinate and condemned the Mormons for what he called their "seeming indifference," and expressed hope that their mute journals would soon begin to speak out.[78] As has been seen, Church journals had not been mute nor indifferent on the issue of slavery. They seemed generally to support its continuation. It is true the Mormon press did not speak for all members on this matter and some, including Joseph Smith, had called for its abolition. However, the Church's official Utah newspaper never did.

Despite its rather forceful position on slavery, the *Deseret News* seldom took strong positions on disputable questions of national interest. More outspoken critics of abolitionism than the *News* often felt the effects of Lincoln's emergency war powers. Commanders of federal troops in occupied territories or states after 1863 silenced opposition newspapers about as readily as they eliminated forts or batteries. Such well-known journals as the Chicago *Times,* New York *World,* and Philadelphia *Evening Journal* were suppressed or suspended by military order as were several newspapers in border states and occupied states in the

South. The Los Angeles *Star* and the Jacksonville, Oregon, *Gazette* were both excluded from the mails by order of postmaster general Montgomery Blair, and the *Star's* editor was arrested for anti-war and anti-Lincoln editorials.

Some evidence indicates that at one time Colonel Connor seriously contemplated gutting the printing office of the *Deseret News*. He did establish a provost guard in Salt Lake City to insure its loyalty.[79] Some of Brigham Young's advisers apparently convinced the prophet that the course being pursued by the *News,* if continued, would provoke difficulty with Connor's federal troops.[80] Perhaps this is what motivated Young to issue the following disclaimer of personal responsibility, which appeared in all issues of the *News* from 28 January to 17 June 1863:

> I hereby inform the public that the *Deseret News* is not and has not been an organ of mine; for, except matter accompanied with my name, I have only occasionally, and that too sometime ago, known any more of the contents of the *News,* until it is published, than I have of the copy furnished to the compositors of the New York *Ledger.*

The *New York Times,* which referred to the *Deseret News* as "Young's Organ," labeled this statement an insincere announcement meant for public consumption, and sarcastically recommended to the editor, "Come, friend Elias . . . round up your shoulders and bear the whole load." The *Times* suggested that Young's disclaimer was perhaps motivated by his disapproval of the general *tone* of the paper or because he objected to some particular article.[81]

A private letter from Brigham Young to editor Elias Smith of the *Deseret News* seems to lend some substance to the conjecture of the New York paper:

> Dear brother:—Upon mature reflection I deem it wisdom to change the tone and policy of the 'Deseret News', and realizing that your health and other important duties will not admit of your giving to its columns that amount of personal attention which its interests demand, I have decided to have bro. A. Carrington take entire charge of the office, calling to his aid such help as may be deemed necessary. Accordingly you will please close your labors on the News with the past issue, and turn the whole business, office, accounts and books and hands over to bro. Carrington immediately.

A postscript at the end signed "B. Y." curtly told Smith that he need not send an answer to the note.[82]

The day after receiving his unceremonious dismissal, Smith confided in his diary that he did not know exactly what influences had brought it about. "If it had been deemed for the good of the saints and there had no one been seeking to tarnish my reputation for uprightness of purpose and honesty of action," which he had some reasons for believing was the case, then he could accept it. He wrote that the decision might have been necessary, but that he did not fully understand the policy of studied reticence. He obviously felt injured and mortified.[83]

Smith was especially hurt that he had been cut off without first having a chance to bid his readers adieu, a courtesy extended to all previous *News* editors.[84] Both Albert Carrington's salutatory and Smith's valedictory appeared in the September 23 issue of the *News*. In his diary Smith expressed grief and dismay that Carrington, a longtime friend, made no allusion to him whatsoever.[85] More importantly, however, in one paragraph of his valedictory Smith shouldered the whole responsibility for any indiscretions. What pressure might have persuaded him to say this is unknown, but he wrote,

> There is one thing to which duty compels reference, and that is that the editorial columns of the *Deseret News,* from the 9th day of March 1859, to the 16th day of September, 1863, were entirely under my control and for their tone no other person is, or has been responsible. Some articles may have been inserted which were not previously duly scanned, but, by whoever, written, no avoidance is pleaded.[86]

Despite its attempted policy of restraint on sensitive issues during the Civil War, the *Deseret News* threatened to offend and provoke certain powers, thereby creating a risk of provoking further coercion from the outside. Realizing this, Brigham Young apparently got himself and the Church off the hook by replacing the editor and changing the tone and policy of the official Mormon newspaper.

As reflected in the pages of the *News,* the Mormons, like many others before and during the War, seemingly felt that the North would not fight to hold the South and that the South would rather easily win its independence. Some Church leaders and the *Deseret News* started out cautiously supporting the South because they saw the advantage to them in a Confederate victory. After Gettysburg and Vicksburg in July 1863, when the tide turned more definitely towards a Northern victory, the sentiments of the

Church paper also shifted in that direction. The Mormons, apparently hoping to profit from the conflict in terms of greater freedom for themselves, did not want to endorse a losing cause. Therefore, since no fundamental Church doctrines were directly involved in the war issues, Mormons could be pragmatic, hoping by a cautious approach to be on the winning side. This pragmatic, cautious approach accounts for the paper's generally moderate and shifting editorial statements on the war.

The influx of gentiles and their increased power because of military occupation in both the Utah War and the Civil War caused a major shift in Mormon policy. Brigham Young's early economic policy of self-sufficiency was needed because of Utah's remoteness from the rest of the country. The same policy now seemed necessary in order to prevent heavy non-Mormon immigration and gentile dominance.

Non-Mormon businessmen, hoping to gain from the Utah War, were accused of encouraging troops to come to the Great Basin. As early as 1857 Brigham Young announced a boycott against such merchants and by 1865 against all "who were considered hostile to the interests of the Latter-day Saints."[87] On 2 January 1867, the *Deseret News* printed a list of the Gentile businessmen considered to be the Church's "enemies" and called for total support of the boycott. The *News* had earlier attacked some non-Mormon Utah merchants for first exploiting the residents of the Territory and then spending their profits outside of Utah.[88] George Q. Cannon, while editor of the *News,* warned the Saints that the same thing had happened in the Midwest and pleaded with them to refrain from supporting their enemies. He stated that the primary purposes of the boycott were to eliminate those who sought to provoke a crusade against the Mormons and to prevent such people from taking over city and territorial offices.[89]

A gentile who worked hard at taking control away from the Mormons was Colonel Patrick Edward Connor. Colonel Connor's *Union Vedette,* a Salt Lake City newspaper described generally as anti-Mormon, grew out of the presence of federal troops during the Civil War. The colonel declared in a letter to his assistant adjutant general in San Francisco that a major policy of his paper was "to invite hither a large Gentile . . . population, sufficient . . . to overwhelm the Mormons by mere force of numbers. . . ."[90] The editorial column of the *Vedette,* employed to this end, boasted of the mineral wealth of Utah, giving exaggerated accounts.

Retaliating, the *Deseret News* editorialized week after week on the speculative dangers of mining, encouraging the Saints to remain on their farms.[91] Consistent with its policy of reducing Mormon-gentile contacts, it labored diligently to discredit reports of rich mineral deposits which otherwise would create a rush to Utah. *News* editor Carrington in 1864 assured his readers that no gold existed in Mormondom and pleaded with those who were thinking of coming to Utah in order to engage in mining to believe him.[92] Criticizing the Helena, Montana, *Herald,* the *News* editor wrote, "The fact is, there is scarcely anything which appears in print setting forth the advantages and richness of new mines that can be relied on."[93]

So consistently did the *News* support the economic policies of Brigham Young that its own editor, introducing an editorial on the subject, wrote in 1872, "This is an old story, and is so familiar as to have become almost trite to our readers."[94] This persistency, even at the risk of boredom, demonstrated the willingness of the *Deseret News* to support Young's goals to the fullest.

One of the Church leader's goals concerned the railroad. The Mormons and the *News* saw that the transcontinental railroad would bring increased economic contact with the East and a dangerous possibility of the destruction of the strong group-consciousness of the Saints. However, unlike their opposition to gentile merchants and mining interests, Mormons fully realized the advantages of the rails. In fact, like most Western newspapers, the *News* had advocated connecting the East with the West in this manner for many years.[95] Church writers were employed in support of the railroad and *Deseret News* editorials often stressed Mormon interest.[96] The Saints welcomed the trancontinental railroad for various reasons. Perhaps as important as any was the hope that improved communications would "cause the East to more truthfully understand the Mormons in Utah" by bringing many people to visit the Great Basin to see the truth, thereby countering the numerous "lies" told by the press.[97]

Between 1850 and 1869, the efforts of the *Deseret News* to keep conflict between Mormons and gentiles to a minimum fell into two parts. First, the paper tended to remain either editorially uncommitted or generally silent on sensitive matters, at times ignoring all anti-Mormon and negative information about Utah and the Saints. Secondly, it "puffed" the positive aspects of Mormondom, at times exaggerating them in hopes of convincing the East that all was well in Zion. Never very successful, this policy proved even less effective with the coming of the railroad. Mormon-gentile antagonism intensified after the rails reached Utah, and the *News* was pressed even further into the role of defender of the faith.

Footnotes

1. Quoted in Howard Roberts Lamar, *The Far Southwest 1846-1912: A Territorial History* (New Haven: Yale University Press, 1966), p. 326.
2. *News,* 22 January 1862.
3. Ibid., 18 November 1851.
4. Ibid., 3 June 1863.
5. For example, *see New York Times,* 18 June and 9 July 1852.
6. Ibid., 18 May 1852, 1 April and 14 July 1859.
7. *News,* 29 September 1858.
8. Ibid., the *News* warned those "professed saints" in Utah who considered the *New York Herald* and *Tribune* to be the only valuable papers and the *News* to be "as dry as a contribution box" that unless they repented they would "drink down error for truth" and "embrace the spirit of Babylon" until they wept and howled in misery without the ability to save themselves; *News,* 23 November 1854.
9. Ibid., 23 March 1859 and 30 December 1871.
10. Brigham Young, Salt Lake City, 22 October 1858, letter to Colonel Thomas L. Kane, photostatic copy at Henry E. Huntington Library.
11. Andrew Jenson, *Church Chronology: A Record of Important Events Pertaining to the History of The Church of Jesus Christ of Latter-day Saints* (Salt Lake City: Deseret News, 1899), pp. 30, 43, 44, 48, 241, 50, 97, 212 respectively.
12. *Seer* [Washington, D. C.], January 1853.
13. Prospectus printed in *News,* 7 December 1854.
14. *The Mormon* [New York City], 6 October 1855.
15. Prospectus printed in *News,* 22 February 1855.
16. Ibid.
17. For example, *see Western Standard* [San Francisco], 12 March 1856. It was printed boldly in every issue from one side of the paper to the other in the masthead.
18. Ibid., 23 February 1856.
19. Ibid., 28 February 1857.
20. *News,* 11 March 1856; on 29 August and 3 October 1860 the *News* spoke well of Richard F. Burton, and on 22 June 1862 of his book, *The City of the Saints, and Across the Rocky Mountains to California* (London: Longman, Green, Longman and Roberts, 1861).
21. Ibid., 24 June 1857.
22. Ibid., 3 February 1858.
23. Ibid., 3 March 1858.
24. Ibid., 2 April 1856.

25. Ibid., 3 September 1857.
26. Ibid., 3 February 1858.
27. Ibid., 24 June 1857.
28. Juanita Brooks, *John Doyle Lee: Zealot, Pioneer Builder, Scapegoat* (Glendale, California: The Arthur H. Clark Company, 1962), pp. 207-12.
29. William B. Rice, *The Los Angeles Star, 1851-1864: The Beginnings of Journalism in Southern California,* ed. John Walton Caughey (Berkeley: University of California Press, 1947), p. 231.
30. *News,* 9 December 1857.
31. Ibid., 26 November 1869.
32. Ibid., 27 July 1850, 7 August 1852, 12 January 1854, 16 April 1856, 19 November 1856.
33. Juanita Brooks, *The Mountain Meadows Massacre* (Palo Alto: Stanford University Press, 1950), p. 31.
34. The *News* on 1 July 1857 first announced the death.
35. Ibid., 22 February 1851, 24 July 1852, 12 August 1857.
36. Smith, *History of the Church,* 6:95
37. Hansen, *Quest for Empire,* p. 80.
38. The *News* claimed that the *New York Herald* clipped and printed large sections of the Mormon paper; *News,* 13 December 1851, 24 July 1852. The *Times* also used the *News* in this way; *New York Times,* 27 July 1857, 14 September 1857.
39. *News,* 23 March 1859.
40. Ibid., 7 February 1852.
41. Ibid., 20 May 1857.
42. Ibid., 4 February 1857.
43. Ibid., 12 August 1857.
44. Ibid., 9 March 1874.
45. Ibid., 24 August 1854.
46. Ibid., 8 March 1855.
47. Ibid., 27 October 1858.
48. Ibid., 21 May 1856.
49. Ibid., 23 September 1857.
50. Ibid., 12 August 1857.
51. Ibid., 17 June 1857.
52. Ibid., 15 July 1857.
53. Ibid., 14 October 1857.
54. Ibid., 29 July 1857.
55. "History of Brigham Young," 7 May 1849; in May 1858, having abandoned the earlier stand-and-fight policy, Mormons virtually evacuated all territory north of a line about fifty miles south of Salt Lake City.
56. "History of Brigham Young," 7 and 15 April 1858; *see also* Elias Smith, diary, 14 October 1861, Utah State Historical Society Library, Salt Lake City, Utah. In a special supplement of the *News* on 16 June 1900, the editor explained that the two southern locations of the press were to conceal from the advancing army the real place where the *News* was printing. This seems erroneous inasmuch as the regular appearance of Fillmore City in the masthead advertised its location.

57. "History of Brigham Young," 15 April 1858.

58. The *News* issued weekly from Fillmore from 5 May 1858 through 1 September 1858, after which it returned to Salt Lake City.

59. The eighteen issues of the *News* published in Fillmore show a definite change in make-up and style of writing. Editorials such as "Education" and "Works of Fiction—Their Effects" in *News*, 14 July and 1 September 1858, respectively, are markedly similar to Cannon's on the same subjects after he became editor in 1867.

60. *News*, 2 March 1859.

61. Ibid., 15 February 1860 and 24 November 1858; *see* Horace Greeley *An Overland Journey from New York to San Francisco in the Summer of 1859* (New York: C. M. Saxton, Barker and Co., 1860), p. 234; and Bancroft, *History of Utah* (San Francisco: Bancroft, 1890), pp. 537-38.

62. *News*, 28 November 1860.

63. Ibid., 24 April 1861.

64. Ibid., 6 March 1861.

65. Ibid., 4 January and 28 November 1860; 7 January and 2 September 1863.

66. Ibid., 1 January 1862.

67. Ibid., 16 May 1860.

68. Greeley, *An Overland Journey*, p. 211.

69. Brigham Young, Speech in Joint Session of the Utah Territorial Legislature, 5 February 1852, Brigham Young Collection, as quoted in Dennis L. Lythgoe's, "Negro Slavery and Mormon Doctrine," *Western Humanities Review* 21 (Autumn 1967): 331.

70. Ibid., p. 338.

71. Bancroft, *History of Utah*, p. 606.

72. Gustive O. Larson, "Utah and the Civil War," *Utah Historical Quarterly* 33 (Winter 1965): 75.

73. T. B. H. Stenhouse, *The Rocky Mountain Saints* (New York: D. Appleton and Co., 1873), p. 610. Copperheads were southern sympathizers during the Civil War.

74. Edward W. Tullidge, *The History of Salt Lake City and Its Founders* (Salt Lake City: Tullidge, 1883), appendix p. xiv.

75. Arlington Russell Mortensen, "The *Deseret News* and Utah, 1850-1867" (doctoral dissertation, University of California, Los Angeles, 1949), p. 66.

76. *Messenger and Advocate*, April 1836; Brigham Young, "Intelligence, Etc.," discourse given 9 October 1859, Salt Lake City, Utah, as published in *Journal of Discourses by Brigham Young, His Two Counsellors, and the Twelve Apostles*, 7:290.

77. *News*, 22 October 1862.

78. Greeley, *An Overland Journey*, p. 243.

79. Stenhouse, *The Rocky Mountain Saints*, p. 610.

80. Ibid.

81. *New York Times*, 22 February 1863. Elias Smith had replaced Albert Carrington as editor of the *Deseret News* on 9 March 1859.

82. Brigham Young, Salt Lake City, 18 September 1863, letter to Elias Smith, Brigham Young Letter Book No. 6, p. 669, LDS Church Historical Department.

83. Elias Smith, diary, 19 September 1863.

84. Ibid.; the right was also respectfully extended to all subsequent *News* editors of the nineteenth century.

85. Ibid., 23 September 1863.

86. *News,* 23 September 1863.

87. Arrington, *Great Basin Kingdom,* pp. 173, 248.

88. *News,* 23 November 1865.

89. George Q. Cannon, "Self-sustaining—Persecutions—Outside Influence," discourse given 7 October 1868, Salt Lake City, as published in *Journal of Discourses,* 12:295-96.

90. As quoted in Arrington, *Great Basin Kingdom,* p. 202; *see Union Vedette* [Camp Douglas, Utah], 11 June 1864, for a statement to this effect by the paper itself.

91. *News,* 22, 29 June, 8 August, and 30 November 1864; 4 January and 14 June 1865; 3 May and 6 September 1866; 6 March and 17 December 1867; 21 March 1868; and 10 March and 18 May 1871.

92. Ibid., 2 March 1864.

93. Ibid., 27 January 1868.

94. Ibid., 31 October 1872.

95. Ibid., 28 April 1858; 10 June 1868; *see* Oliver Knight, *"The Owyhee* [Idaho] *Avalanche:* The Frontier Newspaper as a Catalyst in Social Change," *Pacific Northwest Quarterly* 58(April 1967): 80.

96. *News,* 21 May 1868.

97. Ibid., 28 April 1858; 10 June 1868; 1 July 1869.

5

Mormon Family Newspaper:
A Profile of the
Deseret News

In the thirteen years between 1867 and 1880 the position of editor of the *Deseret News* changed hands four times. In November of 1867 Apostle George Q. Cannon replaced Albert Carrington as editor-in-chief. Like two of his predecessors, Carrington and Willard Richards, Cannon had been Brigham Young's private secretary, a position he held for the three years immediately preceding his appointment as *News* editor. In addition to being well acquainted with Young, Cannon's connection with printing and newspaper work from his youth made him a logical choice. As compositor for the *Times and Seasons* and the *Nauvoo Neighbor,* early Mormon papers edited by his uncle John Taylor, he gained experience and education. He started the *Western Standard* in California in 1856 and for about two years edited and published that Mormon weekly. He was called back to Utah during the Utah War and was appointed to take the *News* press and materials to Fillmore City where he published the paper for four months. Later, while on a mission to England, he edited the *Millennial Star.* The year before he came to the editor's chair of the *News,* Cannon began the *Juvenile Instructor,* a semi-monthly periodical designed expressly for the education and elevation of the youth of the Church.

Despite Cannon's journalistic background and his obvious inclination toward the publishing business, his rather wide range of talents and interests eventually took him away from the paper. On 5 August 1872 he was elected Utah territorial delegate and a year later resigned his post as *News* editor. In his valedictory he explained that during the nearly six years he had been in charge of the *News* it had grown to such proportions that it required "constant supervision" and "undivided care." He said that for the first four or five years he had been able to devote almost exclusive attention to it, but confessed that because other duties claimed his time and a considerable portion of his thoughts he was now unable to attend adequately to the newspaper.[1]

David O. Calder immediately took Cannon's place, but he was no journalist. However, the *News* establishment had become more than just a newspaper. Besides the newspaper, it included a book-and-job office, a bookbindery, a type foundery, and a paper mill. Calder's appointment was apparently because of his long and successful experience in private business and his intimacy with Utah's leading citizens, "especially with President Brigham Young, his counsellors and the Twelve Apostles. . . ."[2] This intimacy resulted from Calder's service as Brigham Young's bookkeeper from 1855 to 1857 and as his "chief clerk" for the following ten years. The actual editorial work could be done by three assistant editors, John Jaques, David Evans, and John Nicholson, all experienced newspapermen.

Calder's association with the *Deseret News* lasted only four years. In 1877 he explained that because of other responsibilities[3] his "directorial connection" with the *News* establishment had come to an end. He no longer had enough time and energy to give the kind of attention to the newspaper that it should receive from the party entrusted with its "direction" and "chiefly responsible" for its condition and conduct.[4]

The night before Calder announced his retirement, Brigham Young, Jr., wrote in his journal, "In evening father instructed Bro C and I to assume editorial ship of D News. I to take charge of the business Bro Cannon senior editor."[5] Because Cannon still continued to serve as Utah's territorial delegate, this second editorial appointment was largely in an advisory capacity and his assistants did the daily work. Cannon confessed that he was only "nominally one of the Editors, Publishers and Managers," and that Charles W. Penrose was the acting editor.[6] Apparently because he was an Apostle and had the confidence of the Church president, Cannon's name remained at the head of the editorial columns of the *News;* and from his residence in Washington he advised his subordinates on questions of employment, wages, advertisements, and editorials.

On 12 July 1879 both Cannon and Brigham Young, Jr., were arrested on a contempt charge for refusing to deliver certain Church property to a court-appointed receiver and they resigned from the *News.* A week later Cannon explained that he was too frequently absent from Salt Lake City and that both he and Young lacked the necessary time to properly superintend the paper.[7] Two days before they entered the penitentiary with sentences of twenty-four days each, their names were dropped from the masthead of the Church paper. No names were substituted for over a year.[8]

A contemporary Mormon historian depicted Cannon as one of the ablest journalists that Utah had ever produced.[9] However, despite his extensive newspaper experience and because he was best-known nationally for advocating Utah statehood, his *New York Times* obituary described him as a politician, statesman, and priest, without mentioning his association with the *Deseret News.*[10]

When Cannon officially began to edit the *News,* the Deseret Store Building, a three-story adobe establishment situated on the northeast corner of South Temple and Main Streets, housed the *News* plant. The attic, or third floor held the composition and editorial rooms. Efforts were made to make the editor's office useful and comfortable. By 1873 it contained separate desks or tables for the editor and his assistants and had been matted and carpeted with twenty dollars' worth of carpet. Along with a clock, maps of Europe and of Utah were hung on the walls of the office, and its bookshelves contained such reference works as Appleton's *New Encyclopedia,* Colton's *Atlas,* Lippincott's *Gazetteer,* a copy of the 1872 *American Newspaper Directory,* and a volume of poetical quotations.[11] However, only one coal-burning stove and a single lamp provided heat and illumination for the whole upper floor,[12] and the cold and dark composition room reduced the quantity of the typesetters' work. In winter it became dark at 5:00 p.m. and at times the candles served as their only light.[13]

How many employees worked directly on the newspaper in this Store Building when Cannon started as editor is not certain, but by 1875 the growing establishment employed fifty-five.[14] They were mostly Mormons, though apparently no firm policy existed against hiring gentiles. Ed Howe, a non-Mormon who later became nationally known as an editor and newspaperman in Kansas, worked as a typesetter for the Mormon paper while eighteen years old.[15]

Compositors, gentile or Mormon, apparently worked many hours. At least this was the case with Joseph Beecroft, who often arrived at the *News* office before sunup and worked after dark by candlelight. Beeecroft packed not only a lunch but breakfast as well, and at times set type and ate simultaneously.[16]

News employees endured not only difficult working conditions and long hours, but also an irritating pay system. Typesetters were compensated according to the quantity of their work, and the weekly take-home pay for one man in 1870 ranged from $2.67 to $19.10. And though they appeared content with the amount they earned, the employees wanted their pay in money rather than in goods. Beecroft recorded in his diary that he told Cannon the *News* hands wanted their wages "paid in better pay." Cannon replied that he could not be dictated to and that he did everything possible to pay with the best kind of resources the office had. The best they had was "store pay," or credit with certain business establishments, and scrip, though sometimes the *News* office itself would dispense wages in the form of goods. Beecroft noted on 27 August 1870 that his week's wages of $10.70 were paid in molasses, eggs, and flour, orders for 75¢ worth of meat, a dollar on the theatre and two dollars on the Church co-operative institution.[17]

Despite the fact that most employees were brothers in the Church and usually stuck together, disharmony was not unknown in the *News* rooms. There were the usual complaints of the compositor having to wait for copy and the editor demanding that the paper come off the presses sooner, but at least one typesetter claimed to have been ridiculed, jeered at, and generally tormented by his colleagues throughout his years of employment. Beecroft reported that on one occasion some of the hands ignited powder under his stand and a month later put salt in his drinking water. Writing of the *News* foreman, Beecroft recorded, "Brother Roberts has proved himself my enemy since the first of my seeking work at the News Office. He has taken every opportunity to insult, harass and humble me. My Father will judge him."[18]

Other early events in the *News* office reveal something about the changing attitudes of the Latter-day Saints. Although today the *News* staff is not permitted to drink or smoke in the city and news rooms,[19] tobacco and alcohol were not always as strictly prohibited as they are now. Beecroft noted that two of his colleagues annoyed him by blowing smoke in his face,[20] and it is clear that some *News* hands drank beer and wine on the job with the express permission of their foreman, Samuel Roberts.[21] Apparently it was excessive drinking that was condemned, as in the case of one Joshua Arthur, whom editor Elias Smith fired after many warnings because of his intemperate use of alcohol.[22]

Just as the *News* reflected in its pages the general problems and concerns of the Church, so its employees reflected the general lifestyle of the community. While frowned upon by the Church, the use of tobacco and alcohol was not totally forbidden until the twentieth century. This was a period of maturation for the Saints in many ways.

Problems of conditions, wages, long hours, and discipline were probably intensified when Cannon took editorial charge of the Church paper in November 1867 and promptly started publishing six days a week. In the masthead the daily carried a new name: *Deseret Evening News.* Evening papers were then becoming more and more popular in the United States, and by 1880 there were more evening than morning papers in the country.

Evening or morning, why did the Church launch a daily paper in 1867, and what were its chances for survival? In an editorial headed "The Daily Newspaper," Cannon explained that improved methods of communication would soon make the daily the most common type of periodical in the United States. He pointed out that although Utah was somewhat isolated from the conveniences of the East, it had not hesitated to avail itself of the "improvements of the age." The territory's northern settlements were already connected by telegraph with those in the south,[23] and it was no longer necessary to send out fatiguing and dangerous horse expresses to gather news. Cannon announced that a daily mail, soon to be established throughout Utah, would bring the daily paper into great demand, especially if the subscription price remained sufficiently low that the masses could pay for it without being burdened economically.[24]

Further explaining why he felt the daily would be successful and subtly trying to enlist subscribers, Cannon wrote:

> We may reasonably expect that there will be developed among all our people a greater anxiety for the news of the day. There is no people in the world who take greater interest in the affairs of the nations and the progress of events than the people of this Territory.

In consequence of their circumstances this disposition has been re-
pressed. But now that there are opportunities afforded for its grati-
fication, it will make itself felt.[25]

The daily replaced neither the weekly nor the semi-weekly,
(begun 3 October 1865); it only supplemented them. Much of the
copy that found its way into the daily also appeared in the other
two papers. The daily appealed essentially to residents of Salt
Lake City, whereas the weekly and semi-weekly interested mostly
the rural population who received the mails only once or twice
a week.

But the *Evening News* was not a daily in the strict sense. Despite
the fact that eagerness for news during the Civil War stimulated
the establishment of Sunday editions of the regular daily papers,
the first *News* "daily" appeared "Every Evening, Sundays Excepted."[26] Nor did the *News* always issue on such national holi-
days as the Fourth of July, Christmas, New Year's, or the Mormon
holiday on July 24.

Selling for ten dollars a year the daily contained a wide variety
of material. Its first issue, for instance, consisted of four 10½-by-15-
inch pages of four columns each, and its contents followed the
general interests of the community. Advertisements appeared
throughout the paper and occupied seven of the sixteen columns.
All advertisements were local except one from a San Francisco
merchant promising Salt Lake City readers delivery of goods by
mule train in forty-five days at freight rates lower than ever
before. National and international news telegraphed from such
cities as Chicago, New York, Memphis, London, Paris, Florence,
and Lisbon filled more than two columns. Local items occupied
only one. On page two, following Cannon's column-long salutatory,
the officials of the University of the State of Deseret announced
the opening in Salt Lake City of the School of the Prophets, which
would teach "in a practical manner" various branches of theology
and science. Correspondence from two missionaries occupied over
half the first page. One, who had been assigned "to the States,"
reported his trip across the plains to Omaha. The other, the Mormon mission president in Hawaii, attached to his letter the minutes
of a recent conference held in the Islands.

Other items in the first issue included a proclamation by Utah's
territorial governor, arrivals and departures at Salt Lake City by
stage, a poem by Eliza R. Snow, and a note on "A Novel Cure
For Sea Sickness." A report of the Paris Academy of Science,

which concluded that ducks produce more eggs than do chickens, also appeared, as did a suggestion on how to keep grapes fresh, a note on the profession of Paris beggars, and a sort of farmers' calendar for November which, in addition to giving various statistics about the moon and sun, contained the signs of the zodiac and their significance.

As the weekly before it, the daily was characteristically a Mormon newspaper. Missionary letters persisted. Moreover, in order for Church members to understand the policies and "partake of the spirit" of the presiding quorums, sermons of ecclesiastical authorities were also published at least once a week.[27] Stake or district quarterly conference reports continued to appear in the columns of the *News,* though the editors noted that if clerks would condense their minutes both the newspaper and the public would be grateful.[28] Church-related announcements of all kinds constantly appeared, albeit an editorial note explained that names of excommunicants would be printed only when an offender was well-known and his dismissal would be of general interest to the whole Church.[29]

The *News* columns themselves reflected Mormon theology. As millenarians, the Mormons wanted their paper to report the "signs of the times" that ancient biblical prophets foretold would precede the second coming of Christ. Cannon reviewed the increasing incidence of earthquakes, volcanic eruptions, typhoons, hurricanes, railway disasters, and steamboat collisions, explaining that the new telegraph was not responsible for the heightened number of reports of catastrophes but that their increasing number represented fulfillment of the words of the Savior, who declared that such signs would herald his second advent.[30]

The Mormons also taught that the restoration of the "ten lost tribes" of Israel must precede the millennium. They believed that the "lost tribes" were located somewhere in the "north country," and the *News* covered with great interest polar expeditions that might result in their discovery.[31] In covering the arctic exploration of the distinguished Finlander Baron Nordenskjold, the paper reported that the icy barriers of the polar region were breaking up. According to the *News,* that phenomenon could not be accounted for scientifically but represented a development which the reporter, thinking of the discovery of the lost Israelites, regarded as the first of a series of events that would startle the whole civilized world.[32]

Perhaps even more important, Mormons strongly felt the Jews would gather and return to Jerusalem before the millennium would come; thus the *News* quite regularly covered events pertaining to the Jewish people.[33] Great interest was expressed in the Crimean War[34] and later, in 1877, in the Turkish-Russian conflict. The Church paper explained that this latter conflict probably interested Mormons more than any community outside the nationalities engaged in the strife itself. Mormon interest, unlike that of England and Austria, was not motivated by the fear that Russia would disturb the European balance of power, but rather by the hope that the war would be the means of opening the way for the restoration of the Jews to Palestine. The *News* did not spell out how the war might do this except to note that an amelioration of the conditions of Jews in the Ottoman Empire had followed the Crimean incident. The paper obviously hoped the Turkish-Russian War would repeat this development.[35]

In 1881 the *Deseret News* described the anti-semitic German government of Bismarck and concluded that because Jews were excelling in all areas of experience in Europe the days of the gentile were nearly fulfilled. It explained that the world was on the eve of important changes and proclaimed: "Judah will come forth to the place and domain decreed by the God of nations, in spite of 'christen' priests, conservative chancellors, popular clamor and the might of Empires."[36]

This concern over zionism and other points of theology, along with its missionary letters, sermons, and Church news generally, made the *News* a distinctively Mormon journal. But it was also a "family" newspaper. Cannon started the *Juvenile Instructor* in 1886 and was appointed the following year as the first general superintendent of the Church's youth-oriented Sunday School Union, suggesting that his particular interest in the young people of Mormondom may have been a major reason for his starting the *Deseret Evening News*. In his 21 November 1867 salutatory, Cannon declared that neither "briskness of the times" nor the "plentiful circulation of money" would of themselves make 1867 a favorable time for starting a daily paper. In his opinion, for some time the youth of Utah had been experiencing an increased desire for knowledge. Later he wrote that as education spread, the daily would become more and more popular, "for the young must have their taste for knowledge gratified."[37] With some obvious hyperbole he argued that "nothing but a judiciously edited daily" would satisfy the minds of inquiring youth and that they would "look for such a paper each day as naturally as they look for their meals."[38] Cannon admitted that newspaper literature was not always deemed "suitable" for young people to read but declared that such an objection could not be used against a "properly conducted paper."[39]

The *News* intended to be a "properly conducted" paper, but it was well aware of the presence of low-caliber journalism in Utah and warned against it. Interesting in light of the editor's earlier suggestion that Mormon youth yearned for expurgated or purified reading, Cannon noted in February 1868 that although highly vulgar and sentimental newspapers were seldom seen in Utah, other journals, "cheap novelettes," and "sensational story papers," which he considered as perhaps even more injurious and dangerous, flooded the territory.[40] Although Cannon criticized these vulgar novels and warned against their pernicious effects, he did not advocate the establishment by the Church of an index of forbidden books. He recognized that the minds of young people were "plastic" and "untrained" and, therefore, could formulate bad as well as good ideas; but as in the Mormon Church of today where the responsibility of censorship is placed largely with the individual and the home, Cannon stressed that parents should monitor their children's reading. It was as much their burden to guard their offspring from improper reading as from bad food.[41] This in no way implied that the Church would not offer direction. The *News* editor continually warned against the sensational printed works that he said abounded in Mormondom and called for moderation, predicting that concentration on such works for primary reading material would lead to demoralization.[42]

The *Deseret News* criticized sensationalism wherever it existed, even beyond the bounds of Utah. In an editorial headed "Disreputable Literature," the *News* editor emphasized what he saw to be the evil in such sensationalism in the American press. He quoted approvingly an editorial from the *Springfield* [Illinois] *Republican,* "Nasty Journalism," which criticized the devotion of certain Eastern newspapers to illustrations of scenes of "violence, crime and lust." The *Republican* declared that such jounals were "more numerous, more filthy, and cheaper than in England or France," and that they were being "sold everywhere."[43] According to the *News,* one of the more notorious of these "nasty" journals was the *New York Herald.* "As long as sensations, true or false, well-founded or baseless, suit the public taste," editorialized the

Mormon paper, "the *Herald* will be sustained, but with the commencement of a different era it will dwindle away."[44] The *News* censured an exchange article that complained about the epidemic character of crimes, especially "personal outrage to females," and blamed the epidemic on newspapers themselves. "It is what might have been expected," wrote the editor. "The newspapers are full of details, highly suggestive to a prurient imagination."[45] Criticizing journalists for not being motivated by high and pure ideals, the Mormon editor claimed that they sold themselves and their influence to the highest bidder.[46] Cannon argued that the liberty of the press, although much lauded as one of the greatest blessings of the times and of the nation, had degenerated into free license. Although avowing his opposition to despotism, he was frustrated enough on this issue to declare that he had often thought that stopping the issue of pornographic material through the exercise of arbitrary authority would be an unmitigated benefit to everybody.[47] In all this the paper reflected a Mormon concern which continues to the present.

Although journalistic sensationalism did not reach its height in the United States until the 1880s, it had been widespread for years, and the Church hoped to discourage Mormons from reading such literature by offering less lurid and more reliable material. To this end it employed the power of the *Deseret Evening News.* But Cannon's first editorial in the new Church journal overestimated the power of a daily newspaper. He declared,

> Within the past few years the whole face of society in our nation has changed; and to the potent influence of the press this is mainly attributable. In a brief space of time it has developed for the American people an entirely new character.[48]

Such extravagant language reflected the importance that Cannon attached to the *News,* and perhaps more credibly the editor stated in the same editorial that the power of the press for good or evil was "very great." He explained that the kind of material that people read daily consciously or unconsciously shaped and colored their thinking. Therefore, he said, to have healthy, sound, and "high-toned" minds, a community must be supplied with quality journalism. This made the position of the journalist a very responsible one, and Cannon concluded, "We view it in this light, and while we fill the position, we sincerely hope that no word may ever drop from our pen that can truthfully be viewed as unworthy of this responsibility."

Cannon's promise to use the power of the daily press for good and his salutatory emphasis on the importance of a wholesome, reliable paper that old and young alike could read with pleasure and satisfaction was not a policy change. The Church sheet had from the beginning been a family paper. Cannon himself claimed that the weekly *News* had always been a safe, sound guide for its readers, that it had always tried to promote the public welfare and that, though it had its faults, unreliability had not been one of them.[49] It was his aim to maintain this same integrity in the daily *Deseret News*—"the highest character, which, in our view, any editor can secure for the journal he conducts. . . ." He concluded, "Honesty of purpose, and truthfulness and diligence, we are convinced will do more towards accomplishing this than any amount of talent, unaccompanied by these other qualities."[50]

Could such a "family" newspaper survive and flourish? Julius Chambers, the New York *World*'s managing editor in the 1880s, argued that "in every case" the successful American journal has been initially built upon sensationalism.[51] Although the *News* did publish advertisements of questionable propriety, it did not depend entirely on circulation and advertisement revenue for its economic existence, and so reliance on yellow journalism was unnecessary. To criticism that he was too sensational, Charles Dana, editor of the New York *Sun,* answered, "I have always felt, that whatever the Divine Providence permitted to occur I was not too proud to report."[52] The *Deseret News,* on the other hand, always subscribed to the idea that "every one in America knows enough about the 'under world' without having it dragged into his notice."[53]

Albert Carrington defended the anti-sensationalist policy of the *News* by suggesting that it was not so hard pressed for variety that it had to outline the method for crime or pander to perverted tastes. As early as 1854 he claimed that Salt Lake City was not "fashionably prolific in duels, murders, assassinations [and] incendiarism. . . ." Moreover, he announced that in reporting such events from other parts of the world the Church paper would omit most or all of the customary detail.[54] Later, under the heading "Another Homicide," Elias Smith explained that the *News* had ignored many recent killings. Unwilling to admit the natural curiosity of man, Smith explained the reason for such omissions by writing, "so far as the [Mormon] people in general . . . [are] concerned, to their great credit we say it, they care very little whether it was Dick that shot Harry, or whether it was Harry that knifed Dick."[55] And after commenting on the 1872 polygamy trial of Brigham Young and the way Eastern newspapers were sensationalizing it, Cannon explained that the *News* tried to "moderate and calm public sentiment, locally and generally," because justice could not be achieved when passions were inflamed.[56]

Perhaps the best example of the *Deseret News*'s policy concerning sensational matters is its coverage of what one historian has called the greatest sensation of the time.[57] On 2 November 1872, Victoria Woodhull and her sister Tennessee Claflin published a story in their *Woodhull and Claflin's Weekly* charging intimacy between Henry Ward Beecher and the wife of Beecher's close friend and protege Theodore Tilton. An eloquent and dramatic preacher, Beecher was a major spokesman and symbol of Protestantism of his time. The Woodhull sisters, who had long advocated free love, exposed what they saw as the hypocrisy of one of the "best" of society practicing in secret what he condemned in public. Explaining that the report startled the whole country, the *Deseret News* called it one of the most dreadful cases of scandal that had ever been publicized in the United States. "Perhaps in view of the tremendous character of the case, in duty to our readers we ought to give them some idea of it," wrote the Mormon editor, "though we shall touch upon it with [an] exceedingly light hand."[58]

The Church paper omitted the names of Beecher and Tilton, referring to them only as "some prominent persons, very extensively known to the public . . . ," and to the language of the allegations as "such unmistakable and unreserved terms as to almost take the hair off one's head."[59] The *News* passed no judgment as to the guilt of the accused, but did deplore the lurid language in which the original exposé had been written. By avoiding the obvious opportunity to lecture critics of Mormon polygamy, the *News* editor displayed commendable restraint in reporting and commenting on the incident.

A similar restraint characterized the *News*'s coverage of politics, and it outspokenly criticized other papers' treatment of political matters. Partisan journalism supposedly reached its peak in the 1840s and 1850s and thereafter declined rapidly, but the *Deseret News,* which claimed to be politically independent, saw little evidence of nonpartisanship in the newspapers on its exchange list. Instead, in its view, national politics "kept seething and boiling, with the press as chief cook and fire-tender."[60] During the 1868 fight for the presidency between Ulysses S. Grant and Horatio

Seymour, Cannon wrote that "in no previous campaign has such low, vulgar and disgraceful language been used by public journalists . . . as now appears in the columns of the various political papers."[61]

Some years later, continuing its criticism of the partisan press, the *News* commented that, on the whole, election matter was "the veriest bosh," not worth the paper on which it was printed and an insult to an intelligent person. "If all the newspapers . . . occupied with this political trash were to cease to exist," wrote the editor, "the number of papers in the country might ' . . . be reduced' by a half or two-thirds, but the country at large would be vastly the gainer."[62] Because the Mormons objected to political parties and Utah citizens were voteless in presidential elections, the *News* naturally reported and editorialized much more on local than on national campaigns. When it did cover national politics in any detail, it felt obliged to apologize to its readers.[63]

Although the *Deseret News* reported politics and the arts less fully than some papers, it boasted in 1889 that for twenty-two years it had preserved a record of events in Utah as well as accounts of the general news of the world. It claimed that it had endeavored to be as complete and reliable as possible in such matters except for avoiding "those offensive features of modern journalism which pander to a taste for sensation. . . ."[64] That same year, Pacific coast historian Hubert Howe Bancroft, judging Utah newspapers in general and the *News* in particular, wrote that "in freedom from journalistic scandal-mongering, they certainly rank among the foremost, and if sometimes dull, they are never silly or obscene." Bancroft concluded, "As a rule, the Mormon journals are less rabid in politics and religion than the gentile newspapers."[65] A more recent historian has observed that whereas the *News* was rarely an exciting paper, it tried to represent Utah and the Mormons in a sober fashion—a policy which generally did it honor.[66]

This moderate, calm policy was perpetuated by George Q. Cannon, who supervised standards of reporting in the *News* even when absent from the territory. For example, on 7 December 1878 the *News* printed an item from the Ogden, Utah, *Junction*: "Salt Lake has had another mysterious foundling. For a settlement with so few inhabitants, 'Briny Pond' [Salt Lake City] has an exceedingly large amount of iniquity." To this the Mormon newspaper added, "Thanks friend *Junction,* the sentiment is indeed Christian." As soon as that issue of the paper came to Cannon's attention in

Washington, D.C., he sent a letter to his subordinates on the *News* rebuking them for printing the item. In his opinion, the Ogden paper had published the story in retaliation against criticisms of Ogden society that had appeared previously in the *News*. Cannon argued that when men "go to slinging filth," the one who owned the shovel with the longest handle would likely win. Scolding his colleagues, he wrote, "The *News* cannot properly indulge in slang."[67]

In the same letter Cannon disagreed with acting editor Charles W. Penrose concerning the wording of certain local columns. "Some of the writing would do well, probably, for the 'Punny Fellow,' " he noted, "but does not adorn the *News*." As an example he cited an editorial headed "Emery Powder," in which the Church paper had berated territorial governor George B. Emery by writing that there was "too much refuse earth in this specimen of Emery powder to have any effect upon the machinery of the Government."[68] Making reference to this editorial and acknowledging the possibility of a certain weakness in his own personality, Cannon wrote, "It may be that I have so much Scotch about me that I cannot appreciate a joke. Sidney Smith, you know, said that before a Scotchman could be made to understand a joke he would have to undergo a surgical operation. But such punning . . . I think unsuited to [the] columns [of the *News*]. The attempt at wit is very bald," he continued. "Besides it is in bad taste to pun in such a way upon a man's name. He is the Governor, and we owe it to ourselves, if not to him, to speak about him, and even to censure him with proper dignity. When we do not," he concluded, "the paper is lowered more than he."

Cannon further suggested that the paper should exercise care as to the kind of advertising it accepted. He objected to an advertisement by a New York banking firm offering information as to how large or small sums of money could be invested on the stock market for a "fabulous profit,"[69] a notice that the absentee editor condemned as an open invitation to gamble. By letting it appear in the columns of the *News,* the editors had tacitly condoned the temptation of some "innocent and unsuspecting person. . . ." Cannon also criticized the *News* for advertising "every quack's nostrums and panacea." He concluded his correspondence by declaring, with some humor, that if the paper's subscribers bought every drug advertised in its columns, death and sickness would prevail in Utah to such an extent that the paper would lose all its readers.

Whatever the amount sold, the purchasing of patent medicines in Utah reveals a good deal about its inhabitants. Advertisements are generally reliable mirrors of a society's moral climate. The *Deseret News* apparently agreed with this axiom, for in 1870 it stated that "the connection between the advertising columns of the press of a country and the social and moral status of its people is very close."[70] One hundred years later, featuring old advertisements from America's past history, the Mormon paper reiterated this judgment and wondered how future generations would interpret the present.[71]

With their shortage of both doctors and medical knowledge, frontier societies naturally attracted medicine vendors. A study of pioneer Minnesota newspaper advertisements revealed that early settlers of that territory were "addicted to the excessive use of patent medicines."[72] The health business in the Southwest was one of the biggest bonanzas in that region's history,[73] and Utah followed the same pattern. The *News* had been carrying patent medicine advertisements since one for Dr. Martieu's "Never Failing Worm Destroying Medicine for Children" appeared on 19 April 1851.[74] At the time of Cannon's criticism in 1878, the paper was carrying advertisements of as many as ten different kinds of patent medicines. These included "Allen's Anti-Fat," a weight reducing concoction; "Lyon's Kathairon," a potion positively guaranteed to prevent grayness and restore new hair to bald heads; and "Stanford's Radical Cure of the foul, thick, bloody discharges of catarrh."[75] Later samples of this type of advertisement in the *News* included Kendall's Spavin Cure "for beast as well as man," "Rupture Permanently cured or no pay," and constipation or indigestion remedied by the use of "Dr. Pierce's Pleasant Purgative Pellets."[76] Perhaps the medicine claiming the greatest power was Dr. E. C. West's Nerve and Brain potion guaranteed to cure

> Hysteria, Dizziness, Convulsions, Fits, Nervous Neuralgia, Headache, Nervous Prostration caused by the use of alcohol or tobacco, Wakefulness, Mental Depression, Softening of the Brain, resulting in insanity and leading to misery, decay and death, Premature Old Age, [and] Barreness, caused by over exertion of the brain.[77]

However, the *News* did not admit to its columns any and every patent medicine advertisement. Mormons held that population determined the strength of a nation. This in part accounts for the absence in the *News* of advertisements for medications designed to bring about abortions or birth control. Nor did the Church paper accept notices of remedies contrived for the treatment of gonorrhea or syphilis, though other papers in the East and West alike had no such compunction,[78] the Denver *Rocky Mountain News*[79] and the *Deseret News*'s major hometown competitor, the *Salt Lake Tribune,* among them. One such advertisement in the *Tribune* claimed that a San Francisco doctor could cure gonorrhea, gleet, stricture, and syphilis in all its forms for only fifteen dollars.[80]

According to one student of patent medicine advertisements, the average Westerner was uncommonly interested in medicines or machinery that would restore or increase his male vigor.[81] Although, as one would expect, the *Deseret News* carried no mention of "Mormon Elders Damiana Wafers," an advertised medication designed to offer men the alleged potency of Mormon polygamists,[82] it did accept advertising of drugs guaranteed to improve virility. From his "editorial office" in Washington, D.C., Cannon criticized the *News* for accepting two such advertisements. "Man's Mission on Earth" and "Nervous Exhaustion," both of which promised to provide purchasers with sex information that would remove "obstacles to marriage" and assure "manhood" for all who applied its wisdom.[83]

Cannon's objection led to the cancellation of the advertisements specifically mentioned by him, but the paper continued to accept much patent-medicine advertising. Such advertising reached flood tide in the United States in the late nineteenth century, and by 1881 the *News* had greatly increased its share in such sales promotion. One issue of that year carried thirty separate medicine announcements, almost twice the number appearing in the *Salt Lake Tribune.*[84]

Nineteenth-century newspapers refrained from vigorously and seriously attacking the patent medicine industry, though William Allen White's anti-nostrum *Emporia* [Kansas] *Gazette* was a stunning exception among country papers.[85] It is somewhat ironic that in spite of its own patent medicine notices the *Deseret News* energetically and consistently warned readers against the fraudulent and dangerous nature of patent medicines. In an 1877 editorial headed "Quack Medicaments" the *News* editor condemned the gullibility of people in Utah, criticizing them for buying and swallowing the pretentious prescriptions of quack physicians who sold worthless and inexpensive drugs at enormous profits, enriching the "ignorant and impudent impostors" and "impoverishing and injuring the people." The Church paper observed that any relief afforded by patent medicines was only temporary and that the after-effects were usually extremely harmful. The editorial explained in some detail that most cure-alls contained no mysterious ingredients, contrary to advertising claims, and that any virtues in them came from common drugs. The *News* directed its readers to heed the advice of the scriptures and send for the Church Elders to pray for the sick or, when medicine was deemed necessary, to call on a skilled and licensed physician. The *News* warned its readers not to "trust to the decoctions called patent medicines or to employ ignorant quacks who are great only in pretension." The editor concluded his rather lengthy criticism with the hope that his editorial might "help to stop the flood into this Territory of the vile stuff" that was becoming universally popular.[86]

In a later editorial in 1888, headed "Worse than Useless," the *News* again criticized patent medicines and the quacks who dispensed them. It tried to convince the public that the so-called specialists sold the same preparations for sick horses and dogs that they prescribed for human ailments, and warned readers of the dangerous consequences that could result.[87] Moreover, the editorial called attention to what seemed to be an injury to the local economy when people purchased patent medicine: the consumption of great quantities of such nostrums in Utah meant the expenditure of large sums of money outside the territory. An unnamed Salt Lake City source was quoted as saying that $25,000 annually were taken out of Utah by one San Francisco patent-medicine establishment alone.[88] At a time when the Church was emphasizing "home industry," such cash outflow was serious.

Although most patent medicines came from outside Utah, not all were imported. In line with Brigham Young's stress on home manufacturing, homemade "Rocky Mountain Pills," highly recommended as a valuable medicine from rare medical plants discovered in the Rocky Mountains, were manufactured by Joseph E. Johnson, a Mormon in the southern Utah town of St. George. According to an advertisement in the *News,* Johnson's pills were guaranteed "if used properly" to cure indigestion.[89] From the same laboratory in St. George, and advertised by the LDS Zion's Cooperative Mercantile Institution (ZCMI), came Johnson's Homemade Family Medicines "Warranted to be Better than the Best Imported" and to "Give Ample Satisfaction." This southern Utah businessman authorized his agents to refund money to dissatisfied customers and to give one-twelfth of the earnings from sales to the poor.[90] Whether early Utah settlers were attracted to patent medicines because their isolated situation demanded self-treatment or because of Brigham Young's outspoken opposition to almost all doctors is difficult to ascertain. Whatever the reason, Mormons apparently were susceptible to the nostrum business both foreign and local.

But why did the *News* accept patent medicine advertisements while at the same time condemning them? Defending the *New York Tribune* for accepting patent medicine advertising in its columns, Horace Greeley claimed that blame should rest on advertisers and not on the newspapers. The newspaper, he argued, accepted advertisements because it needed the money. Operating on the same basis of need, the *News* did not exclude all patent medicine notices simply because they were "bad," as did the *New York Daily Times* and later the *Christian Science Monitor.* In an editorial criticizing patent medicines, the *News* explained why it followed this disharmonious editorial-advertisement policy:

> Quack medicines are advertised more extensively than any other goods offered to the public. And many people confound advertising with endorsement. But it should be understood that newspapers frequently admit into their advertising columns as a matter of business, announcements which they cannot endorse in their editorial columns as a matter of principle.[91]

A later *News* statement suggested a slight shift in policy. Soliciting subscribers in 1891, the Church paper announced that it annually refused thousands of dollars worth of the "best paying advertisements" because it was devoted to the moral interests of its readers instead of to "getting gain at their expense."[92] The *News*'s advertising policy was not based on profit alone; but by accepting notices it could not editorially endorse it showed at least some willingness to make money the way other papers did. And despite the 1891 statement, the Church paper continued to run many patent medicine advertisements.[93]

This advertisement-editorial incongruity was visible in more than just patent medicine. In 1850 the *News* condemned the wearing of corsets as a "pernicious custom" that gave rise to "serious diseases and deformity,"[94] yet later allowed the corset space in its advertising columns.[95] Asked for its opinion on the propriety of masquerade balls, the *News* warned that they were the "cover for intrigue, licentiousness and evil in its worst forms."[96] Three years later the Church paper announced a "Bal Masque," giving all the necessary particulars.[97] Despite the fact that the *News* criticized the New York *Herald* for what it felt was highly vulgar and sensational journalism, it ran advertisements inviting subscription to that newspaper.[98]

The *News* accepted advertising from gentile business and professional people while criticizing them on its editorial page. Brigham Young, particularly after the 1857 Utah War, criticized non-Mormon merchants for refusing to invest their profits in the development of Utah. On 2 January 1867, the Church paper printed the names of some Utah gentile merchants with whom Saints were asked not to trade. By the end of 1868 this boycott had grown into a major Church policy, a policy supported by a series of editorials in the *Deseret News*.[99] Yet despite the boycott the *News* continued to accept local gentile advertisements, even from those businessmen whose names had been blacklisted and who had been described as "enemies" of the Church.[100]

In 1873 the paper published a list of eight Salt Lake City and outstate Utah lawyers who had signed a memorial presented to the United States Congress claiming that legislation in Utah was subversive of the federal authority in the territory and asking that the situation be changed. An editorial in the *News* stated that the names were being published so that Mormons in need of a lawyer would know that the men named were hostile to the Mormon cause.[101] Even so, business cards for at least four of the condemned attorneys were at the same time appearing in the Church paper.

Other examples of incompatibility between advertising and editorial policies concerned such items as liquor, tobacco, tea, and coffee. Although nineteenth-century Mormon policy did not completely prohibit the use of these items as it does now, the *Deseret News* frequently editorialized on their bad effects and warned against their use.

In an 1869 editorial headed "The Evils of Intoxication," Cannon stressed the social and economic rather than physical harm of alcohol and declared that immoderate use of intoxicating drinks constituted one of the greatest evils in the civilized world. While the editor admitted that the older generation in the Church at times still imbibed, he urged young people to adopt complete abstinence. The best rule was "touch not, taste not, handle not."[102] In a later article on the same topic, Cannon observed that the ability to control one's appetites made a person a much more sub-

stantial human being in all his activities and warned that the
habitual use of intoxicants was one of the worst habits one could
adopt and that too often it grew until it completely enslaved its
victim.[103]

Apparently advocating mandatory prohibition, the *News* in 1871
printed the text of a discourse by Apostle Joseph F. Smith on the
subject of alcohol. Smith expressed the hope that he could soon
see the day when no one in Utah, Mormon or Gentile, would be
permitted to touch intoxicating drink:

> It would not be oppression to me, for the proper authorities to
> say—"you shall not take intoxicating liquors; you shall neither
> manufacture nor drink them, for they are injurious to your body
> and mind," nor would it be to any Saint—[104]

As with patent medicine advertisements, those for liquor and
tobacco were accepted simply for commercial reasons, with no
implied Church endorsement. Unfortunately, some modern writers
have tended to perpetuate a misinterpretation of early Utah history
by leaving the impression that such material was never accepted.
Treatment of tobacco and liquor advertisements in the official
centennial biography of the *Deseret News,* for example, is con-
spicuously absent.[105] A *Newsweek* article stated that because of
Mormon principles tobacco and liquor advertisements have never
appeared in the *Deseret News.*[106] Contrary to such assertions, and
unlike such papers as the *Kansas City Star* and the *Christian Science
Monitor,* the *News* in its early years regularly admitted to its
columns advertisements for all kinds of liquors from local as
well as outside merchants, despite its frequent and uniform attacks
on drinking.[107]

Such advertisements found their way into the earliest issues of
the Church paper. On 31 August 1850, a notice by *News* employee
Thomas Bullock offered a good price for hops delivered at his
house. It was not long before *News* advertisements included the
Queen City Hotel's notice of "all kinds of choice Liquors."[108] The
initial issue of the daily had two such advertisements, one an-
nouncing that W. Howard had opened a "Liquor Store" opposite the
Salt Lake Hotel, while the other claimed that Sewell and Company's
Oasis Saloon had the finest and best wines, liquors, and beer in
Salt Lake City.

Representative of this kind of local advertisement, which regularly appeared in the columns of the *News* throughout the nine-

teenth century, is the following notice from William Godbe, an ex-Mormon merchant.

> Pure Wines & Liquors, Fine old Whiskies, Pure Imported Brandies, The Celebrated Red Jacket Bitters, Old Tom Gin, etc. Also Alcohol and Coloque Spirits, to be had at Godbe's Exchange Buildings.[109]

Even ZCMI, owned and operated by the Church, advertised "Liquors, Draught and Case," "Twelve-year-old French Brandy, Lafayette Whiskey, and Genuine Imported Old French Port," as well as the Southern-Utah-brewed "Pure Dixie Port Wine."[110] Liquor advertising came from local liquor stores, from Omaha's Brewer and Bemis Brewing Company, and from Adams McNeill and Company, wholesale grocers of Sacramento.[111]

As with alcohol, the *News* very early began editorial attacks on the use of tobacco. They were aimed directly at the young people and, unlike Church admonitions today, appealed more to the pride of superior man than to the question of health:

> Some people are slaves to tobacco. Only think of it—slaves to that stinking weed! What noble creatures to submit to such vile degradation! . . . They are perfectly helpless in its presence. They almost go crazy in its absence. . . . They are happy only with a pipe or a cigar in their mouths, or a loathsome cud of tobacco between their teeth. What a thing to contemplate—a man, with his vast and exalted powers and capabilities, voluntarily submitting himself to be the slave of a half inch cube of filthy, nauseous, molassesized tobacco![112]

Tobacco advertisements appeared simultaneously with such editorials.

It was easy to detect the coming of the semi-annual Churchwide conferences. Advertisements in most newspapers increase in number around Christmas, but those of the *Deseret News* increased in October and April. Such front-page advertisements as "Special Announcement!" "To Continue During Conference," and "Grand Spring Opening" greeted visiting Church members. In many cases these special notices featured various brands of teas, coffees, and tobacco.[113] A full month before an April Conference, ZCMI began running a long advertisement which included among a long list of items: "Fine cuts, smoking and chewing Tobaccos, Natural leaf, Black and Bright Navy Plugs, in all sizes, including our own and other Brands which we control."[114]

National tobacco companies also advertised in the *News*. Among others were Liggett and Dausman, manufacturers and dealers, and Loker Tobacco Company, both of St. Louis, and the J. B. Pace Tobacco Company of Richmond, Virginia.[115]

All types of advertisements from non-Utah merchants increased in number with the coming of the transcontinental railroad. The first issue of the *News* to reflect the increase in such advertisements appeared 6 August 1868. It contained three full columns headed "Chicago Trade," announcing some twenty-three different items for sale, ranging from hats, paper bags, china, and oil paints to nails, saddles, and wagons. By the end of the year, mercantile advertisements by firms in St. Louis and Chicago filled eight of the seventeen advertising columns in the Church paper.

It was years after the surge in advertising of the late 1860s before the *Deseret News* brought its tobacco and alcohol advertisement policy into closer harmony with its editorials. The last tobacco advertisement appeared on 5 April 1898 and the last liquor advertisement on October 26 of the same year. Later, the *News* even went so far as to retouch comic strips to take cigarette and pipe smoking out of the pictures.[116] Although the Church paper gave no reasons for its policy change, it probably resulted from the increasingly restrictive Church rules concerning such items. However, the *News,* whose business office merged in 1952 with that of the *Salt Lake Tribune,* a paper that does accept tobacco and beer notices, ironically benefits from the prohibited advertisements because it evenly splits all revenue with the *Tribune.*

Despite Church subsidies, the *Deseret News* needed advertising to stay in business. Therefore, even though the *News* was less sensational and more of a family newspaper than most, the advertising was not always in line with the editorial policy. Since the weekly "Church Section" began in 1931, the *Deseret News* itself has become less obviously a religious organ, but it is still generally considered a spokesman for the LDS Church. And its refusal since 1970 to advertise X- and R-rated movies shows that the *News* still takes seriously its goal of being a family newspaper.[117]

Footnotes

1. *News,* 20 August 1873.

2. Ibid.

3. Calder was elected a director of Zion's Cooperative Mercantile Institution in October 1875 and a year later was appointed its secretary and treasurer. Also, a large music business doubtless demanded much of his time. In 1875 he became a councilor for the City of Salt Lake and in 1877 was made first assistant in the presidency of the Salt Lake Stake; Andrew Jenson, *Latter-day Saints Biographical Encyclopedia* (Salt Lake City: Andrew Jenson History Company, 1901), 1:773-74.

4. *News,* 1 August 1877.

5. Brigham Young, Jr., diary, 31 July 1877, LDS Church Historical Department.

6. George Q. Cannon, Washington, D.C., 13 December 1878, letter to Brigham Young, Jr., Brigham Young, Jr., Collection, LDS Church Historical Department.

7. *News,* 2 August 1879.

8. Ibid., 2, 4, and 28 August 1879. Charles W. Penrose continued to edit the *News,* though he was not officially appointed to that position until September 1880.

9. Orson F. Whitney, *History of Utah* (Salt Lake City: George Q. Cannon and Sons Co., 1892), 2:184.

10. *New York Times,* 13 April 1901.

11. Deseret News Company ledger for 1873, LDS Church Historical Department; *see also News,* 28 May 1872.

12. Deseret News Company ledger for 1873.

13. Joseph Beecroft, diary, 7 November and 20 December 1870, LDS Church Historical Department.

14. *News,* 18 January 1875.

15. Edward Howe, *Plain People* (New York: Dodd, Mead and Co., 1929), p. 99.

16. Joseph Beecroft, diary, 29 July, 22 September, and 25 November 1870.

17. Ibid., 23 July, 27 August, 9 and 22 September, 20 October, and 28 December 1870.

18. *See* ibid., 2 and 3 September, 2 November, and 3 and 17 December 1870; 16 March and 1 April 1871.

19. T. C. Liddle, Salt Lake City, April 1970, letter to the author; *see also* "Stern Mormon View," *Time* 90(4 August 1967): 72. "Mormon Spruce-

Up," *Newsweek* 31(24 May 1948): 67, said smoking was prohibited in the editorial and composing rooms of the *News*.

20. Joseph Beecroft, diary, 16 September 1870.

21. Ibid., 10 August 1870 and 6 and 31 January 1871.

22. Elias Smith, diary, 6 September 1861. For a study of the development of Mormon attitudes toward the Word of Wisdom, *see* Paul H. Peterson, "A Historical Analysis of the Word of Wisdom" (master's thesis, Brigham Young University, 1972).

23. By mid-February 1867 the Deseret Telegraph, a Church-owned utility, had stretched and put into operation telegraph lines between Logan and St. George.

24. *News*, 8 April 1868. Yearly subscription rates were ten dollars, a little over three cents a copy. According to Frank Luther Mott, *American Journalism: A History of Newspapers in the United States through 260 Years, 1690-1950* (New York: Macmillan Company, 1950), p. 404, the rates of the leading papers of the country were stabilized at four cents shortly after the Civil War.

25. *News*, 8 April 1868.

26. Ibid., 21 November 1867. The *News* semi-weekly for the first year 8 October 1865 to 8 September 1866 was published every Wednesday and Sunday. The daily *News* issued a Sunday paper between 1948 and 1952, at which time it combined its printing, distributing, and advertising facilities with those of the *Salt Lake Tribune*. After 1952, because Church General Authorities had never felt comfortable publishing on Sunday, the Sunday *News* was terminated and it was decided that the *News* subscribers would receive the Sunday *Tribune* if they wished; William B. Smart, executive editor of the *Deseret News*, Salt Lake City, 17 April 1970, letter to the author.

27. *News*, 25 December 1867.

28. Ibid., 26 February 1878.

29. Ibid., 11 April 1878.

30. Ibid., 2 December 1867; *see also* 1 May 1874.

31. Ibid., 17 January 1868.

32. Ibid., 27 September 1890.

33. Ibid., 20 April 1868.

34. Ibid., March, April, and May 1855.

35. Ibid., 1 August 1877.

36. Ibid., 5 January 1881.

37. Ibid., 8 April 1868.

38. Ibid.

39. Ibid., 21 November 1867.

40. Ibid., 1 February 1868. Similar thinking concerning reading material in Utah was expressed in 1872 by Brigham Young in "The Order of Enoch," discourse given 9 October 1872, Salt Lake City, in *Journal of Discourses,* 15:222-24.

41. *News*, 29 February 1868 and 21 April 1869.

42. Ibid., 1 February 1868.
43. Ibid.
44. Ibid., 25 March 1873.
45. Ibid., 25 August 1874.
46. Ibid., 1 February 1868.
47. Ibid.
48. Ibid., 21 November 1867. He later claimed that public journalists had done more than any other class, politicians not excepted, to bring about the American Civil War; *News*, 11 February 1868.
49. Ibid.
50. Ibid.
51. As quoted in Mott, *American Journalism*, p. 443.
52. Ibid., pp. 386-87.
53. As quoted in *News*, 1 February 1868.
54. *News*, 24 August 1854.
55. Ibid., 18 February 1863.
56. Ibid., 3 January 1872.
57. Alvin F. Harlow, "Victoria Claflin Woodhull," *Dictionary of American Biography*, 20: 493-94.
58. *News*, 7 November 1872.
59. Ibid.
60. Ibid., 11 February 1868.
61. Ibid., 21 October 1868.
62. Ibid., 5 November 1875.
63. Ibid., 9 October 1872.
64. Ibid., 21 November 1889.
65. Hubert Howe Bancroft, *History of Utah* (San Francisco: Bancroft, 1890), p. 715.
66. Dale L. Morgan, "Review of *Voice in the West: Biography of a Pioneer Newspaper,* by Wendell J. Ashton," *Saturday Review of Literature* 30(15 July 1950): 27.
67. George Q. Cannon, Washington, D.C., 13 December 1878, letter to Brigham Young, Jr., George Q. Cannon Collection.
68. *News*, 23 November 1878.
69. Ibid., 22 November 1878.
70. Ibid., 20 December 1870.
71. Ibid., 28 February 1870.
72. Theodore C. Blegen, "Minnesota Pioneer History as Revealed in Newspaper Advertisements," *Minnesota History* #7 (June 1926):101.
73. Billy M. Jones, *Health-Seekers in the Southwest, 1817-1900* (Norman, Oklahoma: University of Oklahoma Press, 1967).
74. The Nauvoo, Illinois, *Times and Seasons,* an earlier official Mormon newspaper, had at intervals carried various patent medicine advertisements; *see* 1 November 1840, and 1 January and 15 September 1841.
75. *News*, 6 and 9 December 1878.
76. Ibid., 13 September 1882, 10 February 1891, and 1 June 1892.
77. Ibid., 10 February 1891.
78. James Harvey Young, *The Toadstool Millionaires: A Social History*

of Patent Medicines in America before Federal Regulation (Princeton: Princeton University Press, 1961), pp. 84, 87. For specific examples *see New York Times,* 1 and 2 July 1869. The *News* claimed that this kind of advertisement was unnecessary in Utah because "secret diseases" were completely unknown among the Mormons; *News,* 24 August 1869.

79. *Rocky Mountain News,* 26 January 1869.

80. *Salt Lake Tribune,* 1 January 1878. This same advertisement ran as late as 3 March 1895.

81. T. H. Watkins, "If You Suffer, It Serves You Right," *The American West Review* 1 (December 1967): 30.

82. Young, *Toadstool Millionaires,* plate 14, between pp. 122-23.

83. *News,* 2 November 1878 and 3 December 1878; and George Q. Cannon, Washington, D.C., 13 December 1878, letter to Brigham Young, Jr., George Q. Cannon Collection.

84. *News,* 3 January 1881; and *Salt Lake Tribune,* 4 January 1881.

85. Young, *Toadstool Millionaires,* pp. 210-11.

86. *News,* July 1877. Similar but not identical advice was given by Brigham Young: "Who is the real doctor? That man who knows by the Spirit of revelation what ails an individual, and by the same Spirit knows what medicine to administer. That is the real doctor, the others are quacks"; Brigham Young, "The Order of Enoch," discourse given 9 October 1872, Salt Lake City, in *Journal of Discourses,* 15:225. Neither the *News* nor Young were alone in their criticism of frontier doctors and patent medicine; *see* Jones, *Health-Seekers in the Southwest,* pp. 28-33.

87. It is interesting to note that despite this criticism the *News* advertisements included "XXX Horse Medicine . . . for Man or Beast"; *News,* 5 October 1889.

88. *News,* 18 January 1888.

89. Ibid.,16 March 1875.

90. Ibid., 22 February 1872. It has been reported that Johnson manufactured no less than twenty kinds of patent medicines in his Valley Tan Laboratory in St. George, Utah; J. Cecil Alter, *Early Utah Journalism: A Half Century of Forensic Warfare, Waged by the West's Most Militant Press* (Salt Lake City: Utah State Historical Society, 1938), p. 230.

91. *News,* 12 July 1877.

92. Ibid., 10 February 1891.

93. Three and one-half columns of such advertisement appeared as late as 2 January 1896.

94. *News,* 6 July 1850.

95. Ibid., 2 January 1872 and 15 November 1884.

96. Ibid., 11 March 1878.

97. Ibid., 4 January 1881.

98. Ibid., 3 January 1885.

99. For example, *see News,* October 1868.

100. *News,* 2 January 1867.

101. Ibid., 17 and 18 February 1873.

102. Ibid., 27 April 1869.

103. Ibid., 23 April 1873.

104. Ibid., 16 September 1871.

105. Wendell J. Ashton, *Voice in the West: Biography of a Pioneer Newspaper* (New York: Duell, Sloan and Pearce, 1950).

106. "Daily Crusader of Mormonism: The *Deseret News* of Salt Lake," *Newsweek* 17(31 March 1941):65.

107. For some further editorials on this subject, *see News,* 23 and 24 November 1895, 8 January 1874, and 2 April 1887.

108. *News,* 18 September 1852.

109. Ibid., 12 December 1868.

110. Ibid., 1 December 1869, 1 September 1870, and 10 July 1875.

111. Ibid., 1 September 1870 and 26 August 1869. It is interesting to note that in 1880 malt liquors constituted the second largest capitalization in Salt Lake City; William Mulder "Salt Lake City in 1880: A Census Profile," *Utah Historical Quarterly* 24(July 1956):236.

112. *News,* 8 June 1876; *see also* 16 March 1853 and 26 December 1874.

113. Ibid., 10 April 1871.

114. Ibid., 2 March 1874.

115. Ibid., 1 September 1870, 14 April 1873, and 1 June 1892.

116. "Daily Crusader of Mormonism: The *Deseret News* of Salt Lake," *Newsweek,* 17(31 March 1941):65 Exactly when this policy started is not yet determined, but it gradually faded out of existence during the mid-1950s. William B. Smart, executive editor, *Deseret News,* Salt Lake City, 23 September 1972, letter to the author. The *Christian Science Monitor* has had a similar policy of editing whiskey drinking and tobacco smoking out of pictures; Erwin D. Canham, *Commitment to Freedom: The Story of the Christian Science Monitor* (Boston: Houghton Miffin Company, 1958), p. 122.

117. For the announcement on movie advertisement policy *see News,* 24 September 1970.

Photographs

Pictures without credit lines were obtained from the Church Archives of the Historical Department of The Church of Jesus Christ of Latter-day Saints.

William Wines Phelps—1832

Oliver Cowdery—1834

John Whitmer—1835

Joseph Smith, Jr.—1837

William Smith—1842

John Taylor—1843

Orson Hyde—1849

Willard Richards—1850-1854

Albert Carrington—1854-1859
and 1863-1867

Elias Smith—1859-1863

George Q. Cannon—1867-1873

David O. Calder—1873-1877

George Q. Cannon—1877-1879

Charles W. Penrose—1880-1892

John Nicholson—1880s

Courtesy of Utah State Historical Society

George C. Lambert—1885

John Q. Cannon—1892-1898

Erastus Snow—1854,
St. Louis Luminary

Orson Pratt—1852, *Seer*
(Washington, D.C.)

Charles Goodwin—1880s,
Salt Lake Tribune

Patrick Connor—1863, *Union
Vedette* (Camp Douglas, Utah)

Courtesy of The New York Historical Society, New York City

George Alfred Townsend—1870s,
Utah correspondent for the
Cincinnati Commercial

Joseph Beecroft—1880s, typesetter
for the *Deseret News*

Courtesy of Kansas State Historical Society, Topeka

Edgar Watson Howe—1870s, typesetter for the *Deseret News*

Deseret Evening News building—1860s

Deseret News building—1890s

Times and Seasons building, Nauvoo, Illinois

DESERET NEWS.

BY W. RICHARDS.   G. S. L. CITY, DESERET, JUNE 15, 1850.   VOL. I.--NO. 1.

LAT. 40° 45' 44". LON. 111° 26' 34"

PROSPECTUS.

DESERET NEWS.

Motto—"Truth and Liberty."

We propose to publish a small weekly sheet, as large as our local circumstances will permit, to be called "Deseret News," designed originally to record the passing events of our State, and in connexion, refer to the arts and sciences, embracing general education, medicine, law, divinity, domestic and political economy, and everything that may fall under our observation, which may tend to promote the best interest, welfare, pleasure and amusement of our fellow citizens.

We hold ourselves responsible to the highest Court of truth for our intentions, and the highest Court of equity for our execution. When we speak, we shall speak freely, without regard to men of party, and when, like other men, we err, let him who has his eyes open, correct us in meekness, and he shall receive a disciple's reward.

We shall ever take pleasure in communicating foreign news as we have opportunity; in receiving communications from our friends, at home and abroad; and solicit ornaments for the "News" from our poets and poetesses.

The first number may be expected as early in June as subscriptions will warrant—waiting the action of 300 subscribers.

Terms, 6 months, $2,50; invariably in advance.

Single copy, 15 cents.

Advertising, $1,50 per square lines, and 50 each succeeding insertion. $1 for half square, or 8 lines.

Travellers and Emigrants, 25 cents per copy, with the insertion of their names, place of residence, time of arrival and leaving.

Companies of 20, and upwards, entered at once, 20 cents each.

A paper that is worth printing, is worth preserving; if worth preserving, it is worth binding; for this purpose we issue in pamphlet form; and if every subscriber shall preserve each copy of the "News," and bind it at the close of the volume, their children's children may read the doings of their fathers, which other wise might have been forgotten; &c. &c.

U. S. SENATE.

"Sketch of debates in the Senate, for Feb. 5, &c., inclusive, 1850, on the subject of Petition; represent Messrs. Seward, Hale & Chase as chief speakers. Mr. Mangum presented the proceedings of a meeting at Wilmington, N. C., denouncing the fanaticism of the North, threatening a dissolution of the Union, in a certain contingency, &c.—Laid on the table.— Several petitions were presented by Mr. Hale, from various sections "for promotion of the abolition of slavery; improving the condition of the free people of color; to prevent the increase of slavery by the non-admission of new State into the Union; for abolishing slavery in the District of Columbia; to prevent the introduction of slavery in the Territories; to prevent internal slave trade between the States; and respectfully ask Congress to propose, without delay, some plan for the immediate and peaceful dissolution of the American Union."

The Germantown ladies address Congress, as "Dear Friends," and after an appropriate prayer, "we bid you an affectionate farewell." Many joined the above gentlemen in debate, which was generally warm, criminative and recriminative; somewhat dramatic, with some symptoms of the tragic.

Query; If the people, the whole people, want the Union peacefully dissolved, why not dissolve it? Why ask Congress to do a thing they have no power to do? Congress did not make the Union; the Union made Congress, and the people made the Union; consequently, on the principles of federal republicanism, the same power that makes must unmake, if unmade at all; and if the Union is ever peacefully dissolved, it will be by the sovereign people who made it; for they alone possess the rightful power of dissolution within themselves, and not in their Senate or Representatives; and we hope we shall never again hear of any portion of the American people petitioning Congress to do what it has no power to do, even if it had the disposition. Let our Union remain forever, peacefully!

TERRIBLE FIRE IN SAN FRANCISCO.

An appalling and destructive fire occurred on the 24th of December, which threatened for a time to reduce the famous city of San Francisco to a heap of smoking ruins. The fire broke out in Dennison's Exchange, and in two hours, nearly a million of dollars worth of property was destroyed. The Parker House was among the buildings burned. All the buildings, except the Delmonico Hotel, on Portsmouth square, and all on Washington street, commencing at the "Eldorado," and running to Montgomery street, were burned.

The Parker House, U. S. Restaurant, Exchange, Eldorado, Merchant's Exchange, Our House, Central House, Washington Arcade, Pollard & Co's. Auction Room, Guerschard & Van Buren's Establishment, and many more valuable buildings were burned, or blown up, to stop the progress of the fire.

First edition, 15 June 1850

First daily edition, 21 November 1867

Editorial answering attacks made on Mormons, titled "The 'Ignorance and Bigotry' of the 'Mormons'," 1 December 1868

Patent medicine advertisements, 3 January 1881

Liquor, tea, coffee, and tobacco ads, 10 April 1871

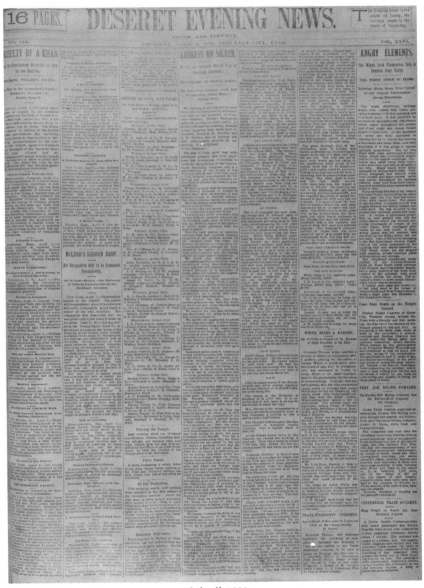

6 April 1893

Sinking of the *Maine*; murder story, 16 February 1898

6

Defender
of the
Kingdom

One and one-half years after the *Deseret News* became a daily, the spike completing the construction of the transcontinental rail-road was driven at Promontory, Utah, greatly facilitating com-munication between East and West. The *News,* which supported the coming of the railroad, anticipated that this improved com-munication would surely quiet the criticisms leveled against the Saints by some Eastern newspapers. This hope, however, was never realized, and the Mormon paper soon had to defend the faith more fervently than ever before.

The intensification of the *Deseret News*'s role of apologist re-sulted from the ever-increasing anti-polygamy campaigns and gen-tile "crusades" against Church economic and political power in Utah during the 1870s and 1880s. The *News* faced the enormous task of correcting distorted reports emanating from residents of and visitors to Utah and of allaying the fears of Mormon rebellion held by policy-makers in Washington and the American public in general.

The gentile "crusades" were largely prompted by Western news-paper reports. Correspondents and reporters have seldom been considered completely reliable, and nineteenth-century Western news published east of the Mississippi was rarely praiseworthy.

Many correspondents denied the hardships and privations associated with Western life. To speed up business and increase land values, local reporters often romanticized and fictionalized news pertaining to mining. Local newspapers notoriously exaggerated the potential of a new town and berated its rivals. Editors suppressed reports of lawlessness because they might hamper immigration. The alarming and overly-colored accounts of Indian raids and massacres by post-Civil War newspaper correspondents foreshadowed the sensational yellow journalism of the 1880s.

Eastern newspapers printed reports from military officers, local newspaper editors, and disappointed office seekers, despite their obvious bias. The *New York Tribune* had the largest staff of special correspondents in "bleeding Kansas" but, because most of them participated in the partisan strife, their reportorial accuracy suffered. Much of this so-called news was, therefore, little more than propaganda to secure a civil appointment or to influence the federal government to send more troops so as to stimulate the business of the tradesman.[1]

Similarly, false reports and malicious slander permeated the treatment of Utah and the Mormons, as shown by a survey of articles dealing with Mormons printed in national periodicals up to 1900 and a study of nineteenth-century anti-Mormon novels.[2] Incorrect statements of fact, if not intentionally libelous, were also typical of reports by some newspaper correspondents in the Great Basin. At least Brigham Young and the editors of the *Deseret News* thought this was the case.

Condemning what he felt to be misguided and misinformed journalists, Brigham Young said that editors published newspapers to have them read and considered anything promoting that end to be legitimate. What the true circumstances might lack, reporters and editors were sharp enough to furnish from their fertile brains. "If one wants to know us, he must come and see us for himself," exclaimed Young. "If he wants to live in perpetual ignorance of us, let him read what is written about us."[3] Ideally, news reports should be free from opinion or bias of any kind, but the *Deseret News* early became outspokenly critical of the correspondents who grossly misrepresented affairs in the territory in order to influence public opinion against the Mormons.

News editor Elias Smith, outraged at gentile reporters, wrote in 1860,

If any country, State or Territory has had a more numerous, worthless, lying corps of correspondents within its borders, during the
last five or six years, than the Territory of Utah, that fact has not
been announced to the public.[4]

In the winter of 1873, the *News* explained that in an anti-Mormon
"crusade" the previous spring, reports from Utah had been "extremely partizan" in character, "exceedingly untrustworthy," and
"wonderfully re-lie-able. . . ."[5] The editor then announced that
a new crusade had started, that the dog had returned to his vomit,
and that the same old intensely partisan and therefore discolored
and untrue reports were being sent out from Salt Lake City.
According to the *News,* many of these reports departed further
from the actual situation at Salt Lake City than if they had been
written by Satan himself.[6]

Whatever the level of accuracy, the gentile press received most
of its Mormon news either from its own Utah reporters or from
those of the Associated Press. Important newspapers all over the
United States at one time or another sent representatives to Utah.
The *New York Times* had a correspondent in Salt Lake City
as early as 1852,[7] and the *New York Tribune* reportedly sent two
in company with Johnston's Army in 1857.[8] Such Eastern, Midwestern and West Coast sheets as the *New York Herald,* the
Chicago Tribune, the *St. Louis Democrat,* the *Cincinnati Commercial,* and the *San Francisco Chronicle* had agents in Utah at
least by the 1870s.[9]

Because these correspondents' names were seldom printed with
their reports, it is difficult to determine their identity and the
length of their stay in Utah, which complicates the question of
reliability. Fortunately, at times a pen name or initials did appear,
and at other times the content of a letter revealed the extent of
their visit. It seems from this evidence that some, and perhaps
many, correspondents came to Salt Lake City on a temporary basis.
In fact, some spent only a day or two, hardly enough time for
adequate observation.

On 16 July 1869, the *Chicago Tribune* published a two-column
condemnation of the moral, social, and political aspects of Mormonism written by a correspondent with the initials *R. W.* Apparently he had only passed through Utah, for the letter was mailed
from San Francisco. Three days later the *Tribune* published a
letter from another agent. This one, with the initials *J. M.,* admitted that his three-day visit to the city of the Saints was not

enough time for anything but a superficial opinion of the state of affairs in the territory. He also admitted that he wrote with inadequate information and did so hesitatingly. On 4 June 1877, the *New York Times* ran a full two-column story on the Mormons, datelined Cheyenne, Wyoming, from a correspondent who had been in Salt Lake City but five days.

The relationship between length of observation and reliability was evaluated by Mark Twain. Though he rarely said anything complimentary about the Mormons, in his report on a short 1861 visit to Salt Lake City Twain explained that, because all his information had three sides to it, he gave up the idea that he could settle the "Mormon question" in two days. He sarcastically noted however, "I have seen newspaper correspondents do it in one."[10]

Correspondents' reliability is questionable, not only because of their brief residence, but also because of their sources of information: gentiles, apostates, federal officials, and devout Mormons, all with definite biases. On 14 April 1872, the *New York Times* ran a front-page three-column letter from its Utah correspondent. The letter, a very critical one, was a dialogue between the correspondent and a gentile informant identified only as "Mr. B." Later, the *Times* printed a long interview between its representative and another anonymous gentile.[11] Unwillingness of reporters to identify such sources—though understandable, since the local informant had to continue living among the Mormons he was criticizing—reduces the historical value of their reports. Another *Times* representative sent a long affidavit exaggerating the involvement of the Mormons in the Mountain Meadows massacre of 1857, signed by an apostate Mormon who, claiming his life was in danger from Mormon authorities, had fled to Nevada.[12] In addition to these sources, the *Times* often reprinted articles from the outspokenly anti-Mormon *Salt Lake Tribune*.[13]

As one would expect, the official apologist for the Church criticized some Utah correspondents for their brevity of residence and their sources of information. In the summer of 1871 the *Deseret News* attacked the *New York Evening Post* for printing a letter that the Church paper described as one of the most remarkable ever published about Utah and the Mormons. The *News* explained that the writer boasted of his "unusual opportunities" for gaining an insight into the affairs in the Mormon capital and of becoming acquainted with the "leading citizens," a boast the *News* editor described as common among such letter writers. He noted, however, that the extent of the correspondent's sources of information could best be judged in light of his twenty-four-hour stay in Salt Lake City. But then, the editor sarcastically pointed out, if Anna Dickinson[14] could obtain enough material during her two-day stay in the city to deliver a thrilling lecture about the evils of Mormonism, then a newspaper correspondent did no credit to his profession if he could not in twelve hours come by enough data for a two-column letter.

In the same editorial, the *News* referred to a recent but very short visit of a Dr. Vincent, who had come to Utah "without prejudice" but, after talking to a federal officer, had left convinced of the truth of all the bad stories he had heard about the Mormons. The Mormon editor claimed that had the *Post* correspondent met this federal officer, or someone else with as little regard for truth and honor and with an imagination equally as fertile, he would have had no difficulty in filling a few columns of an ordinary paper. The *News* concluded that there had been federal judges in Utah who could keep a correspondent busily employed writing stories of this kind even if the reporter wielded as facile a pen as the prolific French writer Alexandre Dumas.[15]

According to the Mormon newspaper, the fabricated stories told by federal officials and their sympathizers and sent out by newspaper agents were designed to overthrow the leaders of Utah and virtually disfranchise the greater part of the citizenry. The *News* charged that many misrepresentations concerning Utah were sent to Washington in order to bring about the enactment of laws to deprive the Mormons of the common rights of American citizens and place them under the domination of those scheming for their overthrow.[16] The presumed conspirators made up a small, locally organized opposition to Brigham Young and the Mormons, sometimes called the "Ring" and composed of apostates and gentiles, including federal officials. They opposed the Mormons for political reasons, with hopes of personal enrichment and economic control as well.

Economic and political power motivated not only Utah-based correspondents affiliated with specific newspapers but also the usually more reliable Associated Press agents, some of whom were assigned to Mormon territory. About 1849, Associated Press Washington bureau chief L. A. Gobright announced that although some independent special correspondents might write to suit the temper of their own newspaper, his organization called for communication of facts without commentary.[17] Reliability, however, seemed about as elusive for the Associated Press correspondent as for newspaper agents. In stressing the need for immediate reform, Victor Fremont Lawson criticized the wire service for pursuing the dollar first and news integrity second.[18] At least one historian, Oliver Gramling, has charged that the AP took liberties with the facts in stories on money, politics, or any other issue with national significance,[19] echoing the sentiments of the *Deseret News*.

The *News* described the Associated Press agent in Utah as a "decided failure" and noted, "for certainly if he endeavored as assiduously to falsify the news he could scarcely be more successful." The Church paper charged that the AP was the fluent instrument of the "Ring" and that the predominant spirit of its dispatches was to glorify that "little intriguing clique of apostates and adventurers" and belittle "the people" of Utah. The *News* concluded,

> In order if possible to prejudice public opinion east and west effectually against the people of this Territory, the most glaring misrepresentations and unwarrantable high colorings are transmitted over the wires, and as they are paid for, they are spread before the world by the duped publishers of papers, commented on by duped editors, and perused by a duped public, duped so far as the dispatches are credited.[20]

In fairness to all concerned, it must be recognized that because of the sharp differences between Mormon and gentile, Utah presented an unusually difficult front for newspaper correspondents to cover. The obvious partisanship of the various newspapers intensified the problem, making it difficult to ascertain the degree of reliability with which Utah correspondents reported the Mormon situation. "Eyewitness" accounts from newspaper agents in Utah varied so widely, often completely contradicting each other, that it seems probable that nobody really had the "correct" picture. The bitter differences in Utah were very much like the Kansas troubles, about which historian James C. Malin concluded there was no such thing as absolute truth: "Each faction . . . had a measure of truth on his side because truth was relative and was conditioned by the interests and position each occupied in the world in which he lived."[21] Naturally, the *Deseret News* portrayed the Mormons as they saw themselves, and they honestly saw themselves as being in the right and their critics as consciously seeking their overthrow.

The *News* and some of its expressed convictions received outside support and corroboration. Various United States newspapers agreed with the *News*'s description of the source and purpose of the anti-Mormon stories. "It looks very much as though the agent of the Associated Press, located at Salt Lake City is doing work for the Federal officials in Utah," reasoned the *Chicago Tribune*. "At all events, scarcely a day passes in which he does not seek to manufacture public sentiment against the Mormons and in favor of the ultra persecution contemplated by some extreme moralists."[22] Under the heading "About Those Dispatches," the *Deseret News* published the following clipping from the *Washington Capital*:

> The Associated Press, organized to gather and transmit through the telegraph important information, is based upon the supposition that its agents are not only active, intelligent, and discriminating, but honest and impartial. The journals composing the association, and the people who read, pay heavily for facts, and they want facts, not opinions. The last named each one is possessed of without price and in the greatest abundance. In opposition to this theory of organization we have a scandalous fact that every day grows more and more offensive. There is an agent at Salt Lake city whose atrocious falsehoods fill the minds of the better informed with utter amazement. With unblushing impudence he openly manufactures barefaced lies while looking his victims in the face, because they are Mormons and supposed to be helpless. . . . But we put it to the managers of the Associated Press whether it is good policy to thus demoralize public confidence in their organization. If it cannot afford to employ a decent, honest, intelligent agent at Salt Lake, the agency had better be dispensed with. We suppose we could exist for several months without hearing from the Saints, and we could live many, many years in peaceful tranquility without hearing from this poor devil of an agent.[23]

The *News* reported that the patience of the people of Utah toward slander and vicious sensational reports elicited admiration, and quoted the *Omaha Bee*:

> If the Gentile and Mormon inhabitants of Utah do not resort to violence, riot and revolution, it is certainly no fault either of the Utah press or the sensational telegraphic press reporters who are making day and night hideous with their constant appeals to passion and prejudice. What, with this class of partisan organs and the rapacity of office hunters . . . the people in Brighamdom evince a great degree of patience and good common sense in keeping their hands off each other's throats.[24]

Because of such Utah newspaper correspondents and Associated Press agents, the *News* felt an exceptional need to relate all public matters connected with the people of Utah with a great deal of caution and candor:

> We . . . say to all readers and hearers of news from Utah, receive everything sensational, exciting, or inflammatory with many, very many grains of allowance. . . . Of much of the news from Utah we may say profitably to all, don't believe it, unless you find it stated or corroborated in the *Deseret News*.[25]

Although the *News* was probably correct in its criticism of many of the reports emanating from Utah, its own self-estimate was not always totally defensible. In 1879, shortly after Albert Carrington, George Q. Cannon, and Brigham Young, Jr., were jailed on contempt charges, the Church paper published an editorial headed, "More Plain Talk." After writing that the Salt Lake "fiend of the wires" was again at work, the editor reprinted the following from the *San Francisco Chronicle* as a sample of the telegrams the "mendacious news-forger" sent out of the city: "The imprisonment of the Apostles seems to have set the Mormon priesthood wild, and the *Deseret News,* the church organ, has teemed with the most violent and incendiary articles for the last two evenings."[26] Despite the fact that the Church paper wrote that this "old stale lie" had done service for Mormon haters for the past thirty years and denied making threats against anyone, it had been sufficiently outspoken, though perhaps with some justification, to have easily led the *Chronicle* to describe it as sinister.

The 8 August 1879 issue of the *News* to which the *San Francisco Chronicle* referred acknowledged a certain degree of unrest in Utah and explained in a rather long editorial that anti-Mormon control of the courts made peaceful redress seem impossible. The editor pointed out that petitions to the powers that appointed the courts in Utah had yielded nothing and warned that the "vampires" who wanted to drain the life-blood from the territory had not taken into account the power of the people nor the power of God. The *News* stated that if carpetbaggers wanted to inaugurate a collision they would be accommodated because the time had come when the Mormons would no longer submit to villainies. "If there is no protection from the Courts," declared the Church paper, "we shall not any longer counsel submission." The Saints were not in Utah to bow down as serfs to government appointees "nor to lick the bribe-stained hands of imported satraps."

> We shall protect our lives as best we may from the murderous assaults of imported assassins; we shall contend for our liberties and resist the incarceration of honorable men in jails while land-sharks, conspirators, murderers, seducers and other vagabonds go at large; and we propose to pursue happiness in our way without the dictation of these corrupt scoundrels.

Moreover, the editorial warned that if the "vile and despicable crew" that had provoked an incident in which a Mormon had killed a gentile did not desist, that incident would be only the "first drop of the drenching shower to come."

The following day the *News* indicated that some non-Mormons had expressed disapproval of the tone of the editorial; but the Church paper did not apologize. On the contrary, it stated that it meant every word it had printed and more. Four days later, the *News* declared,

> We have no war against the law or its officeers, nor animosity against fair-minded people of any sect, party or race. But we wish it to be understood that we have arrived at the firm conclusion that the Latter-day Saints have "turned the other cheek" long enough. . . .
>
> And we [the *News*] have the best reasons for the solid conviction that [the Mormons] mean to defend themselves against the assaults of their adversaries. The kind of weapons to be used will depend upon the nature of the attacks upon us. "Peace" is our motto, as long as there is any virtue in submission. But should there be any tumult, those who have raised the lying cry of "Rebellion against the Government" will no doubt be held in prominent remembrance.

Not all newspaper correspondents were crying Mormon rebellion. In fact, some communications to Eastern journals were quite sympathetic to the Saints. One such report came out of Utah in 1871 during a period in which much of the national press, stimulated by the Brigham Young polygamy trial, actively condemned the Mormons and warned of rebellion against federal authority. In the preface to a report of his interview with Brigham Young, a *New York Tribune* correspondent confessed that he had found Utah dramatically different from what he had expected. He explained that he had been led to believe from purportedly truthful articles in some Eastern newspapers that a stranger in Salt Lake City had to be careful of what he said and did because of constant surveillance from Mormon authorities. This correspondent reported that he had suffered from no such supervision himself and knew of no one who had. Concluding the rather long dialogue which had included such assorted topics as the assassination of Joseph Smith, the Mormon theatre, Utah mining, and Brigham Young and polygamy, the *Tribune* reporter assured the Mormon prophet not only that he would remember the occasion with pleasure, but also that he would be able to correct the many erroneous notions which prevailed as to Young and his work.[27]

The arrest and trial of Brigham Young in 1871, interpreted by the *News* as a deliberate attempt to invite Mormon resistance and thereby lure another federal army, attracted the attention of another newspaper correspondent, the well-known and highly respected George Alfred Townsend. Despite the fact that Townsend opposed polygamy and confessed that he did not believe a "single figment" of the Mormon story, he wrote several letters from Salt Lake City to the reputable *Cincinnati Commercial,* interpreting affairs in Utah and criticizing the exaggerated and sensational stories of Mormon rebellion printed in Eastern papers. Townsend listed and described the prominent members of the "Ring" and characterized United States collector O. J. Hollister as a determined anti-Mormon who flooded the Eastern presses from New York to Chicago with letters of "locums picked up at hearsay, and hardly reliable enough for a comic paper."

Townsend noted that the East was being liberally supplied with inflammatory correspondence charging the Mormons with mutiny despite the fact that Young had peacefully submitted to arrest and appeared in court unattended. Townsend concluded that life in Utah was perhaps safer than anywhere else in civilization, because the motives and causes of murder—avarice, liquor, gambling, quarrelsomeness, and prostitution—existed here in less degree than in other places. "The industrious political vagabonds who write letters from Utah to the East," declared Townsend, "have created the band of 'Danites' and other hobgoblins out of air and foolscap."[28]

But the sympathetic attitude of the *New York Tribune* and the *Cincinnati Commercial* in 1871 did not keep other journals from adversely reporting Utah affairs. The execution of John D. Lee in 1877 for his part in the Mountain Meadows massacre and the convening of a grand jury that Mormons feared would indict other Church leaders for the crime enabled some newspapers to fill their pages with rumors and charges that the Saints were arming, drilling, and otherwise preparing for rebellion against the federal government.

The *Deseret News* claimed that some Utah newspaper correspondents and the "notorious slander mill" in Salt Lake City had deliberately and maliciously "bamboozled" the American press concerning the 1877 situation. The *News* expressed bewilderment that some journals did not require their reporters to record the facts more accurately, and declared that fabrications would not stop until the "lying and venomous correspondents and slander concocters" were kicked out and replaced by more honorable men. Outraged by false reports, the *News* declared that those responsible ought to be punished, threatening that "they will be when justice rules, if not before."[29]

The *News* declared two newspapers responsible for the reports predicting a Mormon insurrection in 1877: the *San Francisco Chronicle* and the *New York Herald*. Files of these two papers seem to substantiate the charges of the Church paper. Throughout the spring of 1877 the California journal filled its columns with specials from Utah and editorial comments.[30] Stacked one-column headlines such as "BRIGHAM'S DEFENDERS ORGANIZING TO PREVENT HIS ARREST BY THE U.S. AUTHORITIES. THE MORMON MILITIA PREPARING FOR AN EMERGENCY. GENTILE EMIGRATION TO ST. GEORGE STRICTLY PROHIBITED" were common.[31] Shorter headings, such as "THE MORMON BUTCHERS" at the top of a statement made by an anonymous ex-Mormon who reportedly had seen orders signed by Brigham Young authorizing the murder of the gentile immigrants in the Mountain Meadows affair, revealed the intensity of the charges being made.[32]

The *New York Herald* crowded its pages with Mormon news even more than did the *Chronicle,* and at one point filled an entire page with telegraphic dispatches and letters from its Salt Lake agent.[33] Like the *Chronicle,* the New York paper got much of its information from questionable sources. Testimony of one James McGuffie, an ex-Mormon who claimed he would have left Utah had Church authorities let him, gave the *Herald* the long story that they topped with the sensational heading "MORMON RASCALITY. Disgusting Rules Which Enslaved Men and Women. ASSASSINATION COUNTENANCED. Putting an Offender 'Over the Rim.' THE PROPHET LIES. Dame's Order to Murder the Arkansas Emigrants."[34] The *Herald* claimed that Brigham Young had called for blood, that all Mormons had taken oaths to defend their prophet and other Church leaders, and that the same Mormon army that had defeated General Albert Sidney Johnston in the 1857 Mormon War was drilling, training, and equipping itself with breech-loading guns shipped in great numbers from the East. Convinced of imminent and widespread Mormon rebellion, the *Herald* pleaded with Washington to do something.[35]

According to the *Deseret News,* the *Herald* reporter responsible for these dispatches and letters was special correspondent Jerome B. Stillson. The Church paper claimed that Stillson could have obtained truthful information had he wished and criticized him for relying almost wholly on the word of apostates.[36] The *News* frequently badgered Stillson and at one time characterized him as the *Herald's* "lunatic special," charging that he must have been under the influence of a jug of whiskey to send such garbled reports over the wires.

In a dispatch to the *Herald,* Stillson claimed that two attempts had been made on his life: a gunshot the night of 30 May 1877 and a stabbing attempt the next afternoon in his hotel. He described the assailant with the knife as a tall, dark man with a black goatee, and explained that several pictures strategically located in his breast pocket and the brass buckle on his suspenders had saved his life. Stillson supposedly only suffered a few sore ribs and a momentary loss of breath. The correspondent's paper quickly charged Mormon officials with the crime, listing the motive as revenge for Stillson's penetrating and revealing reports.[37]

The *Deseret News* said the attempted assassination was a put-up job by Stillson and others to revive sensational stories of Mormon rebellion and murder. It announced that an immediate investigation revealed no sign of an assailant's flight from the hotel by the fire escape and that three maids on duty testified that no one answering to the description given by Stillson had left by the front door. The *News* claimed that Stillson drank a lot and reported that hotel employees swore that the correspondent was already drunk when he left for his room with a quart of whiskey just minutes before he announced the alleged attempt on his life. The Church paper insisted that to blame Mormon leaders was absurd, that instead Old Rye struck Stillson, and that a Grand Jury should be called to make a full and exhaustive investigation.[38]

Nothing beyond an informal hearing conducted by the mayor of Salt Lake City and other Mormons was ever held in the Stillson affair. To charges of the *New York Herald* that the Mormons tried to hush up the assassination attempt, the *News* pointed out that only non-Mormon prosecuting attorney Howard and the mostly gentile grand jury of the district could call a formal hearing.[39]

No formal hearing every took place, but the *News* was active. The Church paper sarcastically chided both Stillson and the *Herald.* It needled Mormon critics with comments like: "WANTED—A little more ingenuity and a little less whiskey, to manufacture another 'Mormon' sensation for the New York *Herald"* and "what you want—when you want to be assassinated, be sure you properly adjust your vest, your mother's photograph, your bandana and your suspender buckle."[40] In reporting a later minor accident of Stillson's, the *News* explained that he had gotten drunk at Wagner's Brewery and, unable to handle his horses, had been thrown from his buggy. "Wonder if the animals were frightened by a 'tall, dark man with a black goatee,' or scared by the spirit of a keg of lager?" taunted the Church paper.[41]

Whether or not Stillson was ever assaulted is questionable, despite Stanley P. Hirshon's acceptance of the *Herald's* story of Stillson's attempted assassination. (Hirshon claimed Brigham Young's true history was to be found not in LDS Church archives, which he was invited to examine, but rather primarily in the columns of the great Eastern newspapers, which he used heavily in his recent biography of Young.[42]) If any attempt was made on Stillson's life it seems unlikely that it resulted from an official order of the Church. Certainly the Mormons, though they obviously preferred a silent Stillson, were aware of the public condemnation that would come from killing or even attempting to kill a newspaperman who had attracted national publicity. A special report to the *New York Times* from its Utah correspondent stated that the supposed assassination attempt seemed to be generally discredited. Staying in the same hotel, the correspondent reported that he could not see how the alleged crime could have been committed and concluded that even in Salt Lake City the attempt was not charged against Mormon agents.[43]

Aside from a few remarks, however, the *Deseret News* tended to follow a policy of restraint. Declaring its unwillingness to dishonor the official organ of the Church, it "refused to sink to the

sensationalism of the *Herald"* in order to answer all the attacks
of that paper.[44] The *News* concluded that except for those addicted
to lurid journalism the American people would ignore the lies of
the *Herald,* and that little could be done with that class of readers
addicted to sensationalism except to let them "revel in their own
slime," and "perish of their own rottenness."[45]

The *News,* however, found it impossible to remain completely
silent. To the *Herald's* charge that Mormons were "drilling and
arming in Utah," it answered humorously,

> The farmers have been drilling wheat, corn, etc., into the earth
> . . . . The miners also do a little drilling in the rocks. We have
> no other drilling. All the arming we have seen is of the arm-in-arm
> variety, which indicates peace, prosperity, sociability.[46]

In an editorial headed "Who Might Say Something," the *News*
stressed that rumors of insurrection in Utah harmed business more
than anything else and urged businessmen to sign a petition swear-
ing to the peaceful conditions in Utah, thus allaying the fears
of those in the East who were ignorant of the situation and who
would remain so as long as they believed the *Herald.*[47]

Much more direct was the *News's* answer to the *Herald's* call
for more troops to put down the supposed Utah rebellion. It warned
the government that this would constitute useless expenditure of
public funds. However, said the *News,* if Washington proved
foolish enough to send troops and the money to maintain them,
the people of Utah would, as had been the case twenty years before, do their best to gather up the money and put it to good use.[48]

The *Deseret News* used other tactics to answer attacks. Stating
that although lies might catch on for awhile, the truth would
eventually come out,[49] the *News* quoted from some newspapers
that described the rumors of rebellion as gross misrepresentations.
A Salt Lake City dispatch to the *New York Sun* stated that in no
place in the United States were the laws more readily obeyed than
in Utah and that the whole issue of Mormon rebellion was the
fake cry of an adventurous few who wanted to take political and
economic power away from well-deserving and industrious Mormons.[50] The *Record,* a gentile newspaper published in the non-
Mormon community of Corinne, Utah, also stated that the rumors
had been manufactured for sensational purposes and that the
charges of Mormon rebellion were groundless.[51]

The *New York Tribune* also discredited claims of rebellion.

This paper's Utah correspondent advised his paper that despite accounts in various journals mentioning trouble in Mormondom, a very little time would show that nothing tangible existed in them.[52] However, no gentile newspaper denied the alleged Utah insurrection of 1877 more faithfully than the *New York Times.* A special dispatch to the *Times* from Salt Lake City, acknowledging that sensational reports of Mormon rebellion appeared almost daily in some Eastern newspapers, stated,

> Those reports are purely sensational with no foundation in fact. No Mormon troops are drilling, no guns or ammunition are being purchased or shipped. There is no active Nauvoo Legion. There is perfect peace in Salt Lake and throughout Utah. . . . The Mormon people are as much startled here by these false reports as you are in New York.[53]

Several months after the rather tense summer of 1877 the *Times* ran another article in defense of Mormon Utah. Its reporter interviewed the widely traveled Captain John Codman, who, unlike most visitors to Mormondom, had spent four entire summers in Utah. Making frequent trips through the length and breadth of the territory, Codman claimed that he had become well acquainted with the character of the various classes of people from the laborer in the field to Brigham Young himself. He called the stories of the previous summer concerning a Utah uprising ridiculous, groundless, and heartlessly false, and blamed the "Gentile ring of office seekers" and their paper, the *Salt Lake City Tribune,* for the sensationalism that other journals printed.[54]

Although it missed the opportunity to use the Codman interview from the *Times,* by the 1870s the *Deseret News* had become very outspoken in answering anti-Mormon attacks. Its role as Church apologist had been somewhat usurped in the 1850s by the quasi-official newspapers discussed earlier. However, the *News,* having "Truth and Liberty" as its motto from the beginning, had never been completely silent in regard to criticism from outside newspapers. By the time it started issuing a daily in 1867, it had wholeheartedly taken upon itself the task of "correcting" the wire releases of the Associated Press, defending the Church against alleged misrepresentations in outside newspapers, and presenting to the public and the policy-makers a positive, if not always completely authentic, picture of Utah and the Mormons.

In the prospectus for the daily *News,* the editor explained that he wanted each subscriber to get more than his money's worth in "good, solid, reliable information." Cannon noted that his aim was to promote the welfare and the various interests of the territory and added that it would be his "province to advocate and defend their rights—social, political and religious [and] to make the Paper the fearless exponent of the truth. . . ."[55] In response to an Idaho paper's judgment that the Utah press ought to be condemned for supporting Mormon religious beliefs, the *News* exclaimed, "If a people really believe anything, that belief is conscientious belief, and to be conscientious people they must defend or stand by that belief. . . . So far as the 'Mormon' or Utah press does this, it is entitled to respectful consideration."[56]

It was not until the completion of the transcontinental railroad in 1869 that the *News* could hope that many people outside Utah would see the paper's defensive arguments and read its answers to gentile critics. In a 13 December 1869 editorial headed "Sensation Stories from Utah—Differences between the Past and the Present," the *News* declared that false reports from Utah had caused the Mormon War of 1857 and, because of wide credence throughout the East, had become firmly rooted in the public mind before any rebuttal appeared. The editor explained that in 1857, because Utah was remote and almost inaccessible, mail communication, even when regular, occurred only monthly. He concluded,

> But now, all this has changed. To-day we have constant telegraphic communication, and the railroad brings us papers and letters three or four days old from the populous cities of the East, and carries news from here and there with equal facility.

The *Deseret News* did not attempt to respond to all charges made against the Mormons by the outside press, nor did it always emphasize them when it did choose to answer. To the frequent query as to why the Utah papers did not "notice, deny, and refute" the many slanders that found their way into the public press, the *News* replied,

> Sometimes we do nail a lie or two to the counter, by way of example and for the sake of variety. But to notice all the calumny that is vomited forth concerning our citizens would be a Herculean task, in which we shall not engage. We have neither taste nor time for such business, nor do we consider it our duty to invest every slanderous report with the importance of a notice in our columns.[57]

When the paper did choose to respond to criticism, it could be very blunt and very sharp. Replying to the *San Francisco Chronicle's* report of Miss Anna Dickinson's two-hour-long censure of Mormonism, Cannon explained that "had the address, sermon or tirade of the fair lecturess been a personal attack merely, gallantry would have forbidden our replying to it; but as it was an attack upon the entire people of Utah, we, as a public journalist, representing that people, feel bound to make some reference to it." Cannon labeled her charge that Salt Lake City was a modern Sodom as nothing more than a lie. As to her lengthy argument against polygamy, Cannon reflected the conservative Mormon philosophy concerning women by calling attention to her feminist ideas and her refusal to marry. He categorized some of her other assertions as "willful misrepresentations," adding that "they would have been lies in a gentleman." He concluded, "But enough on this subject; we have already devoted more time and attention to it than it deserves."[58]

The *Deseret News* was very much aware of its responsibility, and its editors must have believed, as Frank Luther Mott would later write, that a great function of the printing of news was to correct the inevitable abuses of rumor.[59] Also, the Church paper seemed to agree with Alexis de Tocqueville's 1835 judgment of the influence of the press:

> In the United States . . . the power of the periodical press is second only to that of the people. . . . each separate journal exercises but little authority; [but] when many organs of the press adopt the same line of conduct, their influence in the long run becomes irresistible, and public opinion, perpetually assailed from the same side, eventually yields to the attack.[60]

Although not all gentile papers were out to censure Utah, many people in the United States endorsed the anti-Mormon crusades of the 1870s, and their prevailing tone was one of bitterness.

One way the Church paper combatted misrepresentation and corrected rumor was by filling its pages with a positive picture of Utah. A reprint in the *News* of a "sensible letter" written to the *New York Tribune* exemplified this policy. The author of the letter, a gentile who signed himself "Fair Dealing," explained that the editor of the *Tribune* knew him and knew he would not publicize his opinions without first thoroughly examining the subject under consideration. He wrote that Easterners were misled by reports from Utah that he personally knew to be absolutely false and that the current crusade against Brigham Young had been instigated by religious prejudice, bigotry, and the economic envy of gentiles. He argued that Mormons were loyal to the federal government and that nothing but bitter persecution urged on by fanatics would make them raise a hand against their enemies:

> The Mormons as a body are honest, industrious, God-fearing people. Their industry, temperate habits and perseverance have achieved more wonderful results than can be shown from the same causes in any part of your land. They are peaceable, friendly, thrifty and an excessively hard-working people. They are very devotional, and evidently intend and desire to do what is right before God and man. A very large majority of them are not practically polygamists. They tolerate no dramshops, no gambling-saloons, and no houses of ill-fame. They sustain schools and see that all idlers are set to work.[61]

The *Deseret News* published many such letters from people who wrote complimentary reports after visiting Salt Lake City. In an editorial on 2 April 1872 Cannon explained that he was printing extracts from a private letter of this sort from a "most intelligent and worthy citizen of Ohio . . . which indicates, we believe, the tendency of the opinions of just and fair men throughout the country."

Unhypocritically and with total faith in its ability to judge, the *News* admittedly, and perhaps properly, edited many of the extracts it took from its exchanges. In 1872 it listed a number of papers throughout the United States that it felt had been fairly reasonable toward the Mormons in that year's "crusade," and then explained,

> In all cases that have come under our notice, where our contemporaries have spoken, in a candid, fair, and manly way, we have freely done them the best reciprocal honor that we could, in the republication in the News of their articles or extracts, or in a favorable mention thereof, in most instances excluding those portions which might be manifestly misstatements arising from incorrect information or an imperfect apprehension of the circumstances, and in some instances making such comments and corrections as it appeared to us the public had a right to expect at the hands of journalists who were better acquainted with the situation.[62]

The *Deseret News* used more than just extracts from complimentary newspapers to influence its gentile readers. On 12 May 1874 it reviewed in manuscript form John Codman's *The Mormon Country: A Summer with the Latter-day Saints*. The Church paper emphasized that Codman had originally sent his manuscript to a leading magazine for publication but had been turned down because the work was "too impartial" (i.e., pro-Mormon).[63] It is true that Codman generally sympathized with the Saints, though not in every case. He found it hard to believe, for example, that any educated man could have a "real faith" in the inspiration of Joseph Smith or Brigham Young. He wrote that he believed "in the utter absurdity and imposture of the Mormon faith . . ." and that the history of the first Mormon Apostle [Joseph Smith] was developed in fanaticism, and culminated in imposture."[64] Naturally the *News,* although in this case not admitting it publicly, refused to include in its review this outspoken personal disbelief in the divine claims of Mormonism. Nonetheless, George Q. Cannon, whom Codman described as "a man of sterling worth and talent,"[65] declared that while he did not agree with many views and deductions in the book, he personally felt that "its spirit" could not fail to do good.[66]

Rather than endorse the whole book, then, the *News* understandably selected only complimentary material, particularly statements that pictured Mormons to be law abiding and inoffensive, such as,

> In all my voyages and travels about the world, I never before passed three months in a community more industrious, upright, honest in dealing among themselves and with others, quiet, inoffensive, loyal to government, temperate, virtuous and religious, than these Mormons.[67]

The *News* explained that Codman divided the gentiles in Utah into two classes: honorable men who came to stay, and those who sought to set up gambling houses, drinking saloons, and brothels. The book's author wrote that if all were like the first class "there would be scarcely a word of complaint against the Mormons, and no petitions to Congress for relief from the tyranny of the Church."[68] Cannon overlooked Codman's disbelief in the Mormon religion, commenting favorably on the writer's genuine appreciation of the Mormons as a people.

Another method the *Deseret News* employed to allay American fears about Utah was to deny outright, although often without offering evidence, the negative picture of Mormondom presented by books and newspapers and from pulpits. The *News,* after reprinting a column from the *San Francisco Chronicle* which charged that Mormon municipal officers arrested federal soldiers on "frivolous pretexts," responded, "Soldiers are not arrested and detained in this city on frivolous pretexts, though a partizan, subsidized, lying press may make it appear that such is the case."[69] In 1877 the *News* declared that pulpit orators and newspapers had pictured divorce as a common practice among the Saints, claiming it was in accordance with Mormon doctrines. "But we deem it a duty," wrote the *News*, "we owe to the people of Utah, to correct the public mind upon the . . . subject. . . ."[70] A year later, two *News* correspondents complained to the publishers of the *The American Cyclopedia* against what they felt were incorrect articles on Joseph Smith, Brigham Young, and the Mormons. After Appleton and Company, the publishers, wrote back that all articles were true, the editor of the Church journal simply sided with the position of its correspondents.[71]

At times the *News* did present lengthy and logical arguments to counteract criticism from outside Utah. In a 1 December 1868 editorial headlined "The 'Ignorance, Error and Bigotry' of the 'Mormons'," Cannon explained that the San Francisco *Occident*'s correspondent, one "J. S. W.," had admitted in a recent letter to his paper that the Mormons were an industrious, persevering, and frugal people. The California correspondent presented as evidence the well-laid-out city of Salt Lake with its shade trees, streams of water, fine stores, business places, public buildings, and numerous churches. After thus praising the Mormons, however, "J. S. W." characterized them as ignorant bigots who allowed themselves to be enslaved and who degraded women by practising polygamy. Recognizing the inconsistency, the editor of the *News* responded to the *Occident*,

> How ridiculous such correspondents as "J. S. W." make themselves! They come to Salt Lake City, stay here for a few days, see, and are constrained to admire our beautiful metropolis, and to admit the evidences that everywhere present themselves, of the unflagging industry of the people who have built it; they will tell also of the absence of rowdyism, profanity and that squalor and social wretchedness that are so abundant in almost every city within the purview of Christendom and yet they must sing the everlasting song of the degradation, bondage, ignorance, etc., that exist among the Latter-day Saints.

Cannon observed that when writers such as "J. S. W." visited the Shakers or other such communities they could not be too loud in their praises of the good order, sobriety, and morality that prevailed there; and such conditions, instead of being proof of degradation, ignorance, and fanaticism, were attributed to directly opposite causes. On the other hand, argued Cannon, Mormon morality, sobriety, and good order were said to have been founded on ignorance and superstition. And instead of going into great detail on the charge of female debauchery in Utah, the *News* wisely shifted the burden of proof to the accusers and declared that if such men as "J. S. W." were really serious about the degradation of women, they had a much more promising field of study in their own cities. The *News* then concluded its editorial:

> As for us, we are amply satisfied with the workings of our system. We have tried "civilization," and have witnessed its fruits, and infinitely prefer the morality, sobriety, peace and security, which prevail in Zion. And if the latter be the result of ignorance, superstition and degradation, we would to God that all the human family were in that condition!

Although the *News* sometimes argued long and well against alleged misrepresentations, quite often it merely invited public attention to their absurdity by quoting extracts from newspapers. In an 1875 editorial headed "Going Crazy," the Mormon editor exclaimed that newspapers throughout the United States had gone mad on the subject of the Mormons. As proof, he reprinted several statements from the *Territorial Enterprize*. Somewhat like the legendary saying attributed to Andrew Jackson that the only good Indian was a dead Indian, the *Enterprize* exclaimed,

> Every man who is a Mormon . . . should be by law declared a felon, not competent to exercise any right of an American citizen . . . . There is probably no cure for an Old Mormon except death. . . . Of all the dark spots upon our country's history, there is not one, present or past, so black and loathsome as Mormonism.[72]

The *News* explained that the main reason for printing these excerpts was to place on record "some of the furious, the insensate, the maniacal expressions" of the press towards the citizens of Utah. The editor emphasized that they were not quoted to argue their truth or falsity and wrote that it was "entirely unnecessary" to "emphatically deny the assertions . . . of the *Enterprize*" to intelligent people. The excerpts were their own best refutation.[73]

These defensive methods continued to be used over the years as the *Deseret News* tried to explain and justify the social peculiarities of the Mormon people, particularly the practice of polygamy, and to assure America that they were law-abiding citizens, ready for statehood. Both of these subjects, as they related to the *News*, will be discussed in some detail in the last chapter, when we take up the Church's official abandonment of polygamy in 1890 and the achievement of Utah statehood six years later. It is sufficient to say here that after becoming a daily, and after the arrival of the transcontinental railroad, the *Deseret News* answered attacks by some newspaper correspondents by more completely assuming its role of apologist—"in fulfillment of our journalistic duty, in order that the public may be on its guard and not be taken unawares of specious sensational communications."[74]

Footnotes

1. For comments on Western newspaper reliability, *see* Thomas E. Tweito, "The Correspondent in the West, 1850-1860" (unpublished doctoral dissertation, Iowa City, Iowa, 1939), pp. 20-21, 24-27, 58; James F. Willard, "Spreading the News of the Early Discoveries of Gold in Colorado," *The Colorado Magazine* 6(May 1929): 98-104; James Claude Malin, *John Brown and the Legend of Fifty-Six* (Philadelphia: The American Philosophical Society, 1942), pp. 34, 63; and Elmo Scott Watson, "The Indian Wars and the Press, 1866-1867," *Journalism Quarterly* 27(December 1940): 302-3.

2. Richard O. Cowan, "Mormonism in National Periodicals" (unpublished doctoral dissertation, Stanford University, Palo Alto, California, 1962), p. 194; and Leonard J. Arrington and Jon Haupt, "Intolerable Zion: The Image of Mormonism in Nineteenth-century American Literature," *Western Humanities Review* ??(Summer 1968): 244; *see also* Cassie Hyde Hock, "The Mormons in Fiction" (unpublished doctoral dissertation, University of Colorado, Boulder, 1941), pp. 217, 219.

3. *News*, 27 June 1871.

4. Ibid., 12 December 1860.

5. Ibid., 26 February 1873.

6. Ibid. For similar statements by the paper, *see News* 22 July 1857, 3 September 1872, 29 December 1874, and 19 August 1879.

7. *New York Times*, 18 May 1852.

8. Norman F. Furniss, *The Mormon Conflict 1850-1859* (New Haven: Yale University Press, 1960), p. 239. The *New York Tribune*, 9 October 1849, reveals it had a correspondent passing through Salt Lake City.

9. *The New York Herald*, 10 May 1877; *Chicago Tribune*, 8 July 1869; *San Francisco Chronicle*, 3 April 1877. The *New York Times* of 21 November 1868 quoted a special to the *St. Louis Democrat* from the Missouri paper's own Utah correspondent. George A. Townsend of the *Cincinnati Commercial* wrote a number of letters from Salt Lake City to that Ohio newspaper and later published them in his *Mormon Trials at Salt Lake City* (New York: American News Company, 1871).

10. Mark Twain, *Roughing It* (New York: Harper and Brothers, 1871), 1:120-22. Twain was passing through Salt Lake City en route to Virginia City, Nevada, where he served from 1861 to 1864 as a reporter and feature writer for the *Territorial Enterprize*.

11. *New York Times*, 9 September 1877.

12. Ibid., 14 September 1872.

13. *New York Times,* 16 August 1871 and 25 January, 28 May, and 2 August 1873.
14. Miss Anna Dickinson, advocate of women's rights, visited Salt Lake City in June 1869; later she delivered an anti-Mormon lecture in San Francisco.
15. *News,* 16 June 1871.
16. Ibid., 3 February 1874.
17. George H. Manning, "Bennett Fight Opened Senate to Press," *Editor and Publisher,* 67(21 July 1934): 118. The Associated Press, meeting in Louisville, Kentucky, 22 November 1865, adopted the following resolution: "Telegraph reports should above all else be reliable"; Oliver Gramling, *AP: the Story of News* (New York: Farrar and Rinehart, 1940), p. 63.
18. Gramling, *AP,* pp. 110, 115. Lawson had long been in the newspaper business in Chicago and served as president of the Associated Press from 1894 to 1900; Edward A. Duddy, "Victor Fremont Lawson," *Dictionary of American Biography,* 11:60-61.
19. Gramling, *AP,* p. 108.
20. *News,* 29 February 1872. Information pertaining to AP agents in Utah is severely limited as a result of a 1950 "housecleaning" in which virtually all Associated Press records were destroyed; Wes Gallagher, general manager of the Associated Press, New York, N. Y., 24 June 1969, letter to the author.
21. Malin, *John Brown,* p. 32.
22. *Chicago Tribune,* 25 February 1873.
23. *News,* 3 May 1872. This apparently appeared in the *Washington Capital* sometime in April 1872.
24. *Omaha Bee,* 20 March 1873. For *News* citation *see* 26 March 1873.
25. *News,* 24 September 1872.
26. Ibid., 13 August 1879.
27. *New York Tribune,* 2 June 1871.
28. Townsend, *Mormon Trials,* pp. 4, 18, 20, 39-40. For characterization of Townsend and the *Cincinnati Commercial, see* Charles David Abbott, "George Alfred Townsend," *Dictionary of American Biography,* 18:616-17; *New York Times,* obituary, 16 April 1944; and Frank Luther Mott, *American Journalism: A History of Newspapers in the United States through 260 Years, 1690-1950* (New York: Macmillan Company, 1950), p. 459.
29. *News,* 9 and 10 May 1877.
30. For example, *San Francisco Chronicle,* 1, 3, 4, 8, and 30 April and 4, 5, 8, and 13 May 1877.
31. Ibid., 3 April 1877.
32. Ibid., 8 April 1877. In light of Juanita Brooks, *Mountain Meadows Massacre* (Palo Alto, California: Stanford University Press, 1950), it also reveals the unreliability of the *San Francisco Chronicle.*
33. *New York Herald,* 17 May 1877, and almost every day in May and June. For other specific examples of Mormon news *see* 7, 9, and 10 May and 8, 9, 10, and 11 June 1877.
34. Ibid., 10 May 1877.
35. Ibid., 9 and 11 May 1877.
36. *News,* 18 May 1877.

37. *New York Herald,* 1 and 2 June 1877.
38. *News,* 1 and 2 June 1877.
39. Ibid., 14 June 1877.
40. Ibid., 4 June 1877.
41. Ibid., 22 June 1877.
42. Stanley P. Hirshson, *The Lion of the Lord: A Biography of Brigham Young* (New York: Alfred A. Knopf, 1969), p. 319.
43. *New York Times,* 5 June 1877. Immediately before coming to Utah as a *Herald* correspondent in 1877, Stillson had been engaged in western land sales in Denver. Prior to this he had worked for the New York *World.* Stillson left Salt Lake City shortly after the alleged assassination attempt and was assigned by the *Herald,* by whom he was employed until his death in 1880, to General Alfred H. Terry's Peace Commission to Chief Sitting Bull in Canada in the fall of 1877; *see New York Times,* obituary, 27 December 1880; and Mott, *American Journalism,* p. 487.
44. *News,* 16 May 1877.
45. Ibid., 9 May 1877.
46. Ibid., 16 May 1877.
47. Ibid.
48. Ibid., 13 May 1877.
49. Ibid. 17 May 1877.
50. *The Sun* [New York City], 9 May 1877.
51. *See News,* 19 May 1877.
52. *New York Tribune,* 23 May 1877.
53. *New York Times,* 13 May 1877; *see also* ibid., 4 and 5 June 1877.
54. Ibid., 1 October 1877. Codman was an American sea captain, traveler, and author. He distinguished himself in both the Crimean War and the United States Civil War, made extensive trips all over the world, and wrote several books, including *The Round Trip* (1879), a description of a tour of the Western states, and *Mormon Country* (1874); *see* George Harvey Genzmer, "John Codman," *Dictionary of American Biography,* 2:259.
55. *News,* 20 November 1867. The daily was first issued 21 November 1867.
56. Ibid., 15 April 1876.
57. Ibid., 20 December 1871.
58. Ibid., 16 September 1869. For Dickinson's speech *see San Francisco Chronicle,* 4 September 1869.
59. Mott, American Journalism, p. 9
60. Alexis de Tocqueville, *Democracy in America* (New York: Vintage Books, 1945), 1:195. To achieve greater emphasis, the author has slightly rearranged the sequence of de Tocqueville's statements.
61. *New York Tribune,* 18 October 1871. Reprinted in *News,* 31 October 1871.
62. *News,* 6 May 1872.
63. *See* Codman, *Mormon Country* (New York City: John F. Trow and Sons, 1874), foreword, no page number.
64. Codman, *Mormon Country,* pp. 96, 123, 136.
65. Ibid., p. 84.
66. Undated letter to Codman printed in *Mormon Country,* p. 222.

67. *News,* 12 May 1874. *See* Codman, *Mormon Country,* p. 215.
68. Ibid., pp. 215-16.
69. *News,* 15 June 1874. A search of the *Chronicle* did not turn up this alleged charge in its daily issue.
70. *News,* 27 September 1877.
71. Ibid., 19 January 1878.
72. *Territorial Enterprize* [Virginia City, Nevada], circa July 1875, as quoted in *News,* 30 July 1875. A similar example is seen in *News,* 9 November 1875.
73. *News,* 30 July 1875.
74. Ibid., 24 September 1872.

7

The Incorporated
News and
Personal Journalism

Mormons not only were attacked by Eastern and Western newspapers, but also were aggressively assailed by a local press that by
the 1880s had become powerful and influential. As with its dispu-
tations with the outside papers, the *News*'s response to local opposition tended to be quite subdued. This impersonal and restrained
temperament had long been characteristic of the *Deseret News*
when, by the last quarter of the nineteenth century, it began to
typify American newspapers generally.

Nineteenth century newspapers in large American cities, like
many other enterprises of the time, became big businesses. Highly
personalized journalism, feasible only when a paper was small
enough for a single man to dominate it, declined. As greater capital
accumulation permitted enlargement of newspapers, the importance
of the business manager increased, restricting editorial prerogatives.
Corporation-owned papers tended to shift from views to news.
The offensive, flaming editorials were replaced with inoffensive
—and profitable—policy positions. Immensely varied news pro-
grams demanded large staffs with many talents, and the old-time
solitary editor had to yield part of his importance to city and sports
editors.

Technological changes also influenced the newspaper business
of this period. The Western Union Telegraph, the telephone, and

the Atlantic cable made news from all over the world almost instantly available, while faster, better quality presses rapidly prepared it for public reading.

Keeping step with the national trend, the *Deseret News,* both the newspaper and the publishing business, enjoyed a general enlargement and physical improvement. In 1884 a $150,000 three-story stone paper mill was completed. It employed twenty-four workers and produced up to five tons of newsprint, book, and manila paper daily. A used Bullock press, purchased from the Omaha *Republican* in 1890 for $8,500, printed both sides of the paper at once and spun out 14,000 eight-page newspapers an hour. Faster mail service and the introduction into Salt Lake City of the typewriter, telephone, and electric streetcar speeded newsgathering and printing during this period. The old weekly *News* was transformed into a magazine in 1888, and several years later the daily paper employed a city editor and doubled the number of its pages.

However, the *Deseret News* was much less affected by the emergence of newspapers as big business and the resulting decline in personal journalism, for from the beginning the *News* had been, in effect, the organ of a large corporation: the Church. Despite the fact that some editors were gifted and at times spoke out boldly, ecclesiastical authorities controlled and dominated the paper for the benefit of the Church. Although for a time, when feelings ran particularly high between the gentiles and the Mormons in Utah, the *News* did take on some of the trappings of the very personal frontier small-town papers, this was not characteristic of the Church paper and was only a temporary departure from its traditional policy.

This momentary desertion from its customary policy came in the 1880s. The first year of that decade was notable in Utah history. It was the jubilee year of the Mormon Church. John Taylor was officially proclaimed as the new Church President. The gentile-oriented Liberal Party launched a special campaign against the Saints, and presidents Hays and Garfield changed the government's Utah policy to an open assault on the temporal power of the Church.

The beginning of the new decade was also significant in the life of the *Deseret News.* In a city of 20,768, where printing and publishing represented the largest capitalization,[1] the *News* had the largest circulation of the eleven newspapers and quarterlies.[2] In 1880 the Church paper was incorporated under "private"

hands, and Charles W. Penrose was made editor-in-chief, a position
he would hold for the next twelve years.

The incorporated Deseret News Company issued one thousand
shares of stock at one hundred dollars each, with an option to increase the capitalization at a later time. Over one-half of this
stock was purchased by John Taylor shortly before he was officially
named Church President. He was subsequently elected president of
the new newspaper corporation by its stockholders.[3] Perhaps the
News was reorganized in this fashion to keep it in Mormon hands
in the event that Hayes and Garfield carried out the contemplated
policy of confiscating Church-owned property. In 1886 the capital
stock of the Deseret News Company was increased to $250,000.[4] A
year later, just before the Edmunds-Tucker Act disincorporated the
Church and escheated everything over $50,000, John Taylor, who
must have bought a thousand of the new shares as Trustee-in-Trust
of the Church, sold or transferred the Church-owned stock to a
syndicate of Mormon writers and publishers who held them in
trust to avoid confiscation.[5] At any rate, when Penrose announced
the incorporation in the *News,* he noted that the change had been
planned for some time and hoped and expected that it would prove
very beneficial.[6]

The close connection between the *News* and the Church hierarchy
remained essentially the same, for the president of the board of
directors was also the President of the Church, and his two counselors were members of the board. Nevertheless, the incorporation
eventually raised in some minds the question of whether or not
the *News* was to continue as the official spokesman of the Church.
The *Herald,* a Salt Lake paper that began publication in 1870,
was apparently considered by some to have assumed that role.
Commenting on reports from various parts of the territory to that
effect, Thomas E. Taylor, an officer in the Deseret News Company
and the son of President Taylor, expressed some concern about
the future of the *News* if such reports were true:

> We have always understood that the News was the medium
> of communication from the Presidency to the people, and that it
> was the Church Organ. . . . We have no complaint to make against
> any legitimate competition we may have to meet; but we have been
> in the habit of representing the News as the official Church paper,
> and many of the people when only able to have one paper have
> given preference to the News as wishing to keep posted as to
> church matters and the public utterances of the Authorities of the
> Church.[7]

That the *News* was to remain the voice of Mormonism should, however, have been clear from the outset, as Penrose, in publishing the announcement of the incorporation, stated that the paper would "continue to be the official organ of The Church of Jesus Christ of Latter-day Saints. . . ."[8] Later, Penrose further explained that whenever Church leaders had public announcements to make by way of the press they used the *News*. He noted that the paper announced Church meetings, printed discourses of the Church authorities, and advocated and defended Church doctrine against assaults from opponents.[9] Penrose did grant, however, that the *Deseret News* was not owned and published by the Church, but rather by the Deseret News Company.[10]

The *News* not only was still the Church organ, but also began gradually to assume an even more obvious religious role. Because it had been the only Mormon paper in Utah for years, the Saints looked to it for all local, general, and religious news. By the 1880s many of the counties in the territory had their own papers, and the local citizens were counselled by Church authorities to support them. Consequently, those who subscribed to two papers read the *News* not so much for general news as for Church doctrine.[11]

Because John Taylor was both Church president and president of the News Company, the Church also continued to control and, when it was felt necessary, to restrict the *News*. A few years later, during the period when polygamous ecclesiastical officials had gone underground to escape federal marshals, assistant *News* editor George Cannon Lambert recorded in his journal, "The Church authorities were nearly all absent, so that there was little or no chance to consult them about the policy of the paper or the course to be pursued in an emergency."[12] Lambert noted that he occasionally met with new Church President Wilford Woodruff and Apostle Erastus Snow for advice but always clandestinely and usually at night.[13] General Authorities' sermons continued to be submitted for "revision" before they were allowed to be published,[14] and the *News* editors maintained a policy of refusing to print anything they felt the "authorities of the Church would not sanction. . . ."[15]

There was some hedging on the subject of the Church's control of the editorial policy. Penrose publicly denied the *Salt Lake Tribune*'s charge that he had taken solemn oaths to obey his ecclesiastical superiors in all things.[16] However, his assistant, John Nicholson, privately said that *News* editors were not always completely independent. Upon his dismissal from the federal penitentiary, where he had served almost six months for "unlawful cohabitation," Nicholson asked President John Taylor in a letter whether or not he should return to his old position on the *News* staff. Wanting to be completely fair and interested only in the welfare of the Church, Nicholson explained that he hesitated to return for a reason he had felt too delicate to bring up before, but which candor now compelled him to comment on:

> In consequence of not being, in my views, in harmony, occasionally, with the way in which some public questions are handled, there would, in the event of a resumption of my labors, be some danger of the paper appearing inconsistent with itself. . . . There are some positions taken . . . with which I do not believe I could ever coincide, and unfortunately the man in sight is, popularly at least, credited with what happens to appear.[17]

However, as in the paper's earlier history, control and restriction continued to be achieved with an impressive degree of harmony among all concerned. Rather than arbitrary Church domination of the press, it was often a matter of the *News* requesting advice and counsel from the leadership before taking action.[18] Even Nicholson, despite his independent nature, returned to the *News* and served with commendation until 1892.

Although goodwill characterized the relationship between ecclesiastical and newspaper officials, the Church's monitoring of the *News*'s content left little room for personal journalism. In his book *Early Utah Journalism: A Half Century of Forensic Warfare, Waged by the West's Most Militant Press,* J. Cecil Alter argues, as his title suggests, that Utah journalism was highly personal and concludes that most editors in the territory either were confronted by libel suits or were forced to defend themselves with shotgun or fists.[19] But Mormon journalism was usually quite passive, and the 1880s were not pioneer days in Salt Lake City and the editor of the *News* was not in complete control of the paper. Although on one occasion the *News* faced a libel suit, its pages were seldom offensive, and in this one instance the paper settled out of court, paying $1,000 to avoid attracting unwanted attention to the Church journal.[20]

In fact, the *News* called for legislation that would severely punish libelers. Editor George Q. Cannon argued that attacks made on private lives harmed the public rather than helping it, as some papers contended. He said that lies were made to satisfy appetites and sell newspapers, and that if not stopped by legal methods libelers would cause "violence and bloodshed."[21]

Despite the extremely explosive atmosphere in Utah in the 1880s and the outspoken and at all times libelous partisan press in the city, no editor of the *Deseret News* ever suffered physical violence. Before coming to head the *News,* Charles W. Penrose had received a severe canebeating from an unhappy lawyer who took offense at an article in Penrose's Ogden, Utah, *Junction,*[22] but that sort of thing never occurred while he edited the Church paper. In 1884 John Q. Cannon, assistant editor of the *News,* gave a Salt Lake City *Tribune* reporter a lashing with a piece of rawhide for an alleged lie written in the *Tribune.* Reporting the incident, the *News* agreed that assault and battery should not be countenanced—but observed that to anyone knowledgeable of the outrageous course the *Tribune* had for years been pursuing, it was surprising that such things had not happened more often.[23]

Perhaps the paucity of libel suits and the absence of physical violence resulted from the *Deseret News*'s policy of "benign neglect" toward local anti-Mormon newspapers. As in the Midwest, the Mormons in Utah faced newspaper criticism and opposition from within their own "kingdom" as well as from external opponents. Since the birth in 1870 of the *Salt Lake Tribune,* by far the most stable and effective local newspaper opponent of the Church, numerous papers had started in Salt Lake City, most of which chose to antagonize the Mormon establishment.[24] At least three anti-Mormon newspapers in the city prior to 1870—the *Valley Tan* (1858-1860), the *Union Vedette* (1863-1867), and the shorter-lived *Daily Reporter* (1868-1869)—spared little effort in attacking the *Deseret News* and the Mormon Church. But unlike the *News*'s rather outspoken criticism of the gentile newspapers published outside Utah, the editorial tactic used against these local opposition papers was, at least initially, one of almost complete inattention.

The *Valley Tan* was the *Deseret News*'s first local competition.[25] It was begun by former Missouri newspaperman Kirk Anderson and composed at and supported by Camp Floyd, the army post established during the 1857 "Mormon War." The *Tan* explained that it would discuss "fearlessly and fairly" the religious and social questions peculiar to the people of Utah and called for open and fair discussion.[26] The *News,* however, chose to remain silent where this domestic competitor was concerned, and—contrary to common practice among newspapers, be they sympathetic or ardent rivals—

the Church paper ignored both the birth and death of the *Tan.* Apostle John Taylor explained that this silence-is-the-best-policy philosophy was founded on the idea that if ignored, the *Tan,* which Taylor described as a weak and disreputable paper and the avowed enemy of the majority of the citizens of Utah, would soon grow sick and die.[27]

Although the Church chose a policy of silence for the *News,* the overall policy of official and unofficial Mormon journalism was not so silent. The *Tan's* attacks fostered the birth of the Salt Lake City *Mountaineer,* a journal whose motto read, "Do What Is Right; Let the Consequences Follow." The *Mountaineer,* though owned and edited by Mormons, was not the official Church spokesman, and so did not feed the flames of the gentile-Mormon conflict to the same extent that answers from the Church's authorized journal would have done. The *Mountaineer* set the pattern for the Salt Lake City newspapers for the remainder of the territorial period: whenever an anti-Mormon paper appeared, a third paper would pick up the challenge while the *News* serenely ignored it.

Just how successful the *News's* policy of silence as far as the *Tan* was concerned is difficult to assess. The *Tan's* inability to maintain an ample supply of paper and the evacuation of Camp Floyd in 1860 adequately explain its demise. The passing of the *Tan* in 1860, for whatever reason, and the later death of the *Mountaineer* once again left the *News* as the only paper in Salt Lake City.

However, the Church's newspaper monopoly was short-lived. The Third California Volunteers, commanded by Colonel Patrick Connor, was ordered to Utah during the Civil War, presumably to give protection to the overland mail, secure the telegraph, and superintend the Mormons. Connor established Camp Douglas on the east bench overlooking the Salt Lake Valley. From this new army post, as from Camp Floyd, came a competitor for the *Deseret News.*

Named the *Union Vedette,* the new Utah paper had essentially the same objectives as the *Valley Tan.* Colonel Connor, primarily responsible for founding the Camp Douglas newspaper, explained in a communique to his assistant adjutant general that he planned to wrest from the "disloyal and traitorous" Church its absolute control over Utah by starting a mining boom to overwhelm the Mormons by sheer force of numbers.[28] According to the *Vedette,* the paper's mission was to overthrow polygamy and one-man power and to combat heresies which oppressed the Mormon people.[29]

Despite the fact that the *Vedette* was an outspoken anti-Mormon journal, the *Deseret News* maintained its policy of silence and virtually ignored it. This policy was clearly stated: "Our enemies need not flatter themselves that they can induce us to enter their filthy puddle of polemics," wrote the *News* editor in 1864. "Our course is progressive and upward, not retrogressive and downward. We can bear to hear and read their slanders, misrepresentations and falsehoods, unanswered, and smile at them."[30] A year later, in a letter published in the *Millenial Star,* Brigham Young stated and explained this position:

> The *Vedette* has been unusually bitter of late, since the change of editors—too bitter to hold out very long; they will exhaust themselves for want of fuel, for it is very difficult to keep up a one-sided warfare such as they are waging. If we would quarrel with them, or notice them, it would be encouraging, and they would zealously keep on, being fed by the opposition with which they are met; but it is very annoying, after they have exhausted every invective, and every species of vituperation and slander, to find no spot so vulnerable that they can cause us to wince in the least, or to even express the most trifling anger, or vexation. Such contemptuous indifference has more effect upon them, than the most elaborate arguments, and replies would have. . . .[31]

As with the *Valley Tan,* another paper picked up the gauntlet thrown down by the *Vedette.* T. B. H. Stenhouse, assistant editor of the *News* under Albert Carrington, launched the *Daily Telegraph* on 4 July 1864. The paper continued publishing until 26 July 1870.

When and why the *Vedette* stopped publishing is not certain. The fact that the *Daily Reporter,* an avowedly anti-Mormon Salt Lake City paper started in May 1868, was printed on the press of the suspended *Vedette* implies that the *Vedette* did not succumb to the scarcity of newsprint so common among newspapers before the railroad arrived in 1869. Nor did it cease publishing because it had destroyed polygamy or Mormon political power, its major reasons for existence—it had not. Although Utah civilians, Mormons included, did subscribe to the *Vedette,* the great majority of its readers were soldiers. Thus the fact that it survived the evacuation of Fort Douglas by only about a year suggests that its demise was simply the result of the departure of the troops.

Treatment of the new *Daily Reporter* reveals a second reason for the *Deseret News's* policy of silence. In a speech in Church general conference, *News* editor George Q. Cannon criticized the *Reporter* and claimed that it had published "more abominable lies" about the Mormons than even the Nauvoo *Expositor*. However, the *News* itself refused to degrade its columns and made no reference to the *Reporter* at all. In his speech Cannon explained the policy of silence toward anti-Mormon papers generally, and specifically toward the *Reporter*: "We have not noticed it; we have suffered it to go undisturbed. . . . We have never alluded to it; we have deemed it unworthy of allusions [because] it is so utterly contemptible. . . ."[32] This same reasoning was later emphasized in a general statement of *News* policy:

> And above all, those who are connected with the Deseret News should always remember that this paper, as the official organ of the Church of Jesus Christ of Latter-day Saints, must be conducted on a higher plane than other papers. The world expects this, and it has a right to expect it.[33]

Therefore, rather than attack the *Reporter* in the columns of the *Deseret News,* the Church continued to allow Stenhouse's *Daily Telegraph* to perform that function. Wisely refraining from the violent tactics used to stop the *Expositor,* Church leaders advocated economic sanctions against the new paper. Cannon chastisingly told the conference congregation that Mormon money paid for *Reporter* subscriptions, bought its ink, paper, and type, and paid the wages of its editor, compositors, and pressmen. For these reasons he admonished them to stop trading with their gentile enemies.[34]

The *Salt Lake Tribune,* the most successful local anti-Mormon paper, grew out of a line of periodicals edited and published by liberal Mormons who sought specific reforms in the Church. The *Tribune,* first issued on 15 April 1871, and the earlier journals are vivid examples of how individual thought which attempted to obstruct Church goals in Utah at that time was understandably opposed by the Church hierarchy. Papers which countered Brigham Young's ideas and disputed his authority became the object of official Mormon attack.

The *Peep O'Day,* a weekly magazine which began publication on 20 October 1864, was probably the real beginning of the *Tribune.* Despite the fact that the magazine was friendly to Mormonism and that its editors, E. L. T. Harrison and Edward W. Tullidge, were both Mormon converts, the *News* refused to print it because Brigham Young apparently had not sanctioned its publication.[35] This forced Harrison and Tullidge to accept a printing offer from the *Vedette* office at Camp Douglas. Answering an erstwhile Mormon subscriber's complaint that the magazine's editors had resorted to an avowed enemy of the Mormon Church to print their magazine, Harrison and Tullidge pointed out that their critic had confused the editing and publishing of a paper with the printing of it.[36] However, lack of Church backing probably explains the demise of the *Peep O'Day* which ceased publication after only six issues.

Some three years after the failure of the *Peep O'Day,* Harrison and Tullidge, backed by prosperous Salt Lake City merchant William S. Godbe, initiated the *Utah Magazine,* a weekly dedicated to literature, art, science, and education.[37] Unlike *Peep O'Day,* the new journal was started with the approval of Brigham Young,[38] and the *Deseret News,* in whose office it was printed, not only ran its prospectus but from the start welcomed the new weekly and for some time continued to praise it.[39]

However, the *News* stopped praising the magazine when it became apparent that the editors of the new weekly were using it to protest Brigham Young's absolutism. Two *Utah Magazine* articles attacking Young's "depotism" proved very objectionable to Church authorities[40] and led to an ecclesiastical trial involving the continued Church membership of the two editors. During their trial the two men were asked if they would acknowledge Young's right to "dictate" to them "in all things temporal and spiritual."[41] The editors inquired whether it was not possible for them to "honestly differ" with the Church authorities, but were told, allegedly by *News* editor George Q. Cannon,[42] that they might as well ask whether they could honestly differ with the Almighty.[43] Cannon was not as dogmatic as this statement suggests. He later explained in a *Deseret News* editorial that he could "conceive of a man honestly differing in opinion from the authorities of the church and yet not be an apostate." However, he concluded that he "could not conceive of a man publishing such differences of opinion, and seeking by arguments . . . to enforce them upon the people to produce division and strife . . . and not be an apostate. . . ."[44]

Utah Magazine's editors and several of their sympathizers were excommunicated.[45] The Church publicly condemned their journal, printing in the *News* the following signed pronouncement by Brigham Young, his counselors, and several apostles:

Our attention has been called of late to several articles which have appeared in the *Utah Magazine,* a periodical, published in this city. . . .

> The *Utah Magazine* is a periodical that, in its spirit and teachings, is directly opposed to the work of God. Instead of building up Zion, and uniting the people, its teachings, if carried out, would destroy Zion, divide the people asunder, and drive the Holy Priesthood from the earth. Therefore we say to our brethren and sisters in every place, the *Utah Magazine* is not a periodical suitable for circulation or perusal by them, and should not be sustained by Latter-day Saints. We hope this will be sufficient, without ever having to refer to it again.[46]

Whatever the effect of this proscription, it was not a death blow. Although the *Utah Magazine* printed its last issue on Christmas day 1869, it was replaced on 1 January 1870 by the *Mormon Tribune,* whose publishers, the same as those of the *Magazine,* felt that a newspaper was a better medium for the expression and circulation of their views.[47] At first the *Mormon Tribune* professed not to be anti-Church,[48] but by 2 July 1870 it had dropped the word *Mormon* from its official name, and the Church from its friendly consideration.[49] As the newly named *Salt Lake Tribune,* it proclaimed devotion to mental freedom[50] and continued to publish weekly until 10 December 1870, when it stopped, apparently because of financial problems.[51] However, in less than five months it revived in the form of the *Salt Lake Daily Tribune.*[52] The newspaper's ex-Mormon managers soon withdrew in favor of gentile ownership,[53] and the policy changed from trying to reform the Church to attempting to destroy its secular power.

The conflict between Brigham Young and the liberal Mormon press centered around the question of unity or diversity in the social, economic, and political life in Utah. This was a major Mormon-gentile conflict in territorial Utah, the Mormons stressing unity and the Gentiles diversity.[54] In politics, the Mormon ideal of unity meant complete Mormon rule of the territory, a principle which non-Mormons and ex-Mormons in Utah's first opposition party naturally found distasteful. The *Tribune* rapidly became the Liberal Party's organ and remained so throughout the territorial years.

Consistent with its past history, the *News* officially maintained a policy of total abstinence from personal attack.[55] This position, however, was taken only toward a certain kind of newspaper. As seen in its comments on another paper, the Salt Lake City *Indepen-*

dent, the *News* was willing to reply to responsible competition.[56] In announcing the birth of the *Independent,* the *News* welcomed opposition as long as it remained "gentlemanly" and "respectable." Unquestionably having the *Tribune* in mind, the *News* editor further explained,

> And if the *Independent* preserves a tone which will entitle it to recognition and reply, it will be always welcome, and will receive support from a large number of persons who, while delighting in opposition, despise scurrility and low blackguardism which disgraces some aspirants to journalistic fame.[57]

Later in the same year the *News* explained that it welcomed criticism couched in "a proper spirit" and that it always defended itself when the foe was "worthy of attention."[58]

But it apparently felt that like the *Tan,* the *Vedette,* and the *Reporter,* the *Tribune* advanced its opinions in a venomous spirit and did not, therefore, merit consideration. Thus the *News* ignored the *Tribune,* while in the tradition of the *Mountaineer* and the *Telegraph,* a third paper, this time the Salt Lake City *Herald,* was begun on 5 June 1870 to answer the attacks of the *Tribune.*[59]

Despite its intermittent statements that it would not engage in personal criticism and name-calling with the *Tribune,* the *News* occasionally did verge on such activity in the 1870s, though generally without mentioning the *Tribune* by name. For example, in a rather long *News* editorial in 1873 David Calder explained that when local anti-Mormon papers began publication they falsely claimed to be representatives of the entire territory and its people, regardless of creed or party. However, continued Calder, "in a concern that talks as much as a newspaper the lion's skin can not long conceal the fact that an ass wears it. . . ." Referring to the *Tribune,* the *News* editor concluded, "nor can false pretenses and affectations of gentlemen long hide the real character of the coarse, vicious, vituperative scandal-monger, who pours out his nauseous streams of filth periodically, in the hope of besmearing the best and most honored members of the community."[60]

Nine months later, announcing the defeat of the anti-polygamy Poland Bill in 1874, the *Deseret News* took another of its increasingly frequent stabs at the *Tribune:*

> We need go no further back than last winter for evidence of the wicked purposes of this "ring [the Salt Lake City gentile and apostate opposition to the Mormon Church]," nor point to anything but the columns of infamous falsehoods, lies and misrepre-

sentations contained in their organ day by day, to demonstrate what their "great expectations" were.[61]

Commenting on John D. Lee's murder conviction in 1876, the *News,* referring to the *Tribune* as the "ring organ," criticized it for attempting to decide guilt or innocence instead of leaving that matter to juries; and referring to its opponent's editors, declared that they were establishing a record which marked them as asses.[62]

Thus the traditional *News* policy of silence toward local anti-Mormon competitors began to give way in the 1870s. Brigham Young had very early stated that policy but, pragmatist that he was, had also recognized that a change might become advisable in the future.[63] And because of the federal government's enforcement of anti-polygamy laws to the point that the very life of the Church seemed to be jeopardized, the 1880s were a critical time.

Because of its growing number of readers, the *Tribune's* agitation during the 1880s worried the Church much more than anti-Mormon papers had before. By 1883 the combined circulation, daily and weekly, of the *Tribune* had passed the combined circulation of the *News* by a hundred subscribers. A year later its lead had reached 620 and in 1885 the *Tribune* led the *News* by 1,500. It was even more disturbing that the daily *Tribune* by 1886 had reached a circulation three times that of the daily *News.*[64]

News circulation fell behind that of the *Tribune* for a number of reasons. The development of Utah mining led to a considerable increase in the gentile population in the 1870s. Salt Lake City more than doubled in size during the 1880s and the percentage of gentile inhabitants grew significantly. The *News* made little attempt to cater to this rising gentile population. The daily *Tribune,* a larger and less expensive newspaper which also published on Sundays, printed more news than did the Church paper, printed it on a wider variety of subjects, particularly national politics, and did it in a much more lively manner.[65] As a consequence, the *Tribune* attracted Mormon as well as gentile subscribers. Even employees of the *Deseret News* found the *Tribune* interesting despite its almost constant criticism of the Church.[66]

The increased federal attacks on Mormon temporal power, the *Tribune's* rapidly growing circulation, its criticism of the Mormon Church, and the coming in 1880 of the very articulate Charles Carroll Goodwin as its editor[67] combined to eventually have a significant impact on *News* action. Feeling that the *Herald* needed help, the Church paper, in order to vindicate the Saints and their cause, moved closer and closer to a total break with its long-held course of deliberate silence.

In a 21 February 1881 editorial entitled "A Vicious and Ignorant Attack on 'Mormonism'," Penrose finally addressed the *Tribune*'s editor directly and answered the *Tribune*'s name-calling in kind for the first time. The editorial was occasioned not by what Goodwin wrote in the *Tribune,* but by an article, "The Political Attitude of the Mormons," which he had written for the *North American Review,* a monthly which the *News* described as "respectable" but criticized for "spoil[ing] its pages with . . . a mess of trash."

Goodwin argued in his article that the Mormons received very little instruction in worldly knowledge because the policy of the Church was to keep the masses poor and ignorant. He maintained that the Church forbade its members to read books or journals that attacked their faith or appealed to their reason. As an example of the low quality of Church newspapers and periodicals delivered to many Mormon homes, Goodwin wrote that within the past year they had prescribed earnest prayer and punctual obedience to ecclesiastical authorities as certain remedies for diphtheria and blood-poisoning diseases. Goodwin concluded, "Naturally, men so enthralled are mere slaves. Their first and only real allegiance is given to their church and chiefs."[68]

Penrose made no effort to refute Goodwin's specific illustrations. Instead he quoted scripture from the Church's *Doctrine and Covenants* about Mormon belief: "Seek ye out of the best books words of wisdom; seek learning even by study and also by faith. . . . Study and learn and become acquainted with all good books and with languages, tongues and people."[69] Apparently Penrose overlooked the fact that the Church, although for understandable reasons, had at times been known to tell the Saints what constituted a "good" book and what did not.[70]

Seven months later *Harper's Magazine* published a second article by Goodwin, "The Mormon Situation," very similar to the one in the *North American Review.*[71] In commenting on the *Harper's* article, Penrose wrote that the *Tribune*'s editor was a "comparative stranger to the Territory of Utah," that he was "densely ignorant of the system" and knew "nothing of the people" he was attempting to assail and revile, and that he wrote against them and their religion as a businessman "for pay."[72] Referring to an attack Goodwin made on the late Brigham Young, the *News* editor called Goodwin a "cowardly defamer" and said that the "diatribe" would "reflect ineffaceable disgrace upon the petty-minded scribe who penned it." It was "a case of a living dog barking against the dead lion."[73] Penrose professed to grieve to see a man capable of better things descend to the position taken by Goodwin. He expressed hope that Goodwin would become better acquainted with the actual state of affairs before again writing about the Mormons, and concluded that the article displayed "deplorable ignorance as well as contemptible prejudice."[74]

A most significant point in Penrose's response to the Goodwin articles concerns the reason the *News* felt obligated to depart markedly from its former policy of restrained comment. Penrose felt that a "desire to misrepresent" existed throughout both Goodwin's articles, but, totally convinced of the propriety of Mormon activities, Penrose explained that there was no need to say anything about that to the readers of the *News,* who were knowledgeable of Utah and the Mormons. After quoting from the *Harper's* article Penrose commented,

> We need not say to those of our readers who are acquainted with "Mormonism" that the foregoing extracts are entirely devoid of truth. And a simple denial of these allegations ought to be sufficient answer for those who are not familiar with our doctrines and aims and motives.[75]

However, the *News* chose to present an elaborate denial of the allegations because some readers of the *News,* especially those in the East who helped to form public policy, were not familiar with the Mormon system, and also, as the newspaper stated, because *Harper's* is a *popular* and *respectable* monthly, with a *large circulation* and a deservedly high reputation, not because the author of the article is of any particular importance."[76]

The nature of the *News-Tribune* clash in the first half of the 1880s can best be illustrated in two stories: the account of a Salt Lake City lynching in 1883 and the 1884 Irons-Fowler case. These incidents show the extent of the *News*'s name-calling, its momentary sensationalism, and its conspicuous change from a policy of silence, as well as the commitment of the Mormon press to defend the Church and its people.

"Never have we beheld such tremendous excitement," declared the *News* on 25 August 1883 as it described the lynching of a Negro as "one of the most horrible and thrilling tragedies" ever to have taken place in Utah. According to the Church organ, Marshal Andrew Burt and Charles Wilcken answered a complaint from a Negro restaurant operator named F. H. Grice about Harvey, another Negro, who was brandishing a pistol and threatening to shoot. While attempting to disarm the Negro gunman, Burt was shot and killed and Wilcken was wounded. After a short struggle Harvey was taken captive. By then a large crowd, whose "popular rage" was "so dreadful . . . that it looked irresistible," had gathered around the Negro and his captors. A battle ensued between the rabble and the officers who were in charge of Harvey. Finally the mob "tore him away . . . procured a rope . . . dragged him into a shed . . . and strung the writhing wretch up over the beams that support[ed] the roof."

> Hundreds gathered around and gazed at the revolting spectacle presented by Harvey's corpse, the face of which was horrible and repulsive beyond description. The sickening sight and the memory of his awful crime seemed to lash the feelings of the mob into renewed fury, and we never before so vividly realized the terrible frenzy of an unreasoning crowd of enraged people. With a sudden impulse a portion of them rushed up, cut the body down and dragged it along the street rending the air with angry shouts as they went.[77]

Two days later the *News* accused the *Tribune* of trying to further turn Eastern opinion makers against Utah by blaming the Church for the lynching.[78] The *News* stated that the guilt of the Negro was doubted by none, that it was very unlikely that the assassins would ever have been brought to justice, denied the popularity of "Judge Lynch" in Utah, and argued that the general public opposed mob violence. The Mormon paper charged the *Tribune* with encouraging lawlessness in Salt Lake City and blamed it for the violent death of the black man. Although not identifying the *Tribune* by name, the *News* unleashed one of its severest attacks upon that paper, characterizing it as

> the organ of the prostitutes, the apologist for the blackguard and the drunkard, the defamer of women, the slanderer of the dead, the cesspool into which the obscenity, blasphemy and prurient gossip of roughs and loafers and smutty-minded men of the baser sort flows naturally.[79]

Struggling to counter the impression of lawlessness that the *Tribune* was giving to the East, the *Deseret News* properly claimed that the very fact that the "thing"—the *Tribune*—had not been abated as a nuisance, as its "low-lived scribes" had feared, was as great a proof as could be given that the people in Utah respected the law:

> It has been allowed to lie on to its full content. We have taken no notice whatever of its daily libels and scurrilous assaults upon good men and women, living and dead, but have passed them by in silence as we would the yelping of a mangy cur. And we only mention it now because of this dastardly attempt to make capital against the Corporation.[80]

The *News* claimed that a bona-fide investigation would show that the chief actors in the cause of crime in Utah, despite the hints of the *Tribune* to the contrary, were non-Mormons. It also argued that to be fair any investigation into the lynching would have to go to the very roots of the matter and not depend upon the word of those whose only motives were to make anti-Mormon capital.[81] Despite these statements, perhaps fearing a biased investigation and the unwanted attention the case would bring, the *News* did not insist upon a formal inquiry into the violent slaying.

The Irons-Fowler Case involved an abortion in Salt Lake City and illustrated even more than the lynching the temporary break the *News* made from its policy of nonsensationalism. It was also the occasion of the worst of the epithets exchanged by the *News* and the *Tribune,* demonstrating the Mormon journal's almost frantic concern for the defense of the Church and the people for whom it spoke.

The abortion incident came at a most critical time in the struggle to save polygamy, and the *News*'s journalistic extremism over the case can be understood only with reference to the crisis concerning polygamy in the mid-1880s. In an attempt to replace Church power with gentile power, the Edmunds Act of 1882 made those convicted of polygamy ineligible for jury duty, public office, or voting, and subjected them to a $300 fine and/or six months of imprisonment. Rudger Clawson, a citizen of Brigham City and later one of the Church Apostles, had been the first to be convicted (October 1884) under the new law, and his trial created an almost unprecedented amount of excitement in Utah.

The *Tribune*'s reporting and editorializing concerning the legal proceedings offended the Mormons and the *Deseret News*. Stack headlines such as "Colossal Lying by Witness in Clawson Case" and "George Q. Cannon, the Wonderful Know-Nothing" topped columns of the *Tribune,* and its editor described the defendant's relations with women as libertine.[82] However, and perhaps more important in understanding the fury of the *News,* the *Tribune* blamed immorality on the Mormon creed of polygamy, which it described as "Animalism of the grossest kind," and on the Church hierarchy, especially seventy-five-year-old President John Taylor, whom it characterized as an old man "approaching imbecility."[83] Also infuriating to the *News* were the *Tribune* charge that the jury, which refused to bring in a verdict in the first Clawson case, had been bought off with Mormon money, and the epithets that were continually flung at the Church paper and its editor. Penrose was called a "liar" and "a sorry ass" and his journal the "dirty News" and the "vagabond and apologist for crime."[84]

The Irons-Fowler incident came right on the heels of the Clawson trial. A Mr. McCornick, the Salt Lake City banker who employed John W. Irons, one of the accused in the abortionist case, called on assistant *News* editor John Nicholson on Monday morning, 3 November 1884, and asked him to help protect Irons's name and, by not printing the story of the alleged crime, allow the courts to decide his guilt. McCornick explained that all other city papers had agreed to suppress details and names.[85]

The Monday afternoon edition of the *News* announced in a short article the arrest and jailing of "a young man" for accused abortion. While the Church paper noted that the evidence against the accused was rumored to be very damaging, it stated that "we withhold its publication for the present, not only because of its disgusting character, but in order not to prejudge the matter before he has had a fair trial."[86] On Tuesday the *Tribune,* although only very briefly reporting the facts of the abortion case, charged that the Mormons were falsely accusing Irons and Fowler:

> The whole matter is looked upon as a piece of spite work, and people generally believe that the charge was trumped up in order to blacken the characters of the gentlemen as a sort of set-off to the blow given the Church in the Clawson case.[87]

The *Tribune* allegation forced the hand of the Mormon press. The *Deseret News* announced in its Wednesday, November 5, edition that although its Monday issue had only mentioned that the crime had been committed, the *Tribune*'s subsequent charge against the Church was sufficient to call the *News* into action. Concerned with what influence the *Tribune* charge might have in starting an anti-Mormon crusade, the Church paper elected to give a full report so as to show the public that the case was not a put-up by the Church. "The infamous insinuations of the Tribune," explained the Mormon editor, "the apologist of the prostitute and abortionist, and the villifier of the innocent and pure, have rendered it imperative that a position of reticence should no longer be maintained on the subject." The *News* editor explained that in his Monday issue he had purposely suppressed names and details, "the former from motives of fairness and consideration, the latter because too soul-sickening and indecent for the columns of any newspaper having the shadow of a claim to respectability." However, the *News* argued that since Monday's issue, events had occurred which made it essential for the facts and the whole truth to be made known to the public "so far as it can be done without shocking the sensibilities of our readers."

The *News* got its facts from Mr. and Mrs. Milando Pratt, owners of the boarding house in which the alleged crime took place. The accused were Irons, paying teller in the McCornick and Company Bank, and Dr. Allen Fowler, a well-known physician in Salt Lake City. The victim was Miss Lizzie Evans of Brigham City. Irons and Miss Evans had become enamored with each other while she was studying obstetrics in Salt Lake City. After the classes were over and her fellow students had returned to Brigham City, her "lover . . . passed the night with her" in her apartment. Becoming pregnant, Miss Evans went to Dr. Fowler for examination, and when she later became ill the doctor visited her in the Pratt boarding house where he gave her morphine and some "pills." A miscarriage took place, the particulars of which the *News* detailed to the extent of the "terrible pain" and suffering of Miss Evans and a description of the two-month-old fetus. The Church paper noted that remarks made by Irons to Evans, and overheard by Pratt, about how he might have prevented the pregnancy in the first place were "too filthy to repeat." Pratt called the police and both Irons and Fowler were arrested, to be released later on $5,000 bond.[88]

On Thursday, November 6, the *Tribune* rightly questioned the validity of the story of eavesdropping by Pratt that appeared in the Church paper and criticized the *News* for breaking its promise to suppress the story temporarily and for narrating it in all its "filthy and disgusting details." But the gentile paper explained it would remain silent on the issue until a public hearing could be held. Nevertheless, it published a letter addressed to the *Tribune* and signed "S. O. L. Potter, M.D." that raised some reasonable, if not correct, questions about the accuracy of the *News*'s account of the alleged crime. Potter first pointed out that Evans received a certificate of obstetrics and, therefore, needed no doctor to show her how to abort a pregnancy. He then explained that Fowler himself had often spoken out against abortion, that he was a competent doctor, and that only quacks and ignorant women used drugs to cause a miscarriage. Potter contended that Evans caused the abortion herself and only later called in Fowler to attend her. [89]

After sympathizing with Miss Evans, whom the *News* described as a "trusting young girl . . . deceived and seduced from the path of virtue," and after viciously condemning Irons as a "vile wretch," a "moral monster," and a "moral vulture" and calling for his conviction to deter others from committing similar crimes, the *Deseret News* turned on its rival, the *Tribune*:

> The base insinuation of the *Tribune* that this charge has been trumped up to off-set the Clawson case, is truly worthy of that sheet, and a full and scrutinizing examination is rendered necessary by this slanderous innuendo of the organ of seducers and abortionists. That infamous sheet abused and slandered Mr. Rudger Clawson, who was sent to jail on Saturday for conscientiously marrying, living with, providing for and protecting a second wife. No epithet was too virulent to hurl at him. But here is an alleged case of seduction and abortion, committed by one of its own kind, and it immediately attempts to smother up the horrible crime, pat its perpetrator on the back, and insinuate that the damnable outrage against the laws of God, nature and man is a trumpted up charge, instigated and formulated by "Mormons" for an ulterior purpose. The infamy of that vicious sheet can reach no greater depth than this.[90]

The lowest point was yet to come. In a highly emotional editorial headed "The Beast of the News," Goodwin criticized the Church paper for accusing the *Tribune* of concealing the facts about the abortion case and apologizing for the criminals. Goodwin here charged the *News* with hypocrisy and, among other things, called Penrose "the bastard in charge of the *News*," a "psalm-singing male prostitute," and a "God-deformed wretch."[91] Answering back in an almost equally bitter but cynical editorial, the *News* declared that it had been completely overcome with the *Tribune*'s "invincible logic" and "irrestible avalanche of reasoning." However the Church organ did its share of name-calling, too, and described the "Gentlemen of the *Tribune*" as the "advocates and apologists of the libertine, the prostitute and abortionist." The *News* suggested a sedative to calm the troubled nerves of the *Tribune* editors, but warned that they should be sure to wipe their mouths clean with a handkerchief because the "internal filth" that filled them was "oozing from their facial openings." The *News* warned that those interested in the *Tribune* should restrain Goodwin because every time he dipped his pen in filth he obscured his sight by jabbing it right into his own eye and giving himself, the paper, and those who owned it a bad name. Penrose concluded his outburst against the *Tribune* and its editor with:

> Our comments on this case have been made necessary by the malicious course and lying statements of the *Tribune*. Our locker is not exhausted. The conductors of that vile paper make covert threats; we treat them as we do their filthy epithets which, by them, are used as substitutes for facts and argument. We heed them not. They are but a puff of miasmatic vapor from a pile of putrefaction.[92]

The *News-Tribune* conflict never again reached the vitriolic intensity of 1884. Nevertheless, the *News* did not completely ignore its rival, and at times it ventured forth with a few sallies of very outspoken judgments against its constant critic.[93] The rivals finally achieved a semblance of peace near the end of World War I. By 1952 they had reached a point where they formed the Newspaper Agency Corporation to jointly operate printing, circulation, and advertising solicitation for both papers. Though their editorial departments remain separate, they are today all but bedfellows, in contrast to their relations in territorial days.[94]

In the 1880s, however, the *Tribune's* circulation spurred Church leaders to defensive action. Continuing to use the *News* as an apologist, they made intensive efforts to get copies into the hands of influential readers. In 1887, during the implementation of the Edmunds-Tucker Act, the Church paper actively tried to influence national policy makers. The *Deseret News* sent complimentary subscriptions to President Grover Cleveland and his entire cabinet, all territorial delegates, most members of the House of Representatives, and all but one of the Senators. Numbered among those receiving complimentary copies of the *News* from Utah were professors, judges, military men, and newspaper editors in many of the states and territories, including the very influential political cartoonist Thomas E. Nast.[95]

The board of directors of the Mormon paper, in their meeting of 29 May 1889, expressed concern that the *News* did not come off the press in time for passengers on trains through Salt Lake

City to obtain a copy. The *News*'s editor agreed to issue the paper at any hour desired, but complained that he could not publish news before it took place. His assistant explained that the paper came out at an hour that made it difficult to include up-to-date news and still appear in time for sale on the trains. But Board president George Q. Cannon said he favored distributing the paper free of charge on the trains, and Apostle Joseph F. Smith expressed his belief that the Church would assist in paying for such free distribution. All directors voted to publish a train edition, not for any financial consideration but "for the purpose of getting the paper into the hands of the traveling public." The Company held the editor responsible for carrying out these instructions.[96] In the same Board meeting, members voted to send free copies of *News* issues containing important articles to all congressmen and senators during sessions of Congress and to prominent persons all over the country.

The editor of the *Deseret News* at this time was Charles W. Penrose. Penrose was considered to have few equals as a polemical writer; and the public, both Mormon and gentile, regarded him as the "chief journalist of the Church."[97] It is true that Penrose had a great deal of journalistic experience. At two different times he had been associated with the *Millenial Star,* the principal organ of the Church in Europe, first as a writer and then as assistant editor. For the seven years prior to joining the *News* staff in 1877, Penrose edited the Ogden, Utah, *Junction.* But though the *News* board of directors unanimously elected him editor-in-chief of the Church organ in 1880,[98] it seems that for several reasons, foremost among them his continuous absence from Salt Lake City, his assistants did much of the writing and editing in the 1880s.[99]

One of these assistants, John Q. Cannon, complained in his diary that Penrose too often left his work on the Church paper to attend to interests in Ogden. In fact, he privately claimed in 1881 that although Penrose presumably edited the paper the bulk of the work fell upon him. John Q. Cannon's work on the *News* at that time included proofreading, critiquing plays, and doing some editorial writing. In February 1881 he wrote in his diary, "A very busy day in the office. Penrose is officiously running around on all sort of errands instead of attending to business." Cannon described Penrose as a "smart writer," but protested that even when he remained in town he often did not get his work done on time. His journal entry for 19 May 1881 read: "We were very late getting to press owing to Penrose's going home to dinner and returning about 2:30 p.m. when he had not written a line."[100] There was no open clash between these two personalities. Cannon was apparently satisfied to confide his frustrations to his personal diary.

Penrose's absences from the *News* office included more than just a long lunch hour or a day in Ogden. He spent virtually the whole of 1885 as an exile in England and Europe. The Edmunds Act of 1882 provided heavy penalties for the practice of polygamy and "unlawful cohabitation," and the United States Supreme Court's confirmation of the law's constitutionality in 1885 intensified the systematic hunt in Utah for "polygs" and "cohabs." The 20 January 1885 issue of the *News* reported that two deputy U. S. Marshals had that day called at the newspaper office with a warrant for Penrose's arrest on the charge of polygamy. "The officers entered upon an exploring expedition through the establishment," explained the *News,* "but the object of their solicitude didn't happen to be around when they called." The Church, following the policy during the Nauvoo years when Mormons were hunted with writs, had sent Penrose on a "mission." In a letter to George Q. Cannon from New York City dated 10 February 1885, Penrose explained that he was in hiding while awaiting passage to England where he hoped to remain unrecognized.[101] While on his "mission" to England, Penrose editorially assisted the Church's *Millennial Star,* wrote several articles for London papers, and sent commentaries to the *Deseret News* championing polygamy, signed "Exile."[102]

By 10 November 1885 Penrose had clandestinely returned to Salt Lake City and in a letter to Church President John Taylor explained that he thought he could safely resume his duties as editor of the *News* if he lived near the office and went home only rarely.[103]

While he was in England, Penrose's name continued to appear at the head of the editorial columns, though apparently John Nicholson actually edited the paper. Nicholson, a professional journalist, had succeeded Penrose as editor of the Ogden *Junction,* had helped run the *Millennial Star,* and had written off and on for the *Deseret News* since 1868.[104] When it fell his lot to speak for the Church through its official paper, his editorials were articulate and outspokenly critical of those who were arresting polygamists.[105] However, the energetic way in which Nicholson drummed away at mistreatment of the Mormons during the height of the anti-polygamy crusade naturally brought him to the attention of the marshals, judges, and prosecutors his caustic pen had been denouncing. John Nicholson himself was arrested, indicted, tried, and found guilty of unlawful cohabitation. He served almost six months in the Utah Federal Penitentiary. After his prison term Nicholson returned to his editorial responsibilities with the *News.*

Theoretically these responsibilities belonged to Penrose, and Nicholson, unlike John Q. Cannon, soon vocalized his objections. In the spring of 1890 he complained to the Church President that in the previous five years Penrose had done very little work. During the winter of 1887-88 Penrose had lived in the East, where he wrote articles for Eastern papers and lobbied with President Cleveland and nearly all the members of Congress in support of Utah statehood.[106] Nicholson complained that while he had been doing the work, Penrose had been getting both the pay and the credit. He presented a file of the *News* as evidence and two assistants as witnesses. After expressing his displeasure for not receiving proper credit, he tendered his resignation. Recognizing the legitimacy of Nicholson's complaint, the *News* board of directors voted him an additional thousand dollars remuneration for the past five years and raised his annual salary to $2,000. This apparently satisfied Nicholson, and he agreed to continue his work on the *News.*[107]

At the same time that Nicholson registered his grievance, the News Company board discussed whether or not to continue the policy of listing the name of the official *News* editor at the head of its columns. Board members felt that omission of the name would conform more closely to the custom of leading newspapers elsewhere, perhaps increase the influence of the *News,* and relieve the editor from individual responsibility for articles that would attract criticism.[108] When the Board communicated these views to Charles Penrose, he vigorously opposed having his name dropped, arguing that such action was neither customary nor fashionable and that it would reflect upon him personally. He would acquiesce to dropping his name only if the board directly ordered him to do so. Apparently the Board gave no such orders: Penrose's name continued to appear regularly until he left the *News* in 1892.[109]

Despite Penrose's argument to the contrary, to leave off the name of the editor was both customary and fashionable in the United States at this time.[110] The Church organ's vigorous com-

petitor, the *Salt Lake Tribune,* did not post Goodwin's name anywhere in its columns. In fact, some papers, including the *New
York Times,* never did print the name of their editor in this
fashion.[111] Apparently putting the name of the editor in the *Deseret
News* often meant little anyway as far as signifying who actually
edited the newspaper. Although Elias Smith edited the *News* for
a time in 1855 and 1856, Albert Carrington's name continued
to appear as official editor. As we have seen, the same held true
with George Q. Cannon, who did little writing while on his extended visits to Washington, D.C., as Utah's territorial delegate,
and with Charles W. Penrose.

Whatever person or group of persons deserved credit for producing the *News* in the 1880s, it can properly be said that the
corporation-owned newspaper, in the best way it knew how, had
consistently defended the Mormon Church. The 1890s would see
both continuity and change in the *Deseret News.* Despite the fact
that the News Corporation leased the paper to a prominent Salt
Lake City family, it continued its function as Church apologist.
Nevertheless, before the century was ended the official spokesman
for Mormondom found itself altering its policies and defending
the abandonment of traditional Church practices it had vigorously
supported for forty years.

Footnotes

1. $154,660; William Mulder, "Salt Lake City in 1880: A Census Profile," *Utah Historical Quarterly* 24(July 1956): 236. This ranking can in part be explained by pointing out that the Deseret News Corporation, which consisted of a book-and-job office, a bookbindery, a type foundry, and a paper mill, as well as three newspapers, provided almost all the worldwide publication needs of a very vigorous proselytizing Mormon Church.

2. *N. W. Ayer and Son's American Newspaper Annual* (Philadelphia: N. W. Ayer and Son, 1881), 1:569. *See* J. Cecil Alter, *Early Utah Journalism,* pp. 272-384.

3. Deseret News Company Board Meeting Minute Book, 3 September 1880, LDS Church Historical Department; hereafter referred to as Board Meeting Minutes.

4. Thomas E. Taylor, Salt Lake City, 7 June 1886, letter to President John Taylor, Thomas E. Taylor Collection, LDS Church Historical Department.

5. Leonard J. Arrington, *Great Basin Kingdom,* pp. 364-65.

6. *Deseret News,* 4 September 1880.

7. Thomas E. Taylor, Salt Lake City, 9 November 1886, letter to President John Taylor, Thomas E. Taylor Collection.

8. *News,* 4 September 1880.

9. Ibid., 26 January 1892.

10. Ibid.

11. Thomas E. Taylor, Salt Lake City, 31 March 1885, letter to President John Taylor, Thomas E. Taylor Collection.

12. George Cannon Lambert, journal, in Kate B. Carter (comp.), *Heart Throbs of the West* (Salt Lake City: Daughters of the Utah Pioneers, 1948), 9:364.

13. Ibid., p. 366.

14. Board Meeting Minutes, 25 July 1889.

15. George Cannon Lambert, Salt Lake City, 15 December 1887, letter to Wilford Woodruff, George Cannon Lambert Collection, LDS Church Historical Department.

16. *News,* 20 October 1890.

17. John Nicholson, Salt Lake City, 4 May 1886, letter to President John Taylor, John Nicholson Collection, LDS Church Historical Department.

18. Board Meeting Minutes, 21 January 1891. *See also* James Sjodahl,

Manti, Utah, 14 July 1890, letter to Wilford Woodruff, James Sjodahl Collection, LDS Church Historical Department.

19. Alter, *Early Utah Journalism,* p. 10.

20. Legal paper signed by William Thompson Jr. and his attorney, C. S. Farian, Salt Lake City, 27 September 1889, Deseret News Company Collection, LDS Church Historical Department.

21. *News,* 18 January 1878.

22. *Salt Lake Herald,* 28 July 1872.

23. *News,* 10 November 1884.

24. Of some forty major newspapers started in Salt Lake City before 1900, about one-half were outspokenly anti-Mormon and all but three started after the *Salt Lake Tribune;* Alter, *Early Utah Journalism,* pp. 272-384.

25. According to the newspaper's first number (6 November 1858), *Valley Tan* was a name first applied to Utah-made leather. Gradually it began to apply to all articles produced in the territory, and meant "Home Manufactures."

26. *Valley Tan* [Salt Lake City], 22 June 1859.

27. John Taylor, Salt Lake City, 12 January 1859, letter to George Q. Cannon, John Taylor Collection, LDS Church Historical Department.

28. Patrick Connor to R. C. Drum, assistant adjutant general, U. S. Army, 21 July 1864, in Arrington, *Great Basin Kingdom,* p. 202. *See also* Gustive O. Larson, "Utah and the Civil War," *Utah Historical Quarterly* 33(Winter, 1965): 73-74.

29. *Union Vedette,* 22 February 1866 and 22 June and 22 December 1864.

30. *News,* 19 October 1864.

31. Brigham Young, Salt Lake City, 12 January 1865, letter to Daniel H. Wells and Brigham Young, Jr., in *Millenial Star,* 1 April 1865.

32. George Q. Cannon, "Self-sustaining—Persecutions—Outside Influence," discourse given 7 October 1868, Salt Lake City, in *Journal of Discourses,* 12:292.

33. Unsigned, undated statement of *News* policy, *Desereet News* Collection. Internal evidence suggests this statement came as late as 1896, but it seems to be a policy the *News* adhered to from the start.

34. Cannon, "Self-sustaining," p. 294. The *Daily Reporter* had moved to the gentile stronghold of Corinne, Utah, by 21 April 1869. A complete file is located in the LDS Church Historical Department.

35. William J. McNiff, *Heaven on Earth: A Planned Mormon Society* (Oxford, Ohio: Mississippi Valley Press, 1940), p. 97; *see also* T. B. H. Stenhouse, *The Rocky Mountain Saints* (New York: D. Appleton and Co., 1873), p. 630; and *Peep O'Day* [Salt Lake City], 20 October 1864.

36. *Peep O'Day,* 20 October 1864.

37. Prospectus in *News,* 25 November 1867. The *Utah Magazine* started publishing 11 January 1868 in Salt Lake City.

38. *News,* 25 November 1867. It is not clear what accounts for this change of attitude toward Harrison and Tullidge.

39. *See News,* 25 November 1867 and 18 January, 15 February and 28 April 1868.

40. *Utah Magazine* 3(16 October 1869): 376-78 and 3(23 October 1869): 389-91.
41. Ibid., 3(30 October 1869): 406.
42. Roberts, *Comprehensive History of the Church,* 5:266n.
43. Edward Tullidge, "The Godbeite Movement," *Tullidge's Quarterly Magazine* (October 1880), pp. 15-16, as quoted in Roberts, *Comprehensive History of the Church,* 5:265-66n.
44. *News,* 3 November 1869.
45. Roberts, *Comprehensive History of the Church,* 5:268. Godbe, Harrison, and Eli B. Kelsey were excommunicated immediately, and soon afterwards so were Henry W. Lawrence, T. B. H. Stenhouse, William H. Sherman, and Edward W. Tullidge.
46. *News,* 26 October 1869.
47. *Utah Magazine* 3(27 November 1869): 474. The *Utah Magazine* here published the prospectus of the *Mormon Tribune.*
48. *Mormon Tribune* [Salt Lake City], 7 May 1870.
49. *Salt Lake Tribune,* 2 July 1870; hereafter referred to as *Tribune.*
50. Ibid.
51. Ibid., 12 and 19 November 1870.
52. Ibid., 15 April 1871.
53. Oscar G. Sawyer of the outspokenly anti-Mormon *New York Herald* replaced Harrison as editor; Roberts, *Comprehensive History of the Church,* 5:418-19.
54. S. George Ellsworth, "Utah's Struggle for Statehood," *Utah Historical Quarterly* 31(Winter 1963): 63.
55. *News,* 8 December 1873.
56. Ibid., 2 January 1878.
57. Ibid. The *Independent* was anti-Mormon and lasted only about two months.
58. Ibid., 25 September 1873.
59. The *Herald* published until 18 July 1920. It eventually became sufficiently independent from Church influence that ecclesiastical authorities, worried that it might one day follow the anti-Mormon policy of the *Tribune,* bought up *Herald* stock in order, as much as possible, to control it; Abraham H. Cannon, diary, 29 March and 12 April 1894, Brigham Young University Library, Provo, Utah.
60. *News,* 25 September 1873.
61. Ibid., 24 June 1874. *See* such editorials in the *Tribune* as "Polygamy vs. Prostitution," 10 January 1874; "Another Emphatic Falsehood," 7 February 1874; and "Mormon Duplicity and Disloyalty," 18 March 1874.
62. *News,* 12 October 1876.
63. Brigham Young, Salt Lake City, 22 October 1858, letter to Colonel Thomas L. Kane, photostatic copy at Henry E. Huntington Library, San Marino, California. Although this letter specifically relates to Young's policy toward non-Utah anti-Mormon newspapers, it is possible to assume that he held a similar view on local opposition.
64. *Ayer and Son's American Newspaper Annual* (1884-1887), 4:669, 5:687, 6:710, and 7:732.
65. Board Meeting Minutes, 28 May 1891, indicated some concern that

the Church paper had for some time been behind other Salt Lake City dailies in both gathering and presenting the news. *Compare Tribune* treatment of the 1884 national presidential election with that of the *News.*
66. Joseph Beecroft, diary, 2 November 1870 and 14 March 1871. Perhaps some Mormons subscribed to the *Tribune* just to see what was being said about the Church.
67. Originally a New Yorker, Goodwin came west in 1852, first to California, then to Nevada where he for a time edited the Virginia City *Enterprize.* In 1880 he came to Salt Lake City, becoming the editor of the *Salt Lake Daily Tribune* four months before Penrose became *News* editor; *see* Orson F. Whitney, *History of Utah* (Salt Lake City: George Q. Cannon and Sons Co., 1892), 4:341-42.
68. Charles C. Goodwin, "The Political Attitude of the Mormons," *North American Review* 132 (March 1881): 277.
69. As quoted in *News,* 21 February 1881.
70. If Penrose's memory was failing him he could have studied back issues of the *News* and found two such examples: Lucy Mack Smith, *Biographical Sketches of Joseph Smith the Prophet and His Progenitors for Many Generations* (Liverpool, England: S. W. Richards, 1853) was banned from Mormon reading by order of Brigham Young (*News,* 23 August 1865); and the *Utah Magazine* was put on the blacklist in *News,* 26 October 1869.
71. Charles C. Goodwin, "The Mormon Situation," *Harper's New Monthly Magazine* 63 (September 1881): 756-63.
72. *News,* 22 September 1881. Although Goodwin actually arrived in Utah Territory in 1860, one year ahead of Penrose, he resided in the part of Utah that in 1861 became Nevada Territory. He did not come to Salt Lake City until 1880, just one year before writing the *Harper's* article. Therefore his knowledge of the Mormon Church and its people was perhaps somewhat limited, though it may have been an exaggeration to describe him as "densely ignorant."
73. Ibid.
74. Ibid.
75. Ibid.
76. Ibid., emphasis added.
77. Ibid., 25 August 1883.
78. The *Tribune* not only tried to turn Eastern opinion-makers against Utah (*see Tribune,* 25-31 August 1883 and 16 October 1884), but also tried as a major goal to convince the Mormons to give up what the paper judged to be unrealistic notions of setting up a kingdom in the West; *Tribune,* 7 October 1884.
79. *News,* 27 August 1883.
80. Ibid. As seen earlier, the *News* had not been as silent as it here claims.
81. Ibid.
82. *Tribune,* 17, 19, and 26 October and 4 November 1884.
83. Ibid., 26 and 29 October 1884.
84. Ibid., 18, 23 and 25 October 1884.
85. Ibid., 6 November 1884; *News,* 6 November 1884.
86. *News,* 3 November 1884.

87. *Tribune,* 4 November 1884.

88. *News,* 5 November 1884.

89. Although it is not the purpose of this study to determine the truth of the various allegations, abortion techniques are as old as civilization itself. It would, therefore, be illogical to categorically dismiss the possibility that Evans committed feticide.

90. *News,* 5 November 1884.

91. *Tribune,* 7 November 1884.

92. *News,* 7 November 1884. The Grand Jury did not bring an indictment against Irons and Fowler, and the *News* judged that the failure to do so would embolden abortionists; *News,* 22 November 1884.

93. For example *see News,* 10 July 1885, 23 January 1886, 6 January 1887, and 2 January 1891.

94. Illustrative of this close association is the fact that *News* subscribers, because the *News* does not publish a Sunday edition, receive the Sunday issue of the *Salt Lake Tribune.*

95. *Deseret News* subscription list for 1887, LDS Church Historical Department. This list differentiated between paid and complimentary subscriptions.

96. Board Meeting Minutes, 29 May 1889. Board Meeting Minutes of 17 June 1889 revealed that the *News* was pretty regular in meeting the trains and that the directors moved that it be "issued promptly each day." Board Meeting Minutes of 29 November 1889 showed that Robert Aveson's wages were raised to $22 a week because he had been given the job of getting the paper out in time for the train.

97. Edward W. Tullidge, *The History of Salt Lake City and its Founders* (Salt Lake City: Tullidge, 1883), pp. xv (appendix) and 144.

98. Board Meeting Minutes, 3 September 1880.

99. Because editorials were unsigned it is difficult to identify the authors. Penrose's assistants included Nicholson, George Lambert, John Q. Cannon, George J. Taylor, Orson F. Whitney, and James H. Anderson; *see* Tullidge, *History of Salt Lake City,* p. xv (appendix).

100. *See* John Q. Cannon, diary, 21 January, 25 and 28 February, 4, 5, and 7 March, 5 April, and 12 May 1881, typewritten copy, Brigham Young University Library, Provo, Utah.

101. Charles W. Penrose Collection, LDS Church Historical Department.

102. Tullidge, *History of Salt Lake City,* p. 144; and *News,* 27 July 1885.

103. Charles W. Penrose, Salt Lake City, 10 November 1885, letter to President John Taylor, Charles W. Penrose Collection.

104. Hubert Howe Bancroft, *History of Utah* (San Francisco: Bancroft, 1890), p. 716; and *News,* 19 August 1879.

105. *Raids* meant the arrests by U. S. marshals of those acccused of polygamy; *News,* 21 January and 9 and 17 July 1885.

106. Whitney, *History of Utah,* 4:335. *See* Penrose's letters to presidents John Taylor and Wilford Woodruff, 1887 to 1888, written from such Eastern cities as New York and Washington, D.C.; Charles W. Penrose Collection.

107. Board Meeting Minutes, 2 and 16 May 1890.

108. Ibid., 2 May 1890.

109. *News* did not carry the name of its editor between 1 October 1892 and 2 January 1899. The names of both the editor and business manager appeared from 3 January 1899 through 31 January 1907, after which only that of the business manager was printed.

110. John R. Whitaker, "The Influence of the West on the Evolution of Personal Journalism in the United States Since the Civil War" (unpublished doctoral dissertation, University of Texas, Austin, 1947), pp. 234-36.

111. According to Frank Luther Mott, *American Journalism,* p. 279, Henry J. Raymond was the *Times's* first editor and George Jones the first business manager. The *Times,* however, listed both as publishers. Even this type of listing disappeared after the 31 March 1857 issue.

8

Change and Continuity in the Deseret News

By 1891 the Deseret News Company admitted it had real problems. Board members concluded on May 28 of that year that for some time the *News* had been behind the other Salt Lake City dailies in gathering and presenting information and that the editors had generally mismanaged the editorial department. The board suggested employing George Q. Cannon's eldest son, John, and consulted Charles W. Penrose. John Nicholson's recent departure on an English mission left few able journalists on the *News* staff, and Penrose felt that a man like John Q. Cannon would benefit the paper immeasurably. However, George Q. Cannon, a director of the publishing company, did not think the *News* could afford to hire his son and opposed his leaving an economically secure position on the *Odgen Standard* for an uncertain one with the financially shaky *News*.[1] The next day, despite his father's feelings and a ten-dollar cut in salary, young Cannon agreed to take the job for thirty dollars per week. The board immediately approved the arrangement.[2]

Adding Cannon to the editorial staff of the *Deseret News* did not solve the difficulties facing the News Company.[3] Just over a year after young Cannon left the *Ogden Standard* for the Church paper, the Deseret News Company leased its entire operation to the Deseret News Publishing Company, a new corporation formed by members of the Cannon family. The acute financial problems of the Church in general and the News Company in particular forced the lease. Forfeiture of denominational properties under the Edmunds-Tucker Act had shattered Church finances, and solvency changed to a debt of at least half a million dollars.[4] In 1886 the newspaper company's account books showed a loss of $18,659.71. Before this, the publishing establishment had enjoyed an average profit of a little less than four thousand dollars a year since the organization of the Company in 1880.[5] The financial situation of the News Company had become so serious by 1892 that it shut down its big paper mill and even turned delinquent accounts of its own business manager, T. E. Taylor, over to an attorney for collection.[6]

The Deseret News Company notified its employees that after 30 September 1892 their services would no longer be needed, and on October 1, having been leased to the Cannon company, the newspaper underwent a complete change in management.[7] Taking leave after his long association with the *News,* Penrose acknowledged his debt to his "talented, faithful and diligent" corps of assistants. John Nicholson, who had returned in September 1891 from his four-month mission to England, was also leaving the *News,* and retiring chief editor Penrose praised him for his "sound judgment and unswerving faith" and for having "given his whole force and character to the promotion of the public welfare. . . ." After expressing "profound regret" at leaving the *News,* Penrose explained that he did not intend to cease his labors in behalf of Utah and the Church and that his voice and pen would continue to be used in their service.[8]

Penrose and Nicholson had not been fired by an ungrateful Church: once the paper had been leased to the Cannon family the Church apparently lost its power to choose the *News* editor. The president of the new operating company, John Q. Cannon, decided he would edit the newspaper and appointed his brother Abraham as business manager.[9] Although John Q. Cannon's 1881 journal entries suggest some friction between him and Penrose, it appears that Cannon simply wanted the job for himself.[10]

Born in 1857 in San Francisco where his father published the *Western Standard,* John Q. Cannon very early became initiated to newspaper work. By the time he was twenty-four he had hauled rags for the old Salt Lake City paper mill, set type, acted as reporter, and written editorials for the *News*. Although normally connected with the Church's paper, for the three years just prior to returning to the *News* in 1891 Cannon had been associated with the *Ogden Standard*.

The new editor announced in his salutatory that the *News* would continue to be the authorized organ of the Church.[11] Two weeks later, evidently feeling a need for an official statement to that effect, the First Presidency of the Church issued an open letter sanctioning all lease agreements and stating that the *News* continued to serve as their official mouthpiece.[12]

Cannon explained in his first editorial that he could not adequately express nor spare the space to print all the hopes he entertained for the *News* and for the people whose interest the paper had guarded. He hoped to prove worthy of the prestige his predecessors had enjoyed and to preserve what he called the "high character for courage, honesty and reliability" which the *Deseret News* had maintained during "all the years of its existence."[13]

During the years of its existence the *Deseret News* had to one degree or another acted as defender and apologist for the Mormons. The paper had outspokenly championed polygamy and pushed for Utah statehood; both questions virtually disappeared in the 1890s. Polygamy was officially abandoned about two years before Cannon became editor, and statehood in 1896 resolved the other issue. But both questions had swept the *News* through the most colorful period of its history.

On 14 September 1852 the *Deseret News* publicly announced to the world in an "Extra" that the Mormons officially sanctioned polygamy. From that point on, the paper consistently defended plural marriage until shortly before the Church forsook the practice in 1890. The *News* was not alone. Others worked to stop anti-polygamy legislation, particularly the Utah Territorial delegates. However, it seems they could do little to curb them. During the 1870s and 1880s, the period of greatest national concern over the issue, Utah delegates to Congress George Q. Cannon and John T. Caine gave few speeches.[14] Although Caine's speeches generally raised the same issues as the *News*, his presentations, buttressed by statistical and factual information, were more apt to persuade congressmen than were the editorials of the Church paper.[15] The *News*, on the other hand, had the advantage of being a daily newspaper. During the polygamy crisis it packed its pages with reports of arrests and trials of alleged polygamists in Utah, Arizona, and

Idaho, and its editors repeatedly blasted away at federal marshals and judges and the anti-polygamy legislation. The rationale of the Church paper is seen in its many editorials attesting to the sanction of polygamy by the Bible, the sociological and physiological superiority of polygamy over monogamy, and its constitutionality. These arguments are an excellent key to the Mormon mind in the late nineteenth century, so that once again a study of the *News* contributes significantly to an understanding of the Latter-day Saint community.

In an 1866 editorial the *News* republished Joseph Smith's original revelation on plural marriage in order to clarify the position of the Saints and to explain the basis for their belief in the doctrine. The paper pointed out that although the doctrine had all the force of divine sanction and commandment, the Mormons did not have to depend solely on that for authority to practice their marriage customs. "It is sustained by the Bible," wrote the editor, "which all professing Christians . . . receive as their rule of faith, an authority that they declaredly accept as one from which there can be no appeal."[16] The *News* said that although it did not have space for all the Biblical examples of the practice of polygamy, it would elaborate on and document a few of the more obvious and pertinent ones. The editor declared that polygamy was practiced and received approval by God previous to the time of Moses, when the Lord gave Abraham a second wife and promised him great blessings, without offering any reproof, condemnation, or correction. The Church paper also cited David's and Solomon's multiplicity of wives, and in response to the argument that the principles of Christ superseded the Old Testament laws, the *News* pointed out that Jesus spared no word in condemning the adultery and divorce of the day, but nowhere uttered a single word condemnatory of polygamy.[17] The *News* considered itself on firm ground in citing such biblical evidence,[18] but it lost its campaign because Puritan America endorsed the strong anti-polygamy position of the Calvinists and simply refused to accept the newspaper's arguments.[19]

The *News* also argued that polygamy did not constitute a sin against society or a violation of the highest physical and moral standards. Like the antebellum South, which tried to exonerate slavery by stressing the evils of the Northern wage system, the *News,* taking the offensive, argued that monogamy, not polygamy, was the source of many of Christendom's social problems, particularly prostitution. It claimed that prostitution rarely existed in eastern polygamous cultures, but that where monogamy was exclusively legalized that social evil flourished. Without documentation, the Church paper contended that one out of twenty women in Great Britain was a public prostitute, that the morality of France and Germany was lower still, and that America was little better.[20] On the other hand, the *News* argued that prostitution with its resulting diseases had been unknown in Utah before the arrival of those who most vocally described the Mormons as licentious and that it still did not exist among those who believed in the plurality of wives. The paper challenged the Saints' most bitter enemies to prove differently.[21] (It does seem that professional prostitution was relatively unknown in Utah during the polygamous era,[22] though the powerful Church teaching against adultery and fornication may well account for this more readily than simply the practice of polygamy, particularly since the bulk of the Church membership was not polygamous.)

Regardless of the outcome of the monogamy-polygamy debate, the *News* was utterly baffled that some sought to legalize prostitution in the United States. Referring to the report of a committee of the New York State legislature which recommended licensing prostitutes, the Church paper exclaimed that it was curious that, while many in America willingly accepted severe legislation to prohibit polygamy, these same people favored legalized prostitution. "How people can wish to make marriage illegal and prostitution legal," editorialized the *News,* "to have marriage prohibited and punished, and prostitution established and protected by law, and still claim the least shadow of consistency, is incomprehensible to us."[23]

Besides divine sanction, the *News* claimed in support of polygamy that it produced more physically, mentally, and spiritually healthy progeny. It maintained that exclusively legalized monogamy increased the incidence of venereal disease, enfeebled the race physiologically, and shortened the life span. The Church paper asserted that when sexual intercourse continued throughout pregnancy it robbed the future mother of the vigor needed to nourish the embryo and intensified the sensual desires of the offspring.[24] The *Deseret News* insisted that among Mormon polygamous families intercourse ceased from conception until the term of gestation, thus giving the new generation stronger and healthier bodies, purer desires, and a higher condition of physical and mental excellence. One *News* editor even contended that the most stalwart and physically powerful men known came not from Christian monogamous nations but from polygamous Asia and argued that, had he the space, "a host of reliable authorities" could be produced to support the claim.[25] Although these arguments are generally scientifically untenable, they reflect the defensive stance of the Saints at that time.

The *Deseret News* argued that plural marriage was protected by the Constitution. Opponents of polygamy admitted that the Constitution prohibited Congress from making laws forbidding the free exercise of religion, but they also declared that the plurality of wives was unessential to the Mormon faith and, therefore, subject to legislation. The Church paper argued that current and continued revelation had enjoined upon the Mormons the doctrine of polygamy." 'For all those who have this law revealed unto them,' " wrote the *News* editor quoting the original revelation, " 'must obey the same; . . . and if ye abide not that covenant, then are ye damned. . . .' "[26] When anti-polygamists argued that by this same reasoning theft and murder might be adopted as part of a religion and thereby claim constitutional protection, the *News* responded with a rather persuasive series of interrogatories:

> Whom does a man injure by marriage? Himself? We hope not. The woman he marries? That he need not do. Any other woman? Not that we ever heard of. Any other man? How can he? Does he rob anybody? If he does, who is it? Does he destroy life? Why no, marriage naturally increases life. What harm then does he do? What wrong does he do? What crime, morally speaking, does he commit? We have never met with the man who could give an intelligent answer to this question. If there is one, we wish he would stand up and bring forth his strong reasons, and say why, in this enlightened age, in this enlightened country, a man should be threatened with incarceration, confiscation, fire and sword for contracting a marriage common in all ages of the world, among the best men known to history, and among the bulk of the inhabitants of the earth.[27]

The *Deseret News* said that the charge that the majority of the Mormons themselves rejected polygamy was preposterous, and the editor wrote, "The Latter-day Saints, as a people, do most sincerely and honestly believe the doctrine of plurality of wives, recognizing in it a divine injunction. . . ."[28] Opponents contended that while Mormons had a right to believe in polygamy, they should not carry that belief into practice.[29] Countering, the *News* argued that the Mormon people not only believed in polygamy but practiced what they believed.[30] The Church paper considered that limiting religious liberty to belief only bordered on absurdity, pointing out that a man could simply believe even under the most despotic of governments.[31] For editor Charles W. Penrose the very essence of Mormonism was to find out what the Lord wanted done and then to do it, regardless of how hard the world might try to stop it.[32]

Apparently not all Mormon polygamists had the sort of conviction Penrose advocated and tenaciously followed. Despite the determination of Church members to stand fast on the issue of polygamy, as the laws against it became more and more oppressive many Mormons began to vacillate. The *News* was used, both subtly and outspokenly, to counsel and admonish continued loyalty to the doctrine of plural marriage.

Responding to the 1870 House passage of the anti-polygamy Cullom Bill, the *News* published an editorial headed "The Feeling in Town." It explained that the action of the House had made little impression on the people in Salt Lake City, and that contrary to the expectations of some in Congress, the Mormons had not panicked. The Saints had entered into polygamy expecting strong resistance and confrontation from Americans. However, the *News* argued, although plural marriage conflicted with their own traditions, prejudices, and education, it must be obeyed. Although the Mormons knew from the beginning that loss of reputation, world hatred, complete ostracism from society, and even death might result from their practice of polygamy, they had not faltered. Cautiously the editorial noted that the same feeling which had animated the Saints before animated them still: if persecution came, the same kind of heroism that had been shown in Missouri and Illinois would be seen in Utah.[33]

Referring to Reynolds' test case under the 1862 Anti-polygamy Act, and trying to close loopholes that weakening Saints might attempt to crawl through, the *News* editor wrote that anything might be made a crime statutorily but that such did not change the moral nature of the deed.[34] After the United States Supreme Court declared the law constitutional, the Church paper insisted that the law did not and could not make polygamy a crime *per se,* and that those who had practiced their religion could not in reason, justice, or good sense be pronounced criminals.[35] The *News* noted that since one anti-polygamy law had now been declared constitutional, some newspapers were anxious to get the Mormons to make some kind of declaration as to whether or not they would continue to resist the laws. The paper explained that each Mormon could decide for himself. However, hoping to influence the Saints by appealing to their respect for authority, it added that as for the official Church organ, it disagreed with the Court's decision.[36]

The *News* declared to the gentiles that coercion would fail, and to its own people the Church paper exclaimed: "God commands, and obedience to His mandate necessarily requires sacrifice and suffering, who will shrink from duty or cringe and crave for human pardon?" The Saints "must not compromise, in the very smallest degree. . . ."[37]

Despite the attempts of the *News* to keep them in line, some Mormons did compromise. George C. Lambert, acting editor of the Church paper for a time in 1885 and 1886, wrote that the *News* applauded those arrested for polygamy who had the courage to defend their right to marry more than one wife,[38] while it excoriated for their insincerity, cowardice, and weakness those who compromised in order to avoid the penitentiary. Lambert wrote that Henry Dinwoodey, on trial for unlawful cohabitation, had decided to promise to obey the Edmunds Act in the future, and came to the editorial office to try to secure lenient treatment from the *News*. Lambert recorded that he told Dinwoodey, "If you should ever so far forget your duty as to make such a promise I should feel it incumbent upon the News to roast the tar out of you, and you needn't hope for any mercy."[39] Apparently the acting editor persuaded him, for Dinwoodey pled not guilty and silently accepted his six-month sentence.[40]

Claudius V. Spencer and Bishop John Sharp pled guilty to the crime of polygamy and received suspended sentences, but they became the objects of rather severe *News* criticism. Both came to editor John Nicholson to ask for merciful write-ups in the Church paper. Nicholson privately called Spencer a "spineless poltroon" and charged Sharp with being a compromiser, willing to forego the laws of God and obey the laws of the government for selfish personal, economic, and social reasons.[41] In print, the *News* maintained that Spencer's action resulted from "hypocrisy, cowardice or both" and described his compromise as "exceedingly repulsive" and "piteous pleading for judicial clemency."[42] After listing several possible mitigating circumstances for Sharp's disloyalty, the Church paper stated that wealth, influence, social standing, or official position must not be allowed to screen the bishop's public actions from criticism. The *News* felt that silence on its part might give the appearance of endorsement or acquiescence and expressed confidence that Sharp's action would not influence many to follow his example. The Mormon paper, seeming to solidly commit itself to an unretractable position, told the Saints that no matter what stand any one man might take in regard to God's law, polygamy had to be sustained and vindicated regardless of the consequences.[43]

The consequences were more than some wished to take, and solidarity in support of plural marriage cracked in the mid-1880s. With the death of Church President John Taylor in July 1887, the crack began to widen. More and more Mormons, including some leaders, doubted the wisdom of further resistance, and increasing numbers submitted to anti-polygamy laws to escape punishment. An example of the widening break came in December 1887, when Rudger Clawson agreed to sign an oath foregoing polygamy in return for his freedom. Clawson, a prominent Mormon from a prominent family, had been convicted of polygamy in 1884. At that time he refused to compromise and stated that he would always choose the law of God over the law of man,[44] a position the *Deseret News* lauded as noble and consistent.[45] After serving three years and one month of his four-year prison term, Clawson compromised, and President Grover Cleveland issued a pardon. But by then the *News,* reflecting the changing attitude of the Church, had ceased either to heap praise on polygamists who went to the penitentiary or to castigate those who chose freedom. In fact, the paper's policy had so changed that it mildly congratulated Clawson on his restoration to freedom.[46]

One of the first signs that Mormon officials might be preparing to abandon polygamy was the *Deseret News*'s attempt to minimize the extent of the practice of plural marriage among Mormons, of which many gentiles had an exaggerated idea. Lack of official records makes it difficult to determine conclusively the percentage of Mormons practicing polygamy in Utah at any one time. Estimates have run as high as 50 per cent,[47] but closer calculations put it between 15 and 20 percent.[48] However, now struggling to accommodate to the dominant society in the United States, the *News* claimed on 20 May 1890 that no more than two per cent of the Church membership ever engaged in polygamy, a figure that may have been arrived at by counting only the men who had plural wives rather than the total number of Church members who were in polygamous families.[49]

Apparently realizing that polygamy was indefensible before puritanical gentile Americans, the *News* began to prepare the Saints for the possible discontinuance of the doctrine. By 1890 many Mormons began to reason that if their prophets could institute polygamy, surely they could revoke it. A *News* editorial of 18 April 1890 refuted gentile claims that revelation was dead in the Church and that, therefore, no revelation should be expected directing the abolition of polygamy. The Church paper described the growing federal repression of Mormon economic, political, and social rights as the fulfillment of prophecies of Joseph Smith,[50] and began to tell its Mormon readers that they had no alternative but to obey the law, at least until Christ returned to the earth.[51]

On 23 September 1890 a *Deseret News* editorial proclaimed that the Mormons would never be coerced into the renunciation of their belief in plural marriage. However, nothing was said about its practice, and two days later the paper printed Church President Wilford Woodruff's Manifesto announcing the official abandonment of polygamy.

This turnabout in Church policy[52] seems to have resulted from the threat to Mormon political dominance in Utah. On 19 May 1890 the Supreme Court declared that the 1887 Edmunds-Tucker Act was constitutional. Among other things, the Act had abolished woman suffrage in Utah and prescribed a test oath to keep polygamists from voting or holding office. Four months before this court ruling, a test-oath law disfranchising all Mormons in Idaho had been upheld by the same national tribunal, and the Liberal Party in Utah hoped that one of several similar bills would be pushed through Congress to exclude Utah Mormons from the ballot box. However, the *News* explained that because of widespread dislike among Congressmen for such drastic expedients, the bills had been shelved, an action the Church paper claimed had extremely irritated anti-Mormons in Salt Lake City.[53]

The *News* insisted that misleading parts of the 1890 report of the Utah Commission, a five-man board appointed by President James Garfield in 1882 to supervise and conduct all elections in Utah, had been scattered by the Associated Press throughout the United States.[54] It seems these allegedly garbled and deceptive accounts of the Commission's report aroused public opinion and forced Congress to reconsider action on test oaths for Utah.[55]

Besides the threat of disfranchisement, the Church was in financial shambles because of the confiscation of Church property, and as long as the Church practiced plural marriage it seemed that statehood and with it relative independence from the federal government were impossible. President Wilford Woodruff wrote in his journal, "I have arrived at a point in the history of my life as the president of the Church . . . where I am under the necessity of acting for the temporal salvation of the Church." The same day, having prayed to the Lord and "feeling inspired,"[56] Woodruff issued the Manifesto, which he hoped would arrive in Washington in time to offset reports from what the *News* called the "dispatch fiend" in Salt Lake City:[57]

> Press dispatches having been sent for political purposes, from Salt Lake City, which have been widely published, to the effect that the Utah Commission; in their recent report to the secretary of the interior, allege that plural marriages are still being solemnized. . . .
>
> I, therefore, as president of the Church of Jesus Christ of Latter-day Saints, do hereby, in the most solemn manner, declare that these charges are false. . . .
>
> Inasmuch as laws have been enacted by congress forbidding plural marriages, which laws have been pronounced constitutional by the court of last resort, I hereby declare my intention to submit to those laws, and to use my influence with the members of the church over which I preside to have them do likewise.[58]

The *Salt Lake Tribune* called the Manifesto a fraud and the Mormons hypocrites.[59] The *News,* on the other hand, charged that the *Tribune* was infuriated because it had been deprived of the chief subject of its libelous clamor.[60] The Church journal reported that scarcely a paper of prominence in the United States failed to comment on the Manifesto. Some judged it to be a front, some called for a wait-and-see policy, and a few accepted it as an expression of honest intent.[61] Attacks against the Mormons on the issue of polygamy started to decline rapidly, and the *Deseret News* switched from defending polygamy to defending the "Manifesto."[62]

Over the years the *News* has consistently upheld the Manifesto, and now reflects the Church's adamant anti-polygamy stand, as in a 1956 editorial headed "Stamp Out Polygamy," which expressed hope that plural marriage (which small groups of excommunicated fundamentalist Mormons continue to practice) could be entirely ended in Utah.[63] *Truth,* a fundamentalist organ, is highly critical of the *Deseret News* for having abandoned polygamy,[64] but the *News,* far from being inconsistent, has consistently reflected official policy of the Mormon Church. When Church policy changed, so did *News* policy. Mormons had to choose between the practice of an important religious principle and the survival of the Church itself. They chose survival.

The Saints had hoped that sacrificing plural marriage would improve their chances for self-government and statehood, as well as save the Church as an institution by restoring its economic status. However, opposition to polygamy had been but a pretense[65] for some of those opposed to statehood under Mormon political domination. For them the real issue was that of authoritarian government. Thus it still appeared that Utah would remain a territory until its people set up a more republican form of government with a viable two-party system.

Because stories concerning this issue were much harder to get and to sell to the newspapers which had flourished on the fictitious details of the alleged harem-type life in Utah, the reports of this struggle were much less spectacular than those concerning polygamy. And unlike its open defense of plural marriage, the *Deseret News* countered charges of political domination by denying all allegations concerning the political kingdom.[66]

However, that the Mormons hoped to achieve an independent commonwealth is a matter of historical record. It was this issue, rather than polygamy, that led to their expulsion from the Midwest. And in the Far West, when the Saints found themselves again within the borders of the United States, they sought to gain self-government by entering the Union as a state.

The *News* was extremely critical of the territorial system, and maintained this position down to 1896, championing the struggle for statehood. In a 30 September 1869 editorial comparing Utah's nearly twenty years of "territorial tutelage" to "colonial vassalage," the Mormon newspaper called upon its readers to agitate vigorously for entrance into the Union by submitting resolutions and petitions to Congress signed by every citizen in the territory. The editor explained that even if the times did not favor statehood, the subject should be constantly kept before the American people so Congress would not mistakenly assume that Utah was content as a territory.

No movement for statehood materialized on the heels of the 1869 editorial, but shortly after that call to action, Utah citizens presented a number of petitions to Congress, one of which carried 22,000 signatures.[67] Unfortunately, petitions meant little. Utah obviously met every requirement for statehood but one: as the rest of the country saw it, the people of Utah were not ready for democratic self-government. Statehood would allow what was seen as a dictatorship by the Church hierarchy to continue unhampered— indeed protected—by the Constitution.

Thus gentile opposition to Utah statehood usually included attacks on the Mormon Church, as for example in an article in the *New York Herald*. The *News* protested against linking Mormonism with statehood, and argued against such unconstitutional and unrepublican association. Mormons did not generally regard their ecclesiastical leaders as dictators, and with some sarcasm the *News* pointed out that the people of Utah had just as much right to be Mormons as others had to be "Methodist, or Baptists, or Catholics, or Infidels, or Spiritualists, or non discripts, or soreheads."[68]

Of course, the *News* was not alone in urging Utah statehood, but on the few occasions when Utah's territorial delegates argued for statehood on the floor of Congress[69] their reasoning differed little from that of the *News*.[70] Nor did the dialectics of statehood advocates in other Southwestern territories differ from those of Utah.[71] By 1890 arguments for statehood, whatever their nature, crowded the essentially dead issue of polygamy almost entirely out of the columns of the *Deseret News*.[72] If for no other reason, contended the *News,* Utah should be admitted to the Union as a reward for her contributions to the United States. The Mormon organ claimed that, according to the annual statement of Wells, Fargo and Company, a total of $98,421,754 worth of minerals came out of the West in 1877, and that Utah ranked third among the contributors. It described the bounteous mineral wealth in the area, compared it to that of the United States as a whole, and insisted that the Saints were principally responsible for opening up the region to the gentile citizens of the Republic. The *News* maintained that Mormons blazed the trail through the desert, opened the door to California gold, demonstrated that the Great Basin could sustain settlement, and provided a supply depot for surrounding plantations. For Utah's service in developing the wealth of the west and in bringing the prosperous and growing region into close union with the Eastern states, the *News* logically declared that the territory was entitled to something more than what it called the "niggard benefits of a Territorial government, and the cold shoulder. . . ."[73]

Historians concur only in part with the seemingly extravagant claims of the *Deseret News.* Rodman W. Paul estimated that in the latter 1870s Utah's annual output of silver, lead, gold, and copper ran between six and seven million dollars, and suggested that California, Nevada, Colorado, Montana, and Idaho were ahead of Utah in mineral production.[74] It might also be observed here that the Mormon Church could actually take little credit for developing mining in Utah, let alone elsewhere in the West. Gentiles, both American and foreign, not only owned most mineral land in the territory but also had used their capital to develop it.[75] In fact, while the Mormon settlement did provide valuable service to emigrants and settlers, the emigrants, particularly during the gold rushes, substantially helped the Mormon commonwealth survive.[76] But the *News* was most certainly on solid ground in drawing to the attention of the American public the fact that Mormons did achieve great success in settling and developing land that many gentiles considered inhospitable—and that otherwise would likely have remained idle for decades.

In other arguments for statehood the *Deseret News* detailed the requirements set down in the Northwest Ordinance of 1787, claiming that Utah had long since met them.[77] Convinced that the territory had every element necessary to qualify her for entrance into the Union, the *News,* though sincere, was perhaps too self-complacent and boastful for effective argument as it listed them for public consideration. The *News* claimed that Utah had less immorality, prostitution, illegitimate children, drinking and gambling halls than any state or territory in the Union and asserted that it contained the most "quiet, energetic, industrious, persevering, thrifty, public-spirited, peaceable, orderly, law-abiding population" in the United States. According to the Church paper Utah had shown greater forbearance and patience with imported officials, had less Indian blood on her skirts, and set a better example of living within her income than any other community in North America. The *News* also insisted that Utah had excelled all territories and states in respect for the Constitution, in obedience to law, and in the practice of self-government.[78]

The Mormon newspaper was persuaded that Utah deserved to become a state more than some territories that had already been admitted.[79] Agitated to exasperation and possibly revealing some racial bias, it criticized the attempts of President Ulysses S. Grant to annex Santo Domingo to the United States:

> If a country, peopled by half-breed savages, who are in a state
> of almost chronic revolution, can be annexed at the cost of a million
> and a half of dollars, and the annexation be styled . . . a benefit
> to the people of this Republic then surely a Territory like Utah,
> peopled by virtuous, temperate, industrious, intelligent Anglo-Saxons,
> having the groundwork of a great, free, and prosperous state al-
> ready laid, clear of debt, . . . will be welcomed into the sister-
> hood of States without question. . . .[80]

Recognizing the Republican Party's solicitation of blacks in the
American South during Reconstruction, the Church organ sarcastically concluded that if Mormon complexions had more closely
resembled those of the dark people of Santo Domingo, Utah would
probably have been admitted to the Union immediately.[81]

Employing the natural-rights philosophy of Locke and Jefferson,
the *News* argued that it was as normal for territories to want to
become states as for children to want to achieve the status of men
and women. On the other hand, it claimed it was as unnatural for
Congress to attempt to keep the territories in territorial bondage as it
would be for parents to try to keep children from maturing and assuming the duties and responsibilities of an adult.[82] Attempting to appeal to Congress's sense of character, the *Deseret News* wrote that
the national assembly would do itself credit and honor by admitting
Utah. Petty squabbling to obtain humiliating and degrading restric-
tions was unworthy of Congress and those who indulged in it
utterly debased the dignity of such a great body. Appealing to the
patriotic emotions of the people the *News* exclaimed: "No true
American citizen, no lover of the constitution . . . will lift up a
finger to oppose . . . [Utah's] admission."[83]

Regardless of the logic or arguments of the *News*, statehood had
to await a change, not in Congress or the American people, but in
Utah itself. On 26 March 1888 the newspaper reported that in
Congress Cullom's Committee on Territories had unanimously decided that Utah not be admitted until the Church gave up its control over civil affairs.

Of course the Mormon Church had dominated Utah politics
from the beginning of its territorial existence. This was done, at
least at first, with little or no opposition. Under a theo-democratic
system, the early Utah Mormons (much like the founding fathers
of the Republic) felt that political parties were unnecessary and
even undesirable. Brigham Young claimed that to permit political
opposition was to admit the existence of error and corruption some-

where.[84] The notion that political party rivalry assisted in arriving at the truth was rejected in a society that believed in revealed truth.

Announcing in favor of a certain candidate for local office in 1855, the *Deseret News* correctly pointed out that in the United States it was customary for newspapers backing a candidate to praise him excessively and to defame all his opponents. "This singular, unwise, unjust, and rabid course is happily entirely unnecessary in Utah," concluded the *News,* "as our faith, policy, and politics are one, at least with few, if any, exceptions."[85] Admitting the absence of "party-spirit" in the territory in 1860, the Church paper still advised its readers to vote and exercise the inestimable privilege by expressing their preference whether any opposition existed or not.[86]

By the 1860s, however, Church political rivalry had appeared. Reporting the results of the 1862 local election, the *News* confessed that some slight opposition had manifested itself. Some voters erased a few of the names on the regular county ticket and substituted others.[87] As we have already seen, the Liberal Party and its official organ, the *Salt Lake Tribune,* commanded the attention of the Church as early as the 1870s. And in 1889, Liberal candidates gained dominant political power in both Ogden and Salt Lake City.

Although the *News* claimed it was not a political organ, until 1892 it consistently printed the Church—or "People's"—ticket on its editorial pages, energetically lauded its candidates, and openly opposed those of the Liberal Party. On the eve of the 1874 election the Church paper called upon every citizen to go to the polls and, for their own good, vote the People's Ticket. After warning its readers to guard against a Liberal attempt to steal their votes by imitating the People's Ticket, the *News* exclaimed,

> If you are a friend to the people, vote for the "People's Ticket."
> If you have the spirit of '76 in your bosom, vote for the "People's Ticket."
> If you love liberty, not license, vote for the "People's Ticket."
> If you are a genuine, not bogus, patriot, vote for the "People's Ticket."
> If you admire peace, sobriety, morality and good order generally, vote for the "People's Ticket."
> If you wish well to your country, vote for the "People's Ticket."
> If you are a friend to yourself, vote for the "People's Ticket."
> If you want the Territory, country and city to keep out of debt, vote for the "People's Ticket."[88]

In the 1876 Utah campaign for the office of territorial delegate, the *News* detailed the accomplishments of the People's Party candidate, George Q. Cannon, described his abilities, and warned that all voters who had the real welfare of the community at heart should vote for him.[89] The Church paper claimed that although it would have welcomed an honorable and honest opponent to Cannon, it loathed a contest with an opponent of an "irredeemably unscrupulous character," and it asserted that inasmuch as a campaign of this nature had been forced upon Utah, its citizens must not shirk responsibility to vote. The *News* cautioned, however, that if they did not vote for Cannon they would "certainly be misrepresented . . . by a bad man, and a very bad man too."[90]

Fourteen years later, in its 1890 campaign to return John T. Caine to Congress, the *Deseret News* was clearly opposed to *Tribune* editor Charles C. Goodwin, candidate of the Liberal Party. "Of the gentleman personally we have nothing to say," wrote the *News* editor on October 10. "We can only view him in the position he occupies as chief of the vilest paper published on the American continent." The *News* admitted that Goodwin had an exceptional writing ability, but argued that because he prostituted his powers in the interest of a party of fraud it could find no words too condemnatory for him. The paper expressed the belief that conservative gentiles would not vote for Goodwin, and concluded, "Certainly no man connected with the 'Mormon' citizens, could conscientiously support so pronounced an enemy to . . . Utah, and such a malignant foe of the men who laid the foundations of this commonwealth. . . ."

The *News* was not only involved with candidates for national office in 1890. In its January 14 issue of that year it explained that it had received an anonymous letter filled with an array of charges against Theodore Burmester, who, the letter claimed, controlled W. W. Gee, a liberal nominee for justice of the peace. The *News* acknowledged that Gee was disreputable, that he was not its choice, and that the charges were generally true—but noted that not all of them could be authenticated and that the *News* would not participate in any underhanded attack upon Burmester. The letter had suggested that all the allegations could be proved if the *News* reporter would but investigate. To this the Mormon journal replied that it left journalistic "scavengerism" to the *Salt Lake Tribune*. To the plea of the anonymous letter writer that the *News* do something to save the community from such officials as Gee, the Church paper answered, "We expect to do what we can to prevent [his election] by urging sensible people who favor good government to vote for better men, who will be nominated by the People's Party, and thus lay the scrubs under the snow on the 10th of February." The *Deseret News,* although it rejected mudslinging to keep Gee out of office, nevertheless named him, announced that the *News* in nowise supported him, and made it clear that the "good guys" were all in the People's Party.

But the Church had to dissociate itself from the People's Party if it ever hoped to see Utah's territorial status altered. A viable two-party system, separated from Church domination and based on the two national parties, seemed to be the prerequisite for Utah statehood. Thus in 1891 the Church leaders disbanded the People's Party and sent committees throughout the territory telling Mormons to vote either Democratic or Republican. Soon the Liberals also decided to align themselves with the national parties. This formation of political parties on national lines was accompanied by a re-alignment of Utah newspapers. In February 1891 the *Salt Lake Herald* became a Democratic journal and both the *Ogden Daily Standard* and *Salt Lake Evening News* announced that in the future they would be Republican.[91] In a 26 January 1892 editorial headed "The Position of the 'Deseret News'," the Mormon paper revealed the Church's decision to accommodate to traditional American policy on Church-state relations and made it clear where it stood in regard to national parties:

> When this paper expresses its views on political questions it ought to be known by its readers that these are not the enunciations of the Church, for that institution is out of politics. Part of its membership belong to the Republican party, part of it to the Democratic party, and a portion remain yet unconnected with either party.
>
> In politics the DESERET NEWS is INDEPENDENT. It is not a Republican organ. It is not a Democratic organ. It expects to form opinions on public questions which will be its own, and will not ask either party or the leaders of either party permission to express them.

A signed political "Declaration" of the Church leadership, comparable to the 1890 polygamy Manifesto, followed this announcement of the *Deseret News* by less than two months. "As rumors have been circulated and published accusing the Presidency of the Church . . . with interference in political affairs, so as to control elections and to direct members of the Church as to which political party they should support, we hereby declare these rumors to be false and without foundation in fact." The official proclamation counselled the people of Utah to study the principles of both national parties and then, from personal conviction, freely join the one of their choice.[92]

But freedom of choice did not mean that individual Church leaders were nonpartisan. Ecclesiastical authorities continued to play important roles in politics. Jesse N. Smith, a prominent Church leader in Arizona, recorded in his diary on 14 August 1890 that Church President Wilford Woodruff recommended in a private meeting that the Mormons in Arizona affiliate themselves with the Republican Party,[93] which raised a question as to the degree of Church-state separation at this time. A letter from *News* editor Charles W. Penrose to John Taylor suggests a possible answer. Although written five years before the 1892 "Declaration," it reveals the practical strategy Church leaders considered. Penrose wrote privately what he would not have thought of stating in the columns of the *Deseret News*. He contended that statehood was the only real solution for the Church's problems, and to achieve admission to the Union the Church had to at least appear to be separate from Utah government. The acts of the people as citizens of the territory must not be confused with the acts of the Church, and any movement for statehood must be made outside the ecclesiastical body. Penrose reasoned that if legislation disfranchised all Mormons, statehood would come with the anti-Mormon minority in power. However, argued the *News* editor, if Utah came in while the Mormon majority still had the vote, then the influence of the Church could prevail in the new state—not directly, but through those Mormons who occupied civil positions. "It would be 'the power behind the throne,' the spirit controlling the body; but not the body itself."[94]

Whoever was to control the new state, Congress hastened the important day of statehood by passing the Utah Enabling Act. The territory called its seventh and last constitutional convention, which met in Salt Lake City in March 1895. It was made up of many who had formally opposed each other and included forty-eight Democrats and fifty-nine Republicans, twenty-eight of whom were non-Mormons. The resulting constitution was easily ratified and on 4 January 1896 the *News*, with the biggest headlines in its history, joyously announced that Utah had joined the Union. In its editorial column the *News* declared its gratitude to God for delivering the people from territorial status, while acknowledging the accommodation Utah had made in order to achieve its new position. "Utah has entered the domain of Statehood upon the basis of fundamental American institutions [monogamy and the two-party system] and peace and good will to every citizen." Expecting that polygamy and statehood, issues which had occupied so many of its pages, were issues of the past, the Mormon paper expressed its hope that Utah would go on to unparalleled good times and pledged itself, heart and soul, to this policy of common brotherhood, peace, and prosperity.

On 7 September 1898, almost three years after statehood, the Cannon-family-owned Deseret News Publishing Company gave up its lease and turned the *News* and its various departments back to the old News Company.[95] This lease termination resulted primarily from economic difficulties. In the early months of 1893, less than six months after the Cannon company took charge of the indebted News Company, the United States entered a serious depression that lasted until 1897. The Cannon company did not once show a profit during the six-year lease. In fact, by 1898 it had run up a loss of nearly $90,000.[96]

Whereas business manager Abraham Cannon recorded in his diary 24 December 1892 that he had made each employee of the *News* office "a small present of money," a Christmas bonus, within nine months he could not even pay them their wages in full.[97] On 27 November 1893 he admitted the company was "hopelessly in debt."[98] In June of the following year, complaining of his indebtedness, Cannon confided to his journal: "An inability to raise means has worried me so much that my head had ached almost constantly. I try to have faith that the Lord will help me out, but it is difficult to see how He will do so."[99]

The business manager was working and worrying himself to death. In reference to a letter from his brother Frank in New York City urging him to take better care of his health, Abraham wrote in his diary," [Frank] predicts great disaster to me unless I do so. He has urged Father to get me relieved from the News Office."[100] He resigned his *News* position 26 June 1895, after persuading John A. Evans to succeed him. Fearing financial troubles, Evans accepted the job reluctantly, and Abraham wrote, "[Evans] might well be fearful in regard to this, as I have advanced since I came into the office over ten thousand dollars [of my own money] to pay the most pressing bills."[101] The disaster Frank Cannon had predicted for his younger brother came thirteen months after his resignation, when Abraham died in Salt Lake City at the age of 37.[102]

To a lesser degree the lease was terminated because the Cannon family had other involvements that took them from the paper. Three months before the family gave up legal responsibility for the *News,* John Q. volunteered for the United States Cavalry, received the commission of captain, and left Utah to serve in the Spanish-American War.[103] Even before this the military had taken Cannon away from his editorial work: as a member of the Utah National Guard he was sometimes out of Salt Lake City for as long as three weeks attending to military duties.[104]

Abraham, who had to assume editorial responsibilities, expressed dislike for his brother's continued absences, much as John Q. himself had earlier criticized Charles W. Penrose. "He will be gone about ten days," wrote Abraham in his diary. "I do not much like his going, as I think he is needed on the paper, but he prefers excursions of this kind to his regular work, which he too often of late neglects. I told him he had better resign from the military."[105]

The News Company had control of the *Deseret Evening News* for only two months, after which it and all its property, both real and personal, reverted back to the President of the Church.[106] This transfer resulted from the fear that under the old News Company the paper, because of financial difficulties, would soon cease to exist.[107] Because some felt that under the Cannons' ownership the *News* had stopped being the official organ of the Church, it had lost some Mormon support and patronage.[108] Apostle Heber J. Grant, a prominent businessman in Salt Lake City, offered to manage the *News,* but he wanted it strictly understood that the paper belonged to the Church and not to the Grant brothers. Grant wrote,

> In making this proposition it is to be understood that the Deseret News is to be the Church organ; and that the announcement is to be made on each issue that it is published by the Church of Jesus Christ of Latter-day Saints, and under the supervision of the Presidency; and is to have the full support of all the Church officials. . . .[109]

Franklin D. Richards, vice-president of the News Company in 1898, suggested that the Church take the *News* back so that the Mormons would feel that it really did officially represent the Church and so merited the support of all its members regardless of their politics. Richards advocated turning the whole business over to the First Presidency of the Church. He believed that if this happened all Mormons could be persuaded to support the newspaper, making it not only financially solvent but also a profitable investment for the Church as well.[110]

There was reason to believe that the Church might not resume operation of the *Deseret News.* In 1898 Lorenzo Snow, Wilford Woodruff's successor as Church President, initiated a definite policy of retreat from participation in business ventures. But despite this policy, the Church, because of improving financial fortunes and a desire to recapture lost Mormon patrons, bought out the old News Company.[111] Signed by President Snow, an "Official Announcement" to this effect appeared in the *News* every day from 17 December 1898 to 1 January 1899, when a complete change in management took place. Snow returned Charles W. Penrose to the editor's chair and named Horace G. Whitney as business manager.[112] The "Official Announcement" expressed the Church's intent to make the *Deseret News* a first-class family newspaper that would be acceptable to all Mormons. Because the *News,* as the official mouthpiece of the Church, was sustained by the ecclesiastical hierarchy, the newspaper solicited the help of Church leaders in all the stakes and wards. Snow expressed the hope that with this support the *News* would shortly obtain "universal circulation" and become a journal in which all Mormons would have confidence and pride.

The first year of Horace G. Whitney's administration saw a loss of $5,529.49 in the newspaper department of the *Deseret News,*[113] This, Whitney explained, came from the heavy outlay of money needed to bring the paper up to "somewhere near the standard" of its competitors. The new business manager pointed out that the loss was not surprising considering the amount of work expended to bring the *News,* which had fallen into disrepute, back into the favor of the public.[114] However, although the newspaper department of the *News* establishment returned a loss, such other departments as job printing and binding offset this loss and the company showed an overall profit of $5,177.30.[115] Under twenty years of modern, business-like management by Whitney, and with periodical help from the Church, which gave him a clear start by assuming all debts of the old News Company,[116] the growing and increasingly impersonal *Deseret News* became a financially profitable enterprise and saw its daily circulation jump almost 350 percent, from 4,400 in 1898 to over 19,000 in 1918.[117]

As the *News* took upon itself more of the characteristics of big business, the Mormons themselves moved closer to the mainstream of American life, throwing off their past Democratic Party inclinations in favor of voting for big business and Republicanism. By 1896 the issues and related subjects of polygamy and statehood that had so long occupied the columns of the Church paper were gone. After claiming that it had recorded the important daily developments in Utah as well as the principal events in the world, the *News,* celebrating in 1894 its twenty-seventh anniversary as a daily, editorialized,

> But fighting falsehood has been almost as much a part of this paper's work as recording facts. For years and years the weary work of exposing the mendacity of the enemies of the people of Utah went on in its editorial rooms. At times the flood of falsehood seemed greater than any human power could stem, or even perceptibly check; but the paper had a duty to perform, and it did it courageously. . . . The NEWS has lived to see the day when there is litle call for effort from it in this line; when there is comparatively little disposition being shown . . . to slander or misrepresent its constituency, and for such a state of things it feels most thankful.[118]

Like its Midwest predecessors, the Church-owned *Deseret News* had failed to stem the tide of gentile criticism and action against the Latter-day Saint Church. But the Mormons could not realistically abandon Utah as the Saints had abandoned their home in Illinois, and unlike the *Nauvoo Neighbor,* which stopped its press when it had failed in its defense of the Church, the *News* accommodated to reality and continued publishing. With persecution and prosecution subsiding and the collapse of the dream of a Mormon political and economic kingdom, the official organ of the Church began to turn from the vigorous and aggressive journalism characteristic of its pages in the nineteenth century toward more gentle moralizing, reflecting twentieth-century Mormon accommodation to the rest of American society.

Footnotes

1. Board Meeting Minutes, 28 May 1891.
2. Board Meeting Minutes, 29 May 1891.
3. Instead of improving, *News* circulation had dropped by a third from 3,000 in 1891 to 2,000 in 1892. However, by 1896 it had climbed to 4,800.
4. Arrington, *Great Basin Kingdom,* pp. 400-401.
5. Deseret News Company Finances File, LDS Church Historical Department.
6. Board Meeting Minutes, 25 January 1892. The year before, the News Company reported that the paper mill had never paid its way and recommended that it be sold. John A. Evans, secretary of the News Company, Salt Lake City, 21 January 1891, letter to First Presidency and Apostles of The Church of Jesus Christ of Latter-day Saints; News Company Collection.
7. Board Meeting Minutes, 12 and 23 September 1892; and *News,* 14 and 30 September 1892.
8. *News,* 30 September 1892. Penrose soon joined the staff of the *Salt Lake Herald,* a newspaper started in 1870, where he continued his battles with Goodwin and the *Salt Lake Tribune.* He started his new assignment as an assistant editor, but in 1893 became editor-in-chief. He left the *Herald* in the fall of 1895; Andrew Jenson, *Church Chronology: A Record of Important Events Pertaining to the History of the Church of Jesus Christ of Latter-day Saints* (Salt Lake City: Deseret News, 1899), pp. 199, 260.
9. *News,* 1 October 1892.
10. It is of some interest to note that Penrose was named *News* editor in 1880 on the nomination of John's father, George Q. Cannon. However, if he was ever offered an assistant's position by John Q. Cannon, Penrose must have felt too proud to work under his one-time subordinate, for he indicated that he stayed with the *Herald* less than three years because, away from the *News,* he soon lost all desire for newspaper work. *See* Penrose's salutatory when he returned to the Church paper in 1899; *News,* 3 January 1899.
11. Ibid., 1 October 1892.
12. Ibid., 15 October 1892. The *Deseret News* also continued to request and receive direction from the Church leadership; *see* Abraham H. Cannon, diary, 2 June 1893, Brigham Young University Library, Provo, Utah.
13. *News,* 1 October 1892.
14. Of course, it is possible that Utah territorial delegates had some influence in Congress through informal channels.

15. *Congressional Record,* 49th Cong., 2nd Sess., 585-591; and 50th Cong., 1st Sess., 7950-7953.

16. *News,* 8 March 1866. I have relied heavily on a series of pro-polygamy *News* editorials in 1866, which are characteristic of the arguments presented by the paper throughout the 1860s, 1870s, and 1880s.

17. Ibid., 15 March 1866. A similar argument is also found in *News,* 12 May 1879.

18. Polygamy was the rule in biblical day among the ancient Hebrews, permitted and even enjoyed in certain cases by the Mosaic law. Although the Christian Church has always been against plural marriage, certain divines have dissented from this general disapproval; *see* "Polygamy," *Encyclopedia Britannica* (11th ed.), 22(1911): 24.

19. William Graham Cole, Sex in *Christianity and Psychoanalysis* (New York: Oxford University Press, 1966), pp. 130-31. The *New York Times,* 19 April 1881, argued that not all Americans agreed with the morals of the Old Testament. Not only was the *News* unable to persuade Gentiles to accept polygamy, but it also could not even convince all Mormons that it should be practiced. For some Mormon opinions concerning polygamy, *see* Thomas F. O'Dea, *The Mormons* (Chicago: University of Chicago Press, 1957), p. 247; Kimball Young, *Isn't One Wife Enough?* (New York: Henry Holt and Co., 1954), p. 237; and *New York Times,* 14 December 1881.

20. While these *News* figures may seem slightly exaggerated, promiscuity at that time was widespread, despite the stated morals of Victorian England. In the larger cities of England one third to one-half of all babies born were illegitimate. It was thought in the 1830s that in London alone there were some 80,000 regular and occasional prostitutes. It was reported that in certain districts of the English capital in the 1860s a man was approached by twenty harlots in every one hundred steps. An English newspaper in 1857 claimed that one house in sixty in London was a brothel, and one female in sixteen a whore; *see* Walter E. Houghton, *The Victorian Frame of Mind, 1830-1870* (New Haven: Yale University Press, 1957), pp. 365-66; Asa Briggs, *The Making of Modern England, 1783-1867: The Age of Improvement* (New York: Harper and Row, 1959), p. 464; and William Langer, *Political and Social Upheaval, 1832-1852* (New York: Harper and Row, 1969), pp. 195-96.

21. *News,* 22 March 1866. From as early as 1862 Brigham Young and other Church leaders argued that polygamy would destroy prostitution; *see* Brigham Young, "A Knowledge of God Obtained Only through Obedience to the Principles of Truth," discourse given 3 August 1862, Salt Lake City, in *Journal of Discourses,* 5:331; George Q. Cannon, "Influence of the Latter-day Saints . . . ," discourse given 6 April 1879, Salt Lake City, *Journal of Discourses,* 20:200; and George Q. Cannon, "Traveling through the Settlements . . . ," discourse given 2 September 1883, Provo, Utah, *Journal of Discourses,* 25:2.

22. Hubert Howe Bancroft, *History of Utah* (San Francisco: Bancroft, 1890), p. 394; *New York Times,* 19 April 1881; *New York Graphic,* 9 December 1873, as quoted in Young, *Isn't One Wife Enough?,* p. 367; *Omaha Daily Herald,* 24 May 1870.

23. *News,* 15 March 1876.

24. These were common arguments used by Victorian America to put limitations on sexual intercourse within marriage; *see* John S. Haller, Jr., "From Maidenhood to Menopause: Sex Education for Women in Victorian America," *Journal of Popular Culture* (Summer 1972), pp. 61-62.

25. *News,* 29 March 1866.

26. Ibid., 5 April 1866; *see also* Doctrine and Covenants, 132:3-4.

27. *News,* 6 October 1871. Polygamy was approved if not practiced by the majority of the world's population in the 1870s. See "Polygamy," *Encyclopedia Britannica* (11th ed.), 22(1911): 23-24.

28. *News,* 5 April 1866.

29. Ibid., 30 November 1878.

30. Ibid., 3 February 1881.

31. Ibid., 10 January 1879.

32. Charles W. Penrose, "Sincerity Alone Not Sufficient . . . What the Saints Should Do . . . ," discourse given 20 May 1883, Salt Lake City, in *Journal of Discourses,* 25:47.

33. *News,* 25 March 1870.

34. Ibid., 18 July 1876.

35. Ibid., 10 January 1879.

36. Ibid., 3 February 1881.

37. Ibid., 7 January 1879.

38. *See News,* 23 and 26 February 1886, and 13 March 1886 for examples of such praise.

39. George C. Lambert, journal in Carter, *Heart Throbs,* 9:364-65.

40. *News,* 23 February 1886; *see also* 17, 18, and 19 February 1886 for *News* treatment of Dinwoodey and trial.

41. Lambert, journal, in Carter, *Heart Throbs,* p. 364.

42. *News,* editorial "An Abject Spectacle," 2 May 1885.

43. *News,* 19 September 1885. For examples of similar treatment by *News,* see *News* editorial "Another Abject Spectacle," 1 October 1885; *News* editorial "Liberty and Dishonor," 29 September 1885; *News* editorial "God's Will and Man's Law," 1 July 1886; *News,* 4 December 1886. The following *News* editorial and business staff, willing to take the consequences, were arrested and jailed on unlawful cohabitation charges during the 1880s: John Nicholson, John E. Taylor, George C. Lambert, and John Q. Cannon.

44. *News,* 3 November 1884.

45. Ibid., 4 November 1884.

46. Ibid., 12 December 1887. The same issue stated without editorial comment that six convicted polygamists received full terms of six months in the penitentiary, and one, who promised to obey the law in the future, got only sixty days. In 1889 Rudger Clawson was named to the Church's Quorum of the Twelve Apostles.

47. Calculations of some non-Mormon visitors to Utah; *see* O'Dea, *The Mormons,* p. 246. Not all non-Mormons felt polygamy was widely practiced in Utah, though the *New York Times,* 14 December 1881, reported in an editorial headed "The Strength of Polygamy" that monogamous marriages among Mormons were extremely rare.

48. Stanley S. Ivins, "Notes on Mormon Polygamy," *Western Humanities Review* 10(Summer 1956): 230.

49. As Mormons have admitted to fewer and fewer polygamists in order to minimize the importance of a doctrine that brought the Church to the brink of ruin, one Mormon writer has humorously suggested that eventually only Brigham Young and a few of his cohorts will be admitted to have been polygamists; Samuel W. Taylor, "Peculiar People, Positive Thinkers, and the Prospect of Mormon Literature," *Dialogue: A Journal of Mormon Thought* 2(Summer 1967): 20-21.

50. *News*, 20 May 1890.

51. Ibid., 4 February 1890 and 31 May 1890.

52. The Manifesto was not a demonstration of a new policy but rather was issued as an official refutation of charges that polygamous marriages were still being performed. However, it was accepted by the Mormons as an authoritative decision to stop the practice of polygamy; *see News*, 9 October 1890.

53. *News*, 26 September 1890.

54. Ibid.

55. *See St. Louis Globe-Democrat*, 19 September 1890.

56. Wilford Woodruff, journal, quoted in Roberts, *Comprehensive History of the Church*, 3:220.

57. *News.*, 26 September 1890.

58. Ibid., 25 September 1890.

59. *Salt Lake Tribune*, 16 October 1890.

60. *News*, 16 October 1890.

61. Ibid., 15 October 1890. The *New York Times* was among the few who interpreted the Manifesto as sincere. Although the *Times* characterized the Mormons as wily fanatics and their Church as a religious imposter, it stated, "There is really no room for doubt that hereafter polygamy will be discountenanced as much by the Mormons as by the Gentiles"; 3 and 7 October 1890.

62. For a rather extensive study on this development, *see* "The Deseret News and Polygamy," *Truth* 21(March 1956): 289-306.

63. *News*, 28 January 1956.

64. "The Deseret News and Polygamy," *Truth*, 21(March 1956): 289. The slogan "Truth and Liberty," which headed the editorial columns of the *Deseret News* beginning with its first issue, was dropped after 17 August 1918. The present motto, "We stand for the Constitution of the United States as having been Divinely Inspired," first appeared 26 November 1955. The *News* had various mottoes or no motto at all between 1918 and 1955.

65. This is emphasized in Klaus Hansen, *Quest for Empire*, p. 117. It was a position also stressed in the *News; see News*, 26 May 1890 and 9 August 1889.

66. *News*, 15 May 1852.

67. *Congressional Globe*, 41st Cong., 2nd Sess., 616.

68. *News*, 25 March 1872.

69. George Q. Cannon, delegate from 1872-1882, made no speeches from the floor of Congress on statehood. Cannon's diary reveals that he

had personal discussions with members of Congress on these issues, however; George Q. Cannon, journal, 7 January 1879, quoted in Mark W. Cannon, "The Mormon Issue in Congress, 1872-1882: Drawing on the Experience of Territorial Delegate George Q. Cannon" (unpublished doctoral dissertation, Harvard University, Cambridge, 1960), pp. 119-20. I was denied permission to use the George Q. Cannon journals, which are superintended by the First Presidency of the Church; Joseph Anderson, secretary to the First Presidency, Salt Lake City, 18 January 1968, letter to the author.

70. *Congressional Record,* 53rd Cong., 2nd Sess., 176-83.

70. *Congressional Record,* 54rd Cong., 2nd Sess., 176-83.

71. Howard R. Lamar, *Far Southwest, 1846-1912: A Territorial History* (New Haven: Yale University Press, 1966), pp. 497, 499. Religion was more of an issue in Utah, while race dominated as an issue in New Mexico and Arizona.

72. *News,* 9 August 1889.

73. *News,* 4 January 1878. For similar reasoning *see News,* 30 December 1867 and 20 December 1871. It will be recalled that the *News,* in an attempt to preserve Mormon isolation, had discounted gentile claims of mineral wealth in Utah.

74. Rodman Wilson Paul, *Mining Frontiers of the Far West, 1848-1880* (New York: Holt, Rinehart and Winston, 1963), pp. 135, 153. Hubert Howe Bancroft's estimates run slightly lower for this period: about five and a half million a year; Bancroft, *History of Utah,* p. 747. For qualified support of some of the *News* claims *see* Ray Allen Billington, *The Far Western Frontier, 1830-1860* (New York: Harper and Row, 1956), p. 217; O'Dea, *The Mormons,* pp. 87-88; and Arrington, *Great Basin Kingdom,* pp. 52-53.

75. Paul, *Mining Frontiers,* pp. 152-53; Arrington, *Great Basin Kingdom,* p. 252.

76. Paul, *Mining Frontiers,* p. 151.

77. *News,* 16 January 1872.

78. Ibid., 26 December 1871.

79. Ibid., 30 December 1867 and 20 and 26 December 1871.

80. Ibid., 28 March 1871. A somewhat reserved prejudice toward the Negro can be seen in editorials in the following issues of the *News:* 15 February 1869, 23 December 1870, 21 April 1874, and 9 December 1874.

81. *News,* 28 March 1871.

82. Ibid., 31 January 1872.

83. Ibid., 20 December 1871.

84. Brigham Young, "The One-Man Power . . . Priesthood and Government, Etc." discourse given 8 April 1871, Salt Lake City, in *Journal of Discourses,* 14:93.

85. *News,* 11 July 1855. Frank Luther Mott, *American Journalism: A History of Newspapers in the United States through 260 Years, 1690-1950* (New York: MacMillan Company, 1950), p. 253, tends to agree with the *News's* characterization of the political press in the United States at this time.

86. *News,* 1 August 1860.

87. Ibid., 13 August 1862.

88. Ibid., 1 August 1874.
89. Ibid., 10 October 1876.
90. Ibid., 23 October 1876.
91. Lamar, *Far Southwest,* pp. 405-6.
92. *News,* 17 March 1892.
93. Jesse N. Smith, *Journal of Jesse N. Smith* (Salt Lake City: Jesse N. Smith Family Association, 1953), p. 379.
94. Charles W. Penrose and F. S. Richards, Salt Lake City, 16 February 1887, letter to President John Taylor, Charles W. Penrose Collection.
95. Board Meeting Minutes, 7 September 1898.
96. Ibid., 4 November 1898. The Cannon Company had assumed debts of the old News Company, and its interest alone between 1892 and 1898 amounted to $28,471.07.
97. Abraham H. Cannon, diary, 24 December 1892 and 23 September 1893.
98. Ibid., 27 November 1893.
99. Ibid., 23 June 1894.
100. Ibid., 30 March 1895.
101. Ibid., 26 June 1895.
102. A man of much energy and talent, Abraham Cannon had filled his short life with many accomplishments. At 23 he was named to the high church council of the Seven Presidents of Seventies, and when but 30 he was chosen a member of the Quorum of Twelve Apostles. His business activities were wide and varied, but primarily in the publishing field; Andrew Jenson, *Latter-day Saints Biographical Encyclopedia* (Salt Lake City: Andrew Jenson History Co., 1901), 1:167-68.
103. *News,* 14 May 1898. Although Cannon participated in no battle, engagement, or expedition—indeed, never even got to Cuba—he was discharged at Camp Cuba Libre, Florida, 23 October 1898, as a lieutenant colonel. His service was "honest and faithful," and he received for his six months duty $1,183.33; *see* Discharge Papers of John Q. Cannon, John Q. Cannon Collection. J. M. Sjodahl replaced John Q. as editor until 1 January 1899; Jenson, *LDS Biographical Encyclopedia,* 3:714. Cannon twice again edited the *News,* 19 April 1918 to 16 April 1922 and 22 October 1928 to 14 January 1931.
104. Abraham H. Cannon, diary, 4 and 5 January 1895.
105. Ibid., 4 and 8 January 1895. Cannon not only did not resign his military job, but was also named adjutant general of the Utah militia which made him chief of the governor's staff. Even Abraham Cannon, realizing Mormons needed all the influence and power they could get and fearing the post would go to a gentile, was glad John took the job; *see* ibid., 1 April 1895.
106. Board Meeting Minutes, 7 and 21 November 1898. *See also News,* 17 December 1898.
107. Board Meeting Minutes, 6 September 1898.
108. The *News,* for example, had lost most of the patronage of the various missions in the world. The business manager after 1899 suggested that a letter from the Church President to all mission heads informing them that the Church again owned the *News* would be very helpful; H. G.

Whitney, Salt Lake City, 23 March 1899, letter to Lorenzo Snow, *Deseret News* Collection.

109. Heber J. Grant, Salt Lake City, 6 September 1898, written proposition submitted to the board of directors of the Deseret News Company, as reported in Board Meeting Minutes, 6 September 1898. Grant's proposition never materialized.

110. Board Meeting Minutes, 2 November 1898. Although the *News* establishment did become more profitable after 1898, Richards's hopes concerning its circulation were, of course, never met. Even despite a mammoth push in 1948, including the initiation of a Sunday edition, the daily *News* appeals today to only eight per cent of Utah's Mormon population. The *Salt Lake Tribune* seems much more popular. As of 1974 its circulation of 101,981 was nine percent of the total Utah population, whereas that of the *Deseret News* (75,180) constituted only 6.6 percent of the whole.

111. Snow paid $108,364.08; Board Meeting Minutes, 21 November 1898.

112. *News,* 17 December 1898.

113. Financial Report for 1899, *Deseret News* Collection.

114. H. G. Whitney, Salt Lake City, 13 April 1900, letter to Lorenzo Snow, *Deseret News* Collection.

115. Financial Report for 1899, *Deseret News* Collection.

116. Board Meeting Minutes, 7 and 21 November 1898; *see also* H. G. Whitney, Salt Lake City, 23 March 1899, letter to Lorenzo Snow, *Deseret News* Collection.

117. *N. W. Ayer and Son's American Newspaper Annual,* 19:818; 39:975. *See also* Charles W. Penrose, "The *Deseret News,* the Pioneer Newspaper of the West," *Utah Genealogical and Historical Magazine,* 3(July 1912): 143.

118. *News,* 21 November 1894.

Appendix:
Editors of the Deseret News
1850 - 1898

Willard Richards	June 15, 1850–March 1, 1854
Albert Carrington	April 27, 1854–March 9, 1859
Elias Smith	March 9, 1859–September 16, 1863
George Q. Cannon	November 20, 1867–August 21, 1873
David O. Calder	August 21, 1873–August 1, 1877
George Q. Cannon	August 1, 1877–July 19, 1879
Charles W. Penrose	September 6, 1880–September 30, 1892
John Q. Cannon	October 1, 1892–July 1898

John Nicholson	Acting editor for some time during 1880s
George Cannon Lambert	Acting editor during 1885

Bibliography

BOOKS

Alter, J. Cecil. *Early Utah Journalism: A Half Century of Forensic Warfare, Waged by the West's Most Militant Press.* Salt Lake City: Utah State Historical Society, 1938.

Anderson, Nels. *Deseret Saints: The Mormon Frontier in Utah.* Chicago: University of Chicago Press, 1942.

Arrington, Leonard J. *Great Basin Kingdom: An Economic History of the Latter-day Saints, 1830-1900.* Cambridge: Harvard University Press, 1958.

Ashton, Wendell J. *Voice in the West: Biography of a Pioneer Newspaper.* New York: Duell, Sloan and Pearce, 1950.

Atherton, Lewis. *Main Street on the Middle Border.* Bloomington: Indiana University Press, 1954.

Bancroft, Hubert Howe. *History of Utah.* San Francisco: Bancroft, 1890.

Baskin, Robert Newton. *Reminiscences of Early Utah.* Salt Lake City: Tribune-Reporter Printing Company, 1914.

Berrett, William Edwin, and Burton, Alma P., eds. *Readings in L.D.S. Church History From Original Manuscripts.* 3 vols. Salt Lake City: Deseret Book Company, 1954-58.

Billington, Ray Allen. *The Far Western Frontier, 1830–1860.* New York: Harper and Row, 1956.

Book of Mormon. Palmyra, New York. Egbert B. Grandin, 1830.

Briggs, Asa. *The Making of Modern England 1783–1867: The Age of Improvement.* New York: Harper and Row, 1959.

Brodie, Fawn McKay. *No Man Knows My History: The Life of Joseph Smith, the Mormon Prophet.* New York: Alfred A. Knopf, 1945.

Brooks, Juanita. *John Doyle Lee: Zealot, Pioneer Builder and Scapegoat.* Glendale, Calif.: The Arthur H. Clark Company, 1962.
————. *The Mountain Meadows Massacre.* Palo Alto, Calif.: Stanford University Press, 1950.
————. *On the Mormon Frontier: The Diary of Hosea Stout, 1844-1861.* 2 vols. Salt Lake City: University of Utah Press, 1964.
————, and Cleland, Robert Glass, eds. *A Mormon Chronicle: The Diaries of John D. Lee, 1848-1876.* San Marino, Calif.: The Henry E. Huntington Library, 1955.
Burton, Richard F. *The City of the Saints and Across the Rocky Mountains to California.* 2d ed. London: Longman, Green, Longman, and Roberts, 1861.
Canham, Erwin D. *Commitment to Freedom: The Story of the Christian Science Monitor.* Boston: Houghton Miffin Company, 1958.
Cannon, George Q. *The History of the Mormons, Their Persecutions and Travels. Also the Two Manifestoes of the Presidency of the Church of Jesus Christ of Latter-day Saints.* Salt Lake City: George Q. Cannon and Sons Company, 1891.
————. *The Life of Joseph Smith the Prophet.* Salt Lake City: Juvenile Instructor Office, 1888.
————. *Writings from the "Western Standard" Published in San Francisco, California.* Liverpool: George Q. Cannon, 1864.
Cannon, Frank J., and Knapp, George L. *Brigham Young and His Mormon Empire.* New York: Fleming H. Revell Company, 1913.
————, and O'Higgins, Harvey J. *Under the Prophet in Utah: The National Menace of a Political Priestcraft.* Boston: The C. M. Clark Publishing Company, 1911.
Carrington, Irvin Margaret. *AB-SA-RA-KA Land of Massacre: Being the Experience of an Officer's Wife on the Plains, with an Outline of Indian Operations and Conferences from 1865-1878.* Rev. ed. Philadelphia: J. B. Lippincott and Company, 1878.
Carter, Kate B., comp. *Heart Throbs of the West,* vol. 9. Salt Lake City: Daughters of the Utah Pioneers, 1948.
Chandless, William. *A Visit to Salt Lake: Being a Journey Across the Plains and a Residence in Mormon Settlements at Utah.* London: Smith, Elder and Company, 1857.
Codman, John. *The Mormon Country: A Summer with the Latter-day Saints.* New York: John F. Trow and Sons, 1874.
Cole, William Graham. *Sex in Christianity and Psychoanalysis.* New York: Oxford University Press, 1966.
Colton, Ray C. *The Civil War in the Western Territories: Arizona, Colorado, New Mexico, and Utah.* Norman: University of Oklahoma Press, 1959.
de Tocqueville, Alexis. *Democracy in America.* Edited by Phillips Bradley. 2 vols. New York: Vintage Books, 1945.
Dick, Everett N. *The Sod House Frontier, 1854-1890: A Social History of the Northern Plains from the Creation of Kansas and Nebraska to the Admission of the Dakotas.* Lincoln, Neb.: Johnsen Publishing Company, 1954.

Doctrine and Covenants of the Church of Jesus Christ of Latter-day Saints. Salt Lake City: Church of Jesus Christ of Latter-day Saints, 1951. [Originally published as *Book of Commandments for the Government of the Church of Christ* in Zion, Jackson County, Missouri, in 1833.]

Drury, Wells. *An Editor on the Comstock Lode.* New York: Farrer and Rinehart, 1936.

Dwyer, Robert Joseph. *The Gentile Comes to Utah: A Study in Religious and Social Conflict, 1862-1890.* Washington, D. C.: The Catholic University of America Press, 1941.

Encyclopedia Britanica, 9th ed., s.v. "Israel."

Evans, John Henry. *Joseph Smith, An American Prophet.* New York: The Macmillan Company, 1936.

Ferris, Benjamin G. *Utah and the Mormons: The History, Government, Doctrines, Customs, and the Prospects of the Latter-day Saints. From Personal Observation During a Six Months' Residence at Great Salt Lake City.* New York: Harper and Brothers, 1854.

Ferris, Mrs. Benjamin G. *The Mormons at Home: With Some Incidents of Travel From Missouri to California 1852-1853, In a Series of Letters.* New York: Dix and Edwards, 1856.

Flanders, Robert B. *Nauvoo: Kingdom on the Mississippi.* Urbana: University of Illinois Press, 1965.

Fohlin, E. V. *Salt Lake City, Past and Present.* Salt Lake City: E. V. Fohlin, 1908.

Fowler, Gene. *Timber Line: A Story of Bonfils and Tammen.* New York: Friede, 1933.

Furniss, Norman F. *The Mormon Conflict 1850-1859.* New Haven, Conn.: Yale University Press, 1960.

Garrison, Winfred Ernest. *Religion Follows the Frontier: A History of the Disciples of Christ.* New York: Harper and Brothers, 1931.

Goodwin, Charles Carroll. *As I Remember Them.* Salt Lake City: Special Committee of the Salt Lake Commercial Club, 1913.

Gowan, Fred R., and Campbell, Eugene E. *Fort Bridger: Island in the Wilderness.* Provo, Utah: Brigham Young University Press, 1975.

Gramling, Oliver. *AP: The Story of News.* New York: Farrar and Rinehart, 1940.

Greeley, Horace. *An Overland Journey from New York to San Francisco in the Summer of 1859.* New York: C. M. Saxton, Barker and Company, 1860.

Greer, Leland Hargrave. *The Founding of an Empire: The Exploration and Colonization of Utah, 1776-1856.* Salt Lake City: Bookcraft, 1947.

————. *Utah and the Nation.* Seattle: University of Washington Press, 1929.

Greever, William S. *The Bonanza West: The Story of the Western Mining Rushes 1848-1900.* Norman: University of Oklahoma Press, 1963.

Gregory, Winifred, ed. *American Newspapers, 1821-1936: A Union List of Files Available in the United States and Canada.* New York: H. W. Wilson, 1937.

Hafen, LeRoy R. *The Overland Mail, 1849-1869: Promoter of Settlement, Precursor of Railroads.* Cleveland: The Arthur H. Clark Company, 1926.

Hage, George S. *Newspapers on the Minnesota Frontier 1849-1860.* St. Paul: Minnesota Historical Society, 1967.

Hansen, Klaus. *Quest for Empire: The Political Kingdom of God and the Council of Fifty in Mormon History.* East Lansing: Michigan State University Press, 1967.

Harris, Sarah Hollister. *An Unwritten Chapter of Salt Lake, 1851-1901.* New York: privately printed, 1901.

Hirshson, Stanley P. *The Lion of the Lord: A Biography of Brigham Young.* New York: Alfred A. Knopf, 1969.

Houghton, Walter E. *The Victorian Frame of Mind 1830-1870.* New Haven, Conn.: Yale University Press, 1957.

Howe, Edward. *Plain People.* New York: Dodd, Mead and Company, 1929.

Hulbert, Archer Butler, ed. *Letters of an Overland Mail Agent in Utah.* Worcester, Mass.: American Antiquarian Society, 1929.

Hunter, Milton R. *Brigham Young the Colonizer.* Salt Lake City: Deseret News Press, 1940.

Hyde, John, Jr. *Mormonism: Its Leaders and Designs.* New York: W. P. Fetridge and Company, 1857.

Ingraham, Colonel Prentiss, ed. *Seventy Years on the Frontier: Alexander Major's Memoirs of a Lifetime on the Border.* Chicago: Rand McNally and Company, 1893.

Jenson, Andrew. *Church Chronology: A Record of Important Events Pertaining to the History of the Church of Jesus Christ of Latter-day Saints.* 2d ed. Salt Lake City: Deseret News Press, 1899.

————. *Latter-day Saint Biographical Encyclopedia.* 4 vols. Salt Lake City: Andrew Jenson History Company, 1901-36.

Jones, Billy M. *Health-Seekers in the Southwest, 1817-1900.* Norman: University of Oklahoma Press, 1967.

Journal of Discourses by Brigham Young, His Two Counsellors, and the Twelve Apostles. 26 vols. Liverpool: separate volumes issued by different publishers, 1854-86.

Karolevitz, Robert F. *Newspapering in the Old West: A Pictorial History of Journalism and Printing on the Frontier.* Seattle: Superior Publishing Company, 1965.

Kemble, Edward. *A History of California Newspapers 1846-1858.* Reprint. Los Gatos, Calif.: The Talisman Press, 1962.

Kenner, S. A. *Utah As It Is.* Salt Lake City: Deseret News Press, 1904.

Knightley, Philip. *The First Casualty From the Crimea to Vietnam: The War Correspondent as Hero, Propagandist, and Myth Maker.* New York: Harcourt Brace, Javanovich, 1975.

Lamar, Howard Roberts. *The Far Southwest, 1846-1912: A Territorial History.* New Haven, Conn.: Yale University Press, 1966.

Langer, William. *Political and Social Upheaval, 1832-1852.* New York: Harper and Row, 1969.

Larson, Gustive O. *Outline History of Utah and the Mormons.* Salt Lake City: Deseret Book Company, 1958.

Lee, Alfred McClung. *The Daily Newspaper in America.* New York: The Macmillan Company, 1937.

Lee, John D. *Mormonism Unveiled.* St. Louis: J. H. Mason, 1891.

Lingenfelter, Richard E. *The Newspapers of Nevada: A History and Bibliography, 1858-1958.* San Francisco: J. Howell-Books, 1964.

Linn, William Alexander. *The Story of the Mormons, From the Date of Their Origin to the Year 1901.* Reissue. New York: Russell and Russell Inc., 1963.

Lutrell, Estelle. *Newspapers and Periodicals of Arizona, 1859-1911.* Tucson: University of Arizona, 1950.

Lyon, William H. *The Pioneer Editor in Missouri 1808-1860.* Columbia: University of Missouri Press, 1965.

Malin, James Claude. *John Brown and the Legend of Fifty-Six.* Philadelphia: The American Philosophical Society, 1942.

Martin, Douglas D. *Tombstone's Epitaph.* Albuquerque: University of New Mexico Press, 1951.

McMurtrie, Douglas Crawford. *The Beginnings of Printing in Iowa.* Des Moines; printed privately, 1933.

————. *The Beginnings of Printing in Utah, With a Bibliography of the Issues of the Utah Press, 1849-1860.* Chicago: John Calhoun Club, 1931.

————. *Notes on Early Printing in Utah Outside of Salt Lake City.* Los Angeles: Press of the Frank Wiggins Trade School, 1938.

McNiff, William J. *Heaven on Earth: A Planned Mormon Society.* Oxford, Ohio: Mississippi Valley Press, 1940.

Middagh, John. *Frontier Newspaper: The El Paso Times.* El Paso: Texas Western Press, 1958.

Morgan, Dale L. *The Great Salt Lake.* New York: Bobbs-Merrill Company, 1947.

Mott, Frank Luther. *American Journalism: A History of Newspapers in the United States through 260 Years, 1690-1950.* New York: The Macmillan Company, 1950.

Mott, Frank Luther. *A Free Press: The Story of the American Newspaper.* Washington, D. C.: Distributed by U.S. Infomation Service, 1958.

————. *News in America.* Cambridge: Harvard University Press, 1952.

Mulder, William. *Homeward to Zion: The Mormon Migration from Scandinavia.* Minneapolis: University of Minnesota Press, 1957.

Neff, Andrew Love. *History of Utah, 1847-1869.* Edited by Leland H. Greer. Salt Lake City: Deseret News Press, 1940.

Nelson, Lowry. *The Mormon Village: A Pattern and Technique of Land Settlement.* Salt Lake City: University of Utah Press, 1952.

Nelson, Pearl Udall, ed. *Arizona Pioneer Mormon, David King Udall: His Story and His Family 1851-1938.* Tucson: Arizona Silhouettes, 1959.

Nevins, Allan. *The Evening Post.* New York: Boni and Liveright, 1922.

Nibley, Preston. *Brigham Young: The Man and His Work.* Salt Lake City: Deseret News Press, 1936.

————. *Joseph Smith the Prophet.* Salt Lake City: Deseret News Press, 1944.

————. *The Presidents of the Church.* Salt Lake City: Deseret Book Company, 1965.

Noall, Claire. *Intimate Disciple: A Portrait of Willard Richards, Apostle to Joseph Smith—Cousin of Brigham Young.* Salt Lake City: University of Utah Press, 1957.

N. W. Ayer and Son's American Newspaper Annual. 39 vols. Philadelphia: N. W. Ayer and Son, 1881-1919.

O'Dea, Thomas F. *The Mormons.* Chicago: University of Chicago Press, 1957.

Paul, Rodman Wilson. *Mining Frontier of the Far West, 1848-1880.* New York: Holt, Rinehart and Winston, 1963.

Remy, Jules, and Brenchley, Julius. *A Journey to Great Salt Lake City.* 2 vols. London: W. Jeffs, 1861.

Rice, William B. *"The Los Angeles Star, 1851-1864: The Beginnings of Journalism in Southern California.* Edited by John Walton Caughey. Berkeley: University of California Press, 1947.

Roberts, B. H. *A Comprehensive History of the Church of Jesus Christ of Latter-day Saints: Century I.* 6 vols. Salt Lake City: Deseret News Press, 1930.

————. *The Missouri Persecutions.* Reissue. Salt Lake City: Bookcraft, 1965.

————. *The Rise and Fall of Nauvoo.* Salt Lake City: Deseret News Press, 1900.

Roberts, George W. *The Population of Jamaica.* Cambridge, Mass.: Cambridge University Press, 1957.

Rogers, Fred B. *Soldiers of the Overland: Being Some Account of the Services of Patrick Edward Connor and his Volunteers in the Old West.* San Francisco: The Grabhorn Press, 1938.

Romney, Thomas C. *The Life of Lorenzo Snow.* Salt Lake City: Deseret Book Company, 1955.

Salmon, Lucy Maynard. *The Newspaper and the Historian.* New York: Oxford University Press, 1923.

Schindler, Harold. *Orrin Porter Rockwell: Man of God, Son of Thunder.* Salt Lake City: University of Utah Press, 1966.

Shaplen, Robert. *Free Love and Heavenly Sinners: The Story of the Great Henry Ward Beecher Scandal.* New York: Alfred A. Knopf, 1954.

Smith, Jesse N. *Journal of Jesse N. Smith.* Salt Lake City: Jesse N. Smith Family Association, 1953.

Smith, Joseph Fielding. *Essentials in Church History.* Salt Lake City: Deseret News Press, 1953.

————. *The Life of Joseph F. Smith.* Salt Lake City: Deseret Book Company, 1938.

Smith, Joseph, Jr. *History of the Church of Jesus Christ of Latter-day Saints. Period I: History of Joseph Smith the Prophet, by Himself.* Edited by B. H. Roberts. 6 vols. 3d ed. Salt Lake City: Deseret Book Company, 1948-51.

Smith, Lucy Mack. *Biographical Sketches of Joseph Smith the Prophet and His Progenitors for Many Generations.* Liverpool: S. W. Richards, 1853.

Spencer, Seymour Horne. *Life Summary of Orson Spencer.* Salt Lake City: Mercury Publishing Company, Inc., 1964.

Stegner, Wallace. *Mormon Country.* New York: Sloan and Pierce, 1942.

Stenhouse, T. B. H. *The Rocky Mountain Saints.* New York: Appleton, 1873.

Sweet, William Warren. *The Story of Religions in America.* New York: Harper and Brothers, 1930.

Taft, William Howard. *Missouri Newspapers.* Columbia: University of Missouri Press, 1964.

————. *Missouri Newspapers: When and Where, 1808-1863.* Columbia: State Historical Society of Missouri, 1964.

Taylor, P. A. M. *Expectations Westward: The Mormons and the Emigration of Their British Converts in the Nineteenth Century.* Edinburgh: Oliver and Boyd, 1965.

Townsend, George Alfred. *The Mormon Trails at Salt Lake City.* New York: American News Company, 1871.

Tullidge, Edward W. *The History of Salt Lake City and its Founders.* Salt Lake City: Tullidge, 1883.

Turner, Wallace. *The Mormon Establishment.* Boston: Houghton Mifflin Company, 1966.

Twain, Mark. *Roughing It.* 2 vols. New York: Harper and Brothers, 1871.

Wade, Richard C. *The Urban Frontier: The Rise of Western Cities, 1790-1830.* Cambridge, Mass: Harvard University Press, 1959.

Werner, Morris Robert. *Brigham Young.* London: Jonathan Cape, Ltd., 1925.

West, Ray B., Jr. *Kingdom of the Saints: The Story of Brigham Young and The Mormons.* New York: Viking Press, 1957.

Whitney, Orson F. *History of Utah.* 4 vols. Salt Lake City: George Q. Cannon and Sons Company, 1892.

————. *The Life of Heber C. Kimball, an Apostle: The Father and Founder of the British Mission.* Salt Lake City: Kimball Family, 1888.

Winther, Oscar Osburn, ed. *The Private Papers and Diary of Thomas Leiper Kane, A Friend of the Mormons.* San Francisco: Gelber, Lilienthal Inc., 1937.

Young, James Harvey. *The Toadstool Millionaires: A Social History of Patent Medicines in America Before Federal Regulation.* Princeton, N.J.: Princeton University Press, 1961.

Young, Kimball. *Isn't One Wife Enough?* New York: Henry Holt and Company, 1954.

Young, S. Dilworth. *Here Is Brigham: Brigham Young, the Years to 1844.* Salt Lake City: Bookcraft, 1964.

ARTICLES

Abbott, Charles David. "George Alfred Townsend." *Dictionary of American Biography* 18:616-17.

Adeney, Walter F. "Waldenses." *Encyclopedia of Religion and Ethics* 12: 663-73.

Allen, James B. "Ecclesiastical Influence on Local Government in the Territory of Utah." *Arizona and the West* 8(Summer 1966):35-48.

Andrus, Hyrum L. "Joseph Smith and the West." *Brigham Young University Studies* 2(Summer 1960):129-47.

Arrington, Leonard J. "Deseret Telegraph—A Church-Owned Public Utility." *Journal of Economic History* 2(Spring 1951):117-39.

————. "An Economic Interpretation of the 'Word of Wisdom.'" *Brigham Young University Studies* 1(January 1959):37-49.

————. "Religious Sanction and Entrepreneurship in Pioneer Utah." *Utah Academy of Sciences, Arts, and Letters* 70(1952-53):130.

————. "Review of *The Lion of the Lord: A Biography of Brigham Young* by Stanley P. Hirshson." *Brigham Young University Studies* 10(Winter 1970):240-45.

————. "The Transcontinental Railroad and Mormon Economic Policy." *Pacific Historical Review* 20(May 1951):143-57.

————, and Haupt, Jon. "Intolerable Zion: The Image of Mormonism in Nineteenth Century American Literature." *Western Humanities Review* 22(Summer 1968):243-60.

Bagley, Clarence B. "Transmission of Intelligence in Early Days in Oregon." *Oregon Historical Society Quarterly* 13(December 1912):347-62.

Banks, Loy Otis. "The Evening and Morning Star." *Missouri Historical Review* 43(July 1949):319-33.

————. "The Role of Mormon Journalism in the Death of Joseph Smith." *Journalism Quarterly* 27(Summer 1950):268-81.

Blegan, Theodore C. "Minnesota Pioneer History as Revealed in Newspaper Advertisements." *Minnesota History* 7(June 1926):99-121.

Broadbent, Thomas L. "The Salt Lake City 'Beobachter': Mirror of an Immigration." *Utah Historical Quarterly* 26(July 1958):329-50.

Brodie, Fawn M. "Sir Richard F. Burton: Exceptional Observer of the Mormon Scene." *Utah Historical Quarterly* 38(Fall 1970):295-311.

Brown, Ira V. "Watchers for the Second Coming: The Millenarian Tradition in America." *Mississippi Valley Historical Review* 39(December 1952):441-58.

Bushman, Richard L. "The Mormon Persecutions in Missouri, 1833." *Brigham Young University Studies* 3(Autumn 1960):11-20.

Cannon, Mark W. "The Crusades Against the Masons, Catholics, and Mormons. Separate Waves of a Common Current." *Brigham Young University Studies* 3(Winter 1961):23-40.

Clayton, William. "Come, Come Ye Saints." *Hymns of The Church of Jesus Christ of Latter-day Saints.* Salt Lake City: The Church of Jesus Christ of Latter-day Saints, 1948.

Dagenais, Julie. "Newspaper Language as an Active Agent in the Building of a Frontier Town." *American Speech* 42(May 1967):114-21.

"Daily Crusader of Mormonism: The Deseret News of Salt Lake." *Newsweek* 17(March 31, 1941):65.

Daines, Franklin D. "Separatism in Utah, 1847-1870." *Annual Report of the American Historical Association for 1917* 58(1920):333-43.

Davis, David Brion. "Some Themes of Counter-Subversion: An Analysis of

Anti-Masonic, Anti-Catholic, and Anti-Mormon Literature." *Mississippi Valley Historical Review* 47(September 1960):205-24.

"The Deseret News and Polygamy." *Truth* 21(March 1956):289-306. [A monthly magazine of an ex-Mormon fundamentalist group published in Salt Lake City, Utah.]

Duddy, Edward A. "Victor Fremont Lawson." *Dictionary of American Biography* 11:60-61.

Durham, G. Homer. "Administration of the Mormon Church." *Political Science Quarterly* 57(March 1942):51-71.

———. "A Political Interpretation of Mormon History." *Pacific Historical Review* 13(June 1944):136-50.

Ellsworth, S. George. "Utah's Struggle for Statehood." *Utah Historical Quarterly* 31(Winter 1963):60-69.

Elsbree, Oliver W. "The Rise of the Missionary Spirit in New England, 1790-1815." *New England Quarterly* 1(July 1928):295-322.

Fellows, George Emory. "George Quayle Cannon." *Dictionary of American Biography* 3:474-75.

Firebaugh, Dorothy Gile. "The Sacramento Union: Voice of California 1851-1875." *Journalism Quarterly* 30(Summer 1953):321-30.

Gayler, George R. "The 'Expositor' Affair: Prelude to the Downfall of Joseph Smith," *Northwest Missouri State College Studies* 25(February 1961):3-15.

Genzmer, George Harvey. "John Codman." *Dictionary of American Biography* 4.258.

Goodwin, Charles C. "The Mormon Situation." *Harper's New Monthly Magazine* 63(September 1881):756-63.

———. "The Political Attitude of the Mormons," *North American Review* 32(March 1881):266-86.

Halaas, David F. "Frontier Journalism in Colorado." *The Colorado Magazine* 44(Summer 1967):185-203.

Harlow, Alvin F. "Victoria Claflin Woodhull." *Dictionary of American Biography* 20:493-94.

Housman, Robert L. "The End of Frontier Journalism in Montana." *Journalism Quarterly* 12(June 1935):133-45.

Ivins, Stanley S. "Notes on Mormon Polygamy." *Western Humanities Review* 10(Summer 1956):229-39.

Jackson, Richard H. "Righteousness and Environmental Change: The Mormons and The Environment." In *Charles Redd Monographs on Western History: Essays on the American West, 1973-1974.* Charles Redd Monograph Series, no. 5, edited by Thomas G. Alexander. Provo, Ut.: Brigham Young University Press, 1975.

Jennings, Warren A. "Factors in the Destruction of the Mormon Press in Missouri, 1833." *Utah Historical Quarterly* 35(Winter 1967):57-76.

Katz, William A. "The Western Printer and His Publications, 1850-1890." *Journalism Quarterly* 44(Winter 1967):708-14.

Keen, Elizabeth. "The Frontier Press." *Studies in Literature of the West* 20(July 1956):75-101.

Knight, Frank H. "Professor Heimann on Religion and Economics." *Journal of Political Economy* 56(Summer 1948):480-97.

Knight, Oliver. *"The Owyhee* [Idaho] *Avalanche*: The Frontier Newspaper as a Catalyst in Social Change." *Pacific Northwest Quarterly* 58(April 1967):74-81.

Kobre, Sidney. "The Sociological Approach in Research in Newspaper History." *Journalism Quarterly* 22(March 1945):12-22.

Lambert, Neal. "Saints, Sinners, and Scribes: A Look at the Mormons in Fiction." *Utah Historical Quarterly* 36(Winter 1968):64-76.

Larson, Cedric. "Patent Medicine Advertising and the Early American Press." *Journalism Quarterly* 14(December 1937):333-41.

Larson, Gustive O. "The Mormon Reformation." *Utah Historical Quarterly* 26(January 1958):45-63.

————. "Utah and the Civil War." *Utah Historical Quarterly* 33(Winter 1965):55-76.

Linford, Orma. "The Mormons and the Law." *Utah Law Review* 9(Winter 1964):208-70.

Lye, William Frank. "Edward W. Tullidge, the Mormon's Rebel Historian." *Utah Historical Quarterly* 28(January 1960):57-75.

Lythgoe, Dennis L. "Negro Slavery and Mormon Doctrine." *Western Humanities Review* 21(Autumn 1967):327-38.

Manning, George H. "Bennett Fight Opened Senate to Press." *Editor and Publisher* 67(July 21, 1934):116-18.

McMurtrie, Douglas Crawford. "Early Printing in Utah Outside of Salt Lake City." *Utah Historical Quarterly* 5(July 1932):83-86.

Melville, J. Keith. "Theory and Practice of Church and State During the Brigham Young Era." *Brigham Young University Studies* 3(Autumn 1950):33-55.

Miller, George L. "Newspapers and Newspaper Men of the Territorial Period." *Proceedings and Collections, Nebraska Historical Society* 5(1902):31-47.

Morgan, Dale L. "The Changing Face of Salt Lake City." *Utah Historical Quarterly* 27(July 1959):209-32.

Morgan, Dale L. "Review of *Voice in the West: Biography of a Pioneer Newspaper,* by Wendell J. Ashton." *Saturday Review of Literature* 30(July 15, 1950):27.

"Mormon Spruce-Up." *Newsweek* 31(May 24, 1948):67.

Mortensen, Arlington Russell, ed. "Elias Smith: Journal of A Pioneer Editor." *Utah Historical Quarterly* 21(January 1953):1-24; 21(April 1953):137-68; 21(July 1953):237-66; 21(October 1953):331-60.

————. "A Local Paper Reports on the Utah War." *Utah Historical Quarterly* 25(October 1957):298-318.

————. "Main Street: Salt Lake City." *Utah Historical Quarterly* 27(July 1959):275-83.

————. "A Pioneer Paper Mirrors the Break-Up of Isolation in the Great Basin." *Utah Historical Quarterly* 20(January 1952):77-92.

Morton, J. Sterling. "Territorial Journalism." *Proceedings and Collections, Nebraska Historical Society* 5(1902):11-30.

Mulder, William. "Image of Zion: Mormonism as an American Influence in Scandinavia." *Mississippi Valley Historical Review* 43(June 1956): 18-38.

————. "Mormonism and Literature." *Western Humanities Review* 9(Winter 1954-55):85-89.

————. "Mormonism's 'Gathering': An American Doctrine With a Difference." *Church History* 23(September 1954):248-64.

————. "Salt Lake City in 1880: A Census Profile." *Utah Historical Quarterly* 24(July 1956):223-36.

Nelson, Larry E. "Utah Goes Dry." *Utah Historical Quarterly* 41(Fall 1973):341-57.

Nevins, Allen. "American Journalism and Its Historical Treatment." *Journalism Quarterly* 36(Fall 1959):411-22.

Oaks, Dallin H. "Suppression of the *Nauvoo Expositor.*" *Utah Law Review* 9(Winter 1965):862-903.

Pedersen, Lyman C., Jr. "The *Daily Union Vedette*: A Military Voice on the Mormon Frontier." *Utah Historical Quarterly* 42(Winter 1974):39-48.

Penrose, Charles W. "*The Deseret News,* the Pioneer Newspaper of the West." *Utah Genealogical and Historical Magazine* 3(July 1912):140-44.

Persons, Frederick T. "Elias Smith." *Dictionary of American Biography* 17:258-59.

Peterson, V. V. "Early Mormon Journalism." *Mississippi Valley Historical Review* 35(March 1949):627-38.

Piercy, J. W. "The Newspaper as a Source of Historical Information." *Indiana Historical Bulletin* 10(March 1933):387-96.

Poll, Richard D. "The Mormon Question Enters National Politics, 1850-1856." *Utah Historical Quarterly* 25(April 1957):117-31.

————. "A State is Born." *Utah Historical Quarterly* 32(Winter 1964). 9-31.

Ross, Earle D. "Horace Greeley and the West." *Mississippi Valley Historical Review* 20(June 1933):63-74.

Scott, Leslie M. "The Oregonian Newspaper in Oregon History." *Oregon Historical Society Quarterly* 29(September 1927):225-35.

Shipps, Jan. "Utah Comes of Age Politically: A Study of the State's Politics in the Early Years of the Twentieth Century." *Utah Historical Quarterly* 35(Spring 1967):92-111.

Smith, Elbert A. "Forerunners of the Saints' Herald." *Saints' Herald* 57(January 26, 1910):104-19.

Smith, Heman. "Mormon Troubles in Missouri." *Missouri Historical Review* 4(July 1909-10):238-51.

Smith, John H. S. "Cigarette Prohibition in Utah, 1921-1923." *Utah Historical Quarterly* 41(Fall 1973):358-72.

Smith, Walter W. "The Periodical Literature of the Latter Day Saints." *Journal History* 14(July 1921):257-99.

Sorensen, Parry D. "Nauvoo *Times and Seasons.*" *Journal of Illinois State Historical Society* 55(Summer 1962):117-35.

"Stern Mormon View." *Time* 90(August 4, 1967):72.

Tannenbaum, Percy H., and Lynch, Mervin D. "Sensationalism: The Concept and its Measurement." *Journalism Quarterly* 37 (Summer 1960) :391-92.

Taylor, Samuel W. "Peculiar People, Positive Thinkers, and the Prospect of Mormon Literature." *Dialogue: A Journal of Mormon Thought* 2 (Summer 1967) :17-31.

————. "Review of *The City of the Saints and Across the Rocky Mountains to California* by Richard F. Burton." *Dialogue: A Journal of Mormon Thought* 3 (Autumn 1968) :139-42.

Tebbel, John. "Rating the American Newspaper." *Saturday Review* 44 (May 13, 1961) :60-62.

Towne, Jackson E. "Some Suggestive Characteristics of Early Western Journalism." *Arizona and the West* 1 (Winter 1959) :352-57.

Tullidge, Edward W. "The Godbeite Movement." *Tullidge's Quarterly Magazine* 1 (October 1880-July 1881) :14-64.

————. "The Reformation in Utah." *Harper's Magazine* 43 (September 1871) :603-10.

Turner, Frederick Jackson. "Contributions of the West to American Democracy." *The Turner Thesis: Concerning the Role of the Frontier in American History*. Edited by George Rogers Taylor, pp. 19-33. Boston: D. C. Heath and Company, 1956.

Walker, Ronald W. "The Commencement of the Godbeite Protest: Another View." *Utah Historical Quarterly* 42 (Summer 1974) :217-44.

Watkins, T. H. "If You Suffer, it Serves You Right." *The American West Review* 1 (December 1967) :30-31.

Watson, Elmo Scott. "The Indian Wars and the Press, 1866-1867." *Journalism Quarterly* 17 (December 1940) :301-12.

Weigle, Clifford F. "San Francisco Journalism, 1847-1851." *Journalism Quarterly* 14 (June 1937) : 151-57.

Whisenhunt, Donald W. "The Frontier Newspaper: A Guide to Society and Culture." *Journalism Quarterly* 45 (Winter 1968) :726-28.

Whiteman, Susan H. "Mormon Troubles in Carroll County." *Missouri Historical Review* 8 (July 1913-14) :220-22.

Willard, James F. "Spreading the News of the Early Discoveries of Gold in Colorado." *The Colorado Magazine* 6 (May 1929) :98-104.

Wolfinger, Henry J. "A Reexamination of the Woodruff Manifesto in the Light of Utah Constitutional History." *Utah Historical Quarterly* 39 (Fall 1971) :328-49.

NEWSPAPERS

Chicago Democrat, 1840.

Chicago Tribune, June 1869-August 1869, January 1873-February 1873, May 1877-August 1877.

Daily Reporter (Salt Lake City), May 1868-April 1869.

Deseret News (Salt Lake City), June 1850-December 1898.

Elders' Journal (Far West, Missouri), July 1838-August 1838.

Elders' Journal (Kirtland, Ohio), October 1837-November 1837.

The Evening and Morning Star (Independence, Missouri), September 1831-July 1833.

The Evening and Morning Star (Kirtland, Ohio), June 1832-September 1834.
Latter-day Saints' Messenger and Advocate (Kirtland, Ohio), October 1834-September 1837.
The Liberator (Boston), June 1851 and June 1861.
Millennial Star (Liverpool, England), May 1840-June 1840, April 1865-May 1865, November 1874-December 1874.
The Mormon (New York City), 17 February 1855-19 September 1857.
Mormon Tribune (Salt Lake City), January 1870-July 1870.
Mountaineer (Salt Lake City), August 1859-20 July 1861.
Nauvoo (Ill.) Expositor, 7 June 1844. [Only one number issued.]
Nauvoo (Ill.) Neighbor, May 1843-October 1845.
New York Herald, May 1877-August 1877.
New York Times, September 1851-December 1852, January 1863-December 1863, January 1868-December 1868, June 1871-August 1871, August 1872-October 1872, January 1873-December 1873, January 1877-December 1877, January 1881-December 1881, 13 April 1901.
New York Tribune, October 1871-December 1871, May 1877-August 1877.
Omaha Bee, March 1873-April 1873.
Omaha Daily Herald, May 1870-August 1870.
Peep O'Day (Salt Lake City), October 1864-November 1864.
Rocky Mountain News (Denver), January 1869-December 1869.
St. Louis Globe-Democrat, September 1890-November 1890.
St. Louis Luminary, 22 November 1854-15 December 1855.
Salt Lake Herald, July 1872-August 1872.
Salt Lake Tribune, July 1870-December 1870, April 1871-May 1871, January 1874-April 1874, January 1883-December 1883, January 1884 December 1884, October 1890-November 1890.
San Francisco Chronicle, September 1869-November 1869, May 1877-July 1877.
The Seer (Washington, D. C.), January 1853-August 1854.
The Sun (New York City), May 1877-August 1877.
Times and Seasons (Nauvoo, Illinois), November 1839-February 1846.
Union Vedette (Camp Douglas, Utah), November 1863-September 1867.
Utah Magazine (Salt Lake City), January 1868-December 1869.
Valley Tan (Salt Lake City), November 1858-February 1860.
Warsaw (Ill.) Signal, June 1844-July 1844.
Wasp (Nauvoo, Illinois), April 1842-April 1843.
Western Standard (San Francisco), February 1856-October 1857.

GOVERNMENT PUBLICATIONS

U. S., *Statutes at Large,* vol. 22. [Edmunds Act.]
U. S., Congress, House of Representatives. *Congressional Globe,* 41st Cong., 2d sess., 1870, 42:616. [Petition of 22,000 Utah citizens requesting Utah be granted statehood presented to Delegate William H. Hooper.]
U. S., Congress, House of Representatives. *Congressional Record,* 49th Cong., 2d sess., 1887, 18:585-91. [Delegate John T. Caine speaking against an anti-polygamy bill.]

U. S., Congress, House of Representatives. *Congressional Record,* 50th Cong., 1st sess., 1888, 19:7950-53. [Delegate John T. Caine speaking against a resolution pertaining to anti-polygamy laws.]
U. S., Congress, House of Representatives. *Congressional Record,* 53rd Cong., 2d sess., 1893, 26:176-83. [Delegate Joseph L. Rawlins speaking in favor of Utah's admission to statehood.]

UNPUBLISHED WORKS

Anderson, Robert D. "History of the *Provo Times and Enquirer,* 1873-1897." Master's thesis, Brigham Young University, 1951.
Banks, Loy Otis. "Latter Day Saint Journalism." Master's thesis, University of Missouri, 1948.
Barrus, George. "Missouri Newspaper Accounts of the Mormons in Missouri, 1832-1844." Master's thesis, University of Missouri, 1950.
Cannon, Mark W. "The Mormon Issue in Congress, 1872-1882: Drawing on the Experience of Territorial Delegate George Q. Cannon." Ph.D. dissertation, Harvard University, 1960.
Cowan, R. O. "Mormonism in National Periodicals." Ph.D. dissertation, Stanford University, 1962.
Denhalter, Wilson Charles. "A Sociological Analysis of the Official Literature of The Church of Jesus Christ of Latter-day Saints." Master's thesis, University of Denver, 1954.
Fairbanks, Merwin G. "A History of the *Wasatch Wave,* a Weekly Newspaper in Heber, Utah." Master's thesis, Brigham Young University, 1964.
Fielding, Robert Kent. "The Growth of the Mormon Church in Kirtland, Ohio." Ph.D. dissertation, Indiana University, 1956.
Gayler, George R. "A Social, Economic and Political Study of the Mormons in Western Illinois, 1839-1846: A Re-evaluation." Ph.D. dissertation, Indiana University, 1955.
Gentry, Leland H. "A History of the Latter-day Saints in Northern Missouri from 1836-1839." Ph.D. dissertation, Brigham Young University, 1965.
Gibbany, Walter Wright. "Religious Journalism, Its History, Function and Content." Master's thesis, University of Missouri, 1922.
Greenwell, James Richard. "The Mormon–Anti-Mormon Conflict in Early Utah as Reflected in the Local Newspapers, 1850-1869." Master's thesis, University of Utah, 1963.
Halter, Doris Marion. "Mormon Literature of the Nineteenth Century." Master's thesis, New York University, 1946.
Hock, Cassie Hyde. "The Mormons in Fiction." Ph.D. dissertation, University of Colorado, 1941.
Jennings, Warren A. "Zion is Fled: The Expulsion of the Mormons from Jackson County, Missouri." Ph.D. dissertation, University of Florida, 1962.
Knight, Oliver Holmes, Jr. "Reporting by Accredited Newspaper Correspondents of Army Campaigns Against Hostile Indians in the American West, 1866-1891." Ph.D. dissertation, University of Wisconsin, 1959.
Merrill, Harrison R. "The Latter-Day Saint Press, 1830-1930." Master's thesis, Columbia University, 1930.

Morgan, Dale L. "Zion Grows." Unpublished essay, Utah State Historical Society Library, Salt Lake City, Utah.

Mortensen, Arlington Russell. "The *Deseret News* and Utah, 1850-1867." Ph.D. dissertation, University of California at Los Angeles, 1949.

Munn, Bradley. "A Survey and Analysis of Utah's Weekly Newspapers and Their Publications." Master's thesis, Brigham Young University, 1961.

Ollerton, Fay. "The American Periodicals' Treatment of Mormonism Since 1850." Master's thesis, Columbia University, 1927.

Poll, Richard D. "The Mormon Question 1850-1865: A Study in Politics and Public Opinion." Ph.D. dissertation, University of California at Berkeley, 1948.

Ridd, Jay D. "Almon Whiting Babbitt: Mormon Emissary." Master's thesis, University of Utah, 1953.

Smart, Max Neff. "A Study of the Readability of Editorials in Weekly Newspapers of Utah." Master's thesis, Brigham Young University, 1952.

Snider, Cecil A. "Development of Attitudes in Sectarian Conflict: A Study of Mormonism in Illinois in Contemporary Newspaper Sources." Master's thesis, State University of Iowa, 1933.

Snider, Helen Fulton. "Mormonism in Illinois: An Analysis of the Non-Mormon Press Materials 1838-1848." Master's thesis, State University of Iowa, 1933.

Tappan, Paul Wilbur. "Mormon Gentile Conflict: A Study of the Influence of Public Opinion on In-Group Versus Out-Group Interaction With Special Reference to Polygamy." Ph.D. dissertation, University of Wisconsin, 1939.

Tweito, Thomas E. "The Correspondent in the West, 1850-1860." Ph.D. dissertation, State University of Iowa, 1939.

Whitaker, John R. "The Influence of the West on the Evolution of Personal Journalism in the United States Since the Civil War." Ph.D. dissertation, University of Texas at Austin, 1947.

MANUSCRIPT COLLECTIONS

Beecroft, Joseph. MS Diary. HDC [HDC, as used here and below, refers to Historical Department of The Church of Jesus Christ of Latter-day Saints, Salt Lake City. Library and Archives, Salt Lake City, Utah.]

Cain, Joseph. MSS. HDC.

Calder, David. MSS. HDC.

Cannon, Abraham H. MS Diary. Brigham Young University Library, Provo, Utah.

Cannon, George Q. MSS. HDC.

Cannon, John Q. MS Diary, typewritten copy. Brigham Young University Library, Provo, Utah.

Carrington, Albert. MSS. HDC.

Deseret News. MSS. HDC.

———. MS Subscription List for 1887. HDC.

Deseret News Company. Board Meeting MS Minute Book. HDC.

———. Finances File. HDC.

———. MS Ledger for 1873. HDC.

————. MSS. HDC.

"Journal History of the Church." HDC. [Unpublished day-by-day history of The Church of Jesus Christ of Latter-day Saints from 1830 to the present.]

Lambert, George Cannon. MSS. HDC.

Nicholson, John. MSS. HDC.

Penrose, Charles W. MSS. HDC.

Richards, Willard. MSS. HDC.

Sjodahal, James. MSS. HDC.

Smith, Elias. MS Diary. Utah Historical Society Library, Salt Lake City, Utah.

Stenhouse, T. B. H. MSS. HDC.

Taylor, Thomas E. MSS. HDC.

Whitney, Horace G. MSS. HDC.

Young, Brigham. MS. Letter Books. HDC.

————. MSS. HDC.

————. Letter to Colonel Thomas L. Kane, Salt Lake City, Utah, October 22, 1858, photostatic copy. Henry E. Huntington Library.

Young, Brigham, and others. "History of Brigham Young." HDC. [1847-77.]

Young, Brigham, Jr. MSS. HDC.

————. MSS Diary. HDC.

INTERVIEWS AND PERSONAL CORRESPONDENCE

Anderson, Joseph, Secretary to the First Presidency of The Church of Jesus Christ of Latter-day Saints, Salt Lake City, Utah. Letter to the author, 18 January 1868.

Graham, C. M., Secretary to William B. Smart, Editor and General Manager, *Deseret News,* Salt Lake City, Utah. Letter to the author, 9 October 1974.

Gallagher, Wes, General Manager of the Associated Press, New York City, New York. Letter to the author, 24 June 1969.

Hawkes, E. E., Publisher of the *Deseret News,* Salt Lake City, Utah. Personal interview with the author, 17 January 1968.

Haycock, Arthur, Secretary of the Deseret News Corporation and Member of the Board of Editors, Salt Lake City, Utah. Personal interview with the author, 16 January 1968.

Lamar, Howard Roberts, New Haven, Connecticut. Letter to the author, 21 August 1968.

Liddle, T. C., Managing Editor of the *Deseret News,* Salt Lake City, Utah. Letter to the author, April 1970.

Seifert, Marilyn, Research Assistant, Historical Department of The Church of Jesus Christ of Latter-day Saints, Salt Lake City, Utah. Letters to the author, 24 March 1970 and 14 July 1970.

Smart, William B., Executive Editor of the *Deseret News,* Salt Lake City, Utah. Personal interview with the author, 17 January 1968.

————. Letter to the author, 17 April 1970.

Index